T4-AHG-827

Bc

WESTERN EUROPE IN KISSINGER'S GLOBAL STRATEGY

Western Europe in Kissinger's Global Strategy

Argyris G. Andrianopoulos
The George Washington University

St. Martin's Press   New York

D
1065
.U5
A874
1988

© Argyris Gerry Andrianopoulos, 1988

All rights reserved. For information, write:
Scholarly and Reference Division,
St. Martin's Press, Inc., 175 Fifth Avenue, New York, NY 10010

First published in the United States of America in 1988

Printed in Hong Kong

ISBN 0-312-01544-5

Library of Congress Cataloging-in-Publication Data
Andrianopoulos, Argyris G.
Western Europe in Kissinger's global strategy.
Bibliography: p.
Includes index.
1. Europe—Foreign relations—United States.
2. United States—Foreign relations—Europe.
3. Kissinger, Henry, 1923–   . 4. World politics–
1965–1975.   I. Title.
D1065.U5A874   1988   327.7304   87–26528
ISBN 0-312-01544-5

For my parents, Sotirios and Katina, and my
uncle, Kimon

Contents

Preface

The US–West European relationship is continually plagued by conflicts over recurring policy issues. These include strategic doctrine, nuclear weapons control, the role of conventional forces, burden-sharing, West European unity, and the future of Germany. Most studies in the 1960s attributed intra-Alliance conflicts to President de Gaulle's nationalist perspective and intransigence. Kissinger's writings, however, rejected the prevailing view that de Gaulle caused conflicts in the Alliance, stressing that sovereignty and nuclear weapons imposed structural constraints which made the solution of these issues unlikely for the foreseeable future regardless of who governed in Paris or in Washington. Kissinger urged the forging of a common Atlantic policy, concluding 'there is [an American] price to be paid'.

Kissinger's global strategy, intellectualism or imperious and secretive diplomatic style were cited as causes of the bitter controversy between the US and Western Europe in the early 1970s. During the first Nixon Administration he devoted his diplomatic energies to US–Soviet detente, US–PRC (People's Republic of China) rapprochement, and the Vietnam War, and as a result the US–West European relationship (which had been the focus of his writings) drifted from his range of vision. The critics maintained that the spectacular breakthroughs with the USSR and the PRC were based on an unsound view of geopolitics, and were achieved only by weakening the more durable alliances with Western Europe (and Japan).

Rejecting the current thesis, this study maintains that the conflicts were caused by the misinterpretation and/or disregard of Kissinger's writings, and the exaggerated expectations created on both sides of the Atlantic when he was appointed Assistant to the President for National Security Affairs. A more thorough examination of Kissinger's writings would have indicated that despite his advocacy of a common Atlantic policy he would not have dealt with the dilemmas of the Alliance, given his conviction that these could not be resolved due to the limits imposed by sovereignty and nuclear weapons.

Having urged the forging of a common Atlantic policy, as a policymaker Kissinger was expected to 'pay the price' and establish that common policy. This study examines the relationship between Kissinger-the-scholar and Kissinger-the-policymaker.

ARGYRIS G. ANDRIANOPOULOS

x

Acknowledgements

I am indebted to several individuals and organizations who were particularly helpful in the preparation of this book. Their help was of great value in many ways, from reassuring me that what began to appear patently persuasive had not been said before, to offering incisive critiques that led to my rethinking some basic concepts and arguments. For their patience in reading through the entire manuscript I am most grateful to Professors J. L. Black, Harald von Riekhoff, and John H. Sigler, of Carleton University. For their help with particular parts of the manuscript I want to thank Professors Burton M. Sapin, William H. Lewis, and Michael J. Sodaro of The George Washington University. I am particularly indebted to Professor Linda P. Brady of Emory University whose insightful observations and critiques allowed me to progress much more efficiently than would have otherwise been possible. Several institutions and individuals helped to make this research possible and I wish to express my appreciation to them: The Norman Paterson School of International Affairs at Carleton University and its Director, B. W. Tomlin, and former Director, J. H. Sigler; the Department of Political Science at The George Washington University and its Chairman, Hugh L. LeBlanc, and former Chairman, Bernard Reich; and The Institute for Sino–Soviet Studies at The George Washington University and its Acting Director, Carl A. Linden, and former Director, Gaston J. Sigur.

Francis C. Barrineau was a source of unwavering encouragement and assisted with the typing and editing of the final manuscript. Spyros C. Philippas facilitated its completion by acquainting me with the contemporary scholar's technological companion, the computer, and teaching me the latest word-processing skills. Alexander J. Bennett made helpful observations and critiques. Kim Moloughney and Brenda Sutherland of Carleton University, and Marcia L. Sleight and Suzanne Stephenson of The George Washington University provided their administrative assistance. Kay Beach, Betty Burton, Marti L. Melzow, Leila Sanders, and Dorothy Wedge helped to create an environment conducive to research. Finally, I owe a very special debt to my parents Sotirios and Katina, to my sisters Dimitra and Beth, and to my brothers Lambros and George. Their xii* Acknowledgements*

understanding, assistance, and patience made this book possible.

A.G.A.

author and the publishers are also grateful to the following for permission to reproduce copyright material in the text:

The New York Times, for the extracts from 'Partial Transcript of an Interview with Kissinger on the State of Western World' 10/13/74 (Copyright © 1974 by The New York Times Company).

Council on Foreign Relations, for permission to use quotes from *The Troubled Partnership* by Henry Kissinger (Copyright © Henry A. Kissinger, 1965).

Harper & Row, Publishers, Inc., and Chatto & Windus for extracts from *The Necessity for Choice* by Henry Kissinger (Copyright © 1960, 1961 by Henry A. Kissinger).

Little, Brown and Company and Henry A. Kissinger for the extracts from Henry Kissinger's *White House Years* (Copyright © 1979 by Henry A. Kissinger).

Det Norske Nobelinstitut (The Norwegian Nobel Institut) for permission to use two quotes from the Nobel Lecture given by Willy Brandt in 1971.

Every effort has been made to trace all the copyright-holders, but if any have been inadvertently overlooked the publishers will be pleased to make the necessary arrangements at the first opportunity.

Glossary

ABM	Anti-ballistic Missile
COCOM	Coordinating Committee on Export Controls (NATO)
CSCE	Conference on Security and Cooperation in Europe
DEFCON	Defense Condition (states of alert of US nuclear forces)
DPRC	Defense Programme Review Committee
EEC	European Economic Community
EDIP	European Defense Improvement Programme
EFTA	European Free Trade Association
FBS	Forward Based Systems
FRG	Federal Republic of Germany
GDR	German Democratic Republic
ICBM	Intercontinental Ballistic Missile
IRBM	Intermediate Range Ballistic Missile
MBFR	Mutual and Balanced Force Reductions
MFR	Mutual Force Reductions
MIRV	Multiple Independent Re-entry Vehicles
MLF	Multilateral Force
MRBM	Medium Range Ballistic Missile
NATO	North Atlantic Treaty Organization
NPG	Nuclear Planning Group (NATO)
NSC	National Security Council
NSSM	National Security Study Memorandum
OPEC	The Organization of Petroleum Exporting Countries
PRC	People's Republic of China
SAC	Strategic Air Command
SACEUR	Supreme Allied Commander Europe
SALT	Strategic Arms Limitations Talks
SLBM	Submarine-Launched Ballistic Missile
SIG	Senior Interdepartmental Group
WSAG	Washington Special Actions Group

1 Introduction

OVERVIEW

The Atlantic Alliance is one of the most thoroughly researched subjects in world affairs. The continuous interest in the Alliance is generated by factors such as: (a) the perception that the Alliance has helped to keep the peace in the postwar period; (b) the recurrence of the insoluble problems that have plagued the Alliance since the early 1960s – strategic doctrine, control of nuclear weapons, West European unity, and the problem of Germany; and (c) the hope that changes in administrations on both sides of the Atlantic (and particularly in Washington) would help to resolve these problems. Most 1960s' studies of the Alliance concluded that major causes of intra-Alliance conflict were President de Gaulle's policies and intransigence. The 1970s' studies claimed that the causes were Henry Kissinger's policies and imperious diplomatic style.

Kissinger contributed to the voluminous research on the subject through his writings during the 1950s and 1960s which were devoted to the Atlantic Alliance and Western Europe. Yet Kissinger rejected the prevailing view that de Gaulle was the cause of the bitter controversy between the US and Western Europe. He criticized American policies toward the Allies and underlined the false premises on which these policies were based. Kissinger concluded that structural constraints and the nature of the issues to be resolved imposed limits on statesmen, therefore making the solution of the beleaguering problems of the Alliance unlikely in the foreseeable future regardless of who governed in Paris or in Washington. In *The Troubled Partnership*, published four years before his appointment as Assistant to the President for National Security Affairs, Kissinger considered the forging of a common Atlantic policy with Western Europe as one of the most urgent tasks confronting American foreign policy.[1] In his view the 'American policy [had] suffered from an unwillingness to recognize that there is a price to be paid,[2] if the dilemmas confronting NATO were to be resolved. Hence, it was not at all surprising that many on both sides of the Atlantic (and especially in Western Europe) saw Kissinger's appointment as a manifestation of the new Administration's commitment to resolve

1

some of the dilemmas that were threatening the cohesion of the Alliance.

During the first Nixon Administration Kissinger paid little attention to the Allies (and even less to Japan). His diplomatic energies were devoted to US–Soviet detente, US–PRC rapprochement, and the Vietnam War. The US–West European relationship, which had been the major focus of Kissinger's academic writings, had virtually disappeared from his range of vision. By 1973, it was quite clear that America's main military alliance was in serious disrepair; the relationship with Western Europe was drifting from respect and friendship into mutual resentment and hostility. Many Americans and West Europeans blamed this deterioration on Kissinger's global strategy, lofty attitude, and imperious diplomatic style, accusing him of placing the interests of US–Soviet detente, and US–PRC rapprochement before the interests of the Alliance, which he did. The critics maintained that the spectacular breakthroughs with the PRC and the USSR were based on an unsound view of geopolitics, and were achieved only by weakening the more durable alliances with Western Europe (and Japan).[3]

Kissinger, like de Gaulle, is a controversial world statesman. The controversy that surrounds him stems from factors such as his conceptions of war, peace and the contemporary international system on which his policies were based; the policies he conceived and implemented; his secretive negotiating style; and his relationship with the US foreign policy bureaucracy, the Congress, and the media. Kissinger's official policymaking role ended in 1977, but his impact on American foreign policy continues, and in turn the controversy that surrounds him. This study examines the US–West European relationship between 1969 and 1973 because this was a time of fundamental change in American diplomacy. American policies toward the Allies during this period – and in particular Kissinger's handling of these policies – generated the misperception that Kissinger was responsible for the disruption of the relationship. This misperception contributed to the controversy that surrounds him.

The examination of de Gaulle's role within the Alliance in the 1960s led Kissinger to conclude that 'no one man could have disrupted the Alliance by himself'.[4] Those who have examined Kissinger's foreign policies never asked whether Kissinger disrupted the Alliance by himself. They simply implied and/or claimed that he did, even though the question was posed: who was the principal architect of America's global strategy, Nixon or Kissinger?[5]

NIXON AND KISSINGER: A 'SPECIAL RELATIONSHIP'?

The question of who the architect of American foreign policy was in the Nixon Administrations has not been answered, and it seems unlikely that it will be answered unequivocally. A brief survey of the Nixon–Kissinger relationship manifests that their foreign policy views were highly compatible, as were their basic conceptions of the style in which foreign policy should be formulated and implemented.[6]

Kissinger acknowledged that his major foreign policy achievements from 1969 to 1973 were inextricably linked to President Nixon. In his words,

> I . . . am not at all sure I could have done what I've done with him with another president. Such a special relationship, I mean the relationship between the President and me, always depends on the style of both men . . . Really, some things depend on the type of president. What I've done was achieved because he made it possible for me to do it.[7]

President Nixon also admitted many times that much of his foreign policy success depended heavily on Kissinger.[8]

Sorting out the credit or debit is not the real issue in this study. The matter that will be addressed in this section is the Nixon–Kissinger 'special relationship' that made possible some fundamental changes in American foreign policy. This analysis will focus on some of the policy and style concerns of the two men, and on the decisionmaking structure in which these concerns were reflected.

Until his first meeting with the President-elect on 25 November 1968, Kissinger shared the prevailing view in the Council on Foreign Relations, and in the minds of many intellectuals, that Nixon was 'shallow, power-mad, unscrupulous, so compulsively anti-Communist that he would lead the United States into nuclear confrontations with Moscow and Peking'.[9] To his anti-Nixon friends Kissinger would say, 'Nixon is not fit to be president'.[10]

In *A World Restored*, Kissinger equated institutionalized diplomacy with bureaucratic statesmanship, something he deplored. He was convinced that a large bureaucracy, however organized, tends to stifle creativity because 'the spirit of policy and that of bureaucracy are diametrically opposed. The essence of policy is its contingency . . . the essence of bureaucracy is its quest for safety . . . Profound policy thrives on perpetual creation . . . Good administration thrives on routine . . . The attempt to bureaucratically conduct policy leads to a quest for calculability which tends to become a prisoner of events'.[11] Kissinger was determined to free American foreign policy 'from its violent historical fluctuations between euphoria and panic, from the illusion that decisions depended largely on the idiosyncrasies of decision-makers. Policy had to be related to some basic principles of national interest that transcended any particular Administration and would therefore be maintained as presidents changed'.[12] President Nixon shared Kissinger's dislike for the bureaucracy, although for different reasons, and was determined to run foreign policy from the White House.[13]

Kissinger's views on foreign policy were highly compatible with those of the President. In his memoirs President Nixon states that both 'shared a belief in the importance of isolating and influencing the factors affecting worldwide balances of power ... [and] agreed that whatever else a foreign policy might be, it must be strong to be credible – and it must be credible to be successful'.[14] In addition, both had a penchant for secrecy; their basic conceptions of the 'style' in which foreign policy should be formulated and implemented were thus similar, thereby strengthening their relationship. But there were differences, and as the President wrote, 'the combination was unlikely – the grocer's son from Whittier and the refugee from Hitler's Germany, the politician and the academic. But our difference helped make the partnership work'.[15]

The mechanism through which Kissinger exercised his control over foreign policy was the National Security Council (NSC). The NSC, as envisioned by the President and organized by Kissinger, cut deeply into the jurisdictions of the Departments of State and Defense – the traditional foreign policymakers – and both challenged Kissinger. Kissinger consistently maintained that it was President Nixon, not he, who made the decisions. 'There is no "Kissinger policy" on questions of substance', he said. 'My task is to convey the full range of policy options to the President'.[16] Subsequent developments, however, brought into question Kissinger's claim.[17]

Kissinger and President Nixon agreed that the purpose of the NSC was to coordinate foreign and defence policy, and to develop policy options for President Nixon to consider before making decisions. The focus of the NSC should be on long-term planning since Kissinger wanted to avoid involvement in short-term crises generated by specific events. But this plan was quickly abandoned, and Kissinger became involved in every crisis.

To dominate the NSC system, Kissinger chaired every key inter-agency committee: the Senior Review Group, the Forty Committee, the Defense Program Review Committee, the Intelligence Commit-tee, the Washington Special Actions Group (WSAG), the Verifica-tion Panel, and the Vietnam Special Studies Group. Few (if any) foreign policy decisions could be made without going through Kissinger's elaborate system. Hence, since Kissinger controlled the NSC system, he controlled the decisionmaking process.

The foreign policy decisionmaking process began with a National Security Study Memorandum (NSSM) on a wide range of specific long-range policy issues. Wanting to avoid a 'bureaucratic policy proposal', which Kissinger defined as 'the present policy bracketed by two absurd alternatives',[18] he asked each agency to respond separately. Kissinger's staff would summarize the options presented by the agencies and then present them to the Senior Review Group. The Group's responsibility was to ensure that all realistic options were presented to the President. But unless chairman Kissinger considered an option realistic – a word he defined in different ways depending on the circumstances – it would never reach the President. The 'realistic' options were formally submitted to Presi-dent Nixon (and the other statutory members of the NSC) with Kissinger presenting the various options. Thus, though the President made the final decision, it was only on the basis of the options presented to him by Kissinger, and in terms of the way Kissinger presented them.

Once a decision was made by President Nixon, it would be handed down to Kissinger, who relayed it to the Under-Secretaries Commit-tee which implemented the decision. However at the President's request, to avoid endless confrontations with the bureaucracy, many times Kissinger dealt with key foreign leaders through 'backchan-nels', thus disassociating himself from the foreign policy ventures of the Departments of State and Defense.[19]

The preceding discussion suggests that given the compatibility of the personalities and policy concerns of the two men, Kissinger's greatest diplomatic feat was not to get the President's trust but 'to survive the bureaucratic struggle in the White House without being irretrievably knifed'.[20] Kissinger admits that 'until the end of 1970 I was influential but not dominant. From then on, my role increased as Nixon sought to bypass the delays and sometimes opposition of the departments' and 'tactical decisions were increasingly taken outside the system in personal conversations with the President'.[21]

Persistent efforts have been made to distinguish between policies that were assumed to be Kissinger's and those that might more reasonably be attributed to President Nixon. All such theorizing, while justifiable, has not contributed anything to resolving the one question that ought to have been asked: Was foreign policy under President Nixon shaped by concepts and influenced by operational procedures that had some significant resemblance to what Kissinger had advocated in his academic writings?[22]

HYPOTHESIS AND ANCILLARY PROPOSITIONS

This study explores the hypothesis that Kissinger's West European policies were consistent with conceptions advanced in his academic writings.[23] It will be argued that mutual resentment and hostility within the Alliance in the early 1970s were not generated by Kissinger's global strategy, lofty attitude or imperious and secretive diplomatic style, but by the misinterpretation and/or disregard of his writings, and the exaggerated expectations this created on both sides of the Atlantic when he was appointed Assistant to the President for National Security Affairs. A more thorough knowledge of Kissinger's writings might have made it easier for others to anticipate many of his policies, making it possible for them to look somewhat more critically at the 'spectacular achievements and failures' he produced.

While serving as Assistant for National Security Affairs, the fact that Kissinger did not really systematically explain the overall conceptual design of the Administration's foreign policy contributed to the misunderstanding (or disregard) of his views. Political observers and the public were largely left to infer Kissinger's concepts of international relations from the short statements made during press briefings and background sessions with selected media members and congressional leaders, and from the annual Presidential Reports to Congress on Foreign Policy. Although they were prepared by him, their official and standardized format could not fully convey Kissinger's conceptions. The paucity of policy statements by Kissinger during the 1969–73 period accounts for much of the confusion in attempts to interpret Kissinger's intentions.[24]

In the case of Kissinger, neither private correspondence nor classified documents needed to be consulted by those who wanted to know what he thought about American foreign policy. His writings provide a running commentary on the foreign policy achievements and failures of three Administrations – Truman's, Eisenhower's, and Kennedy's – and all are public record. Kissinger did not simply write to set the record straight; his goal was to influence policy. Those who examined Kissinger's work focused primarily on his views about three nineteenth-century statesmen (Metternich, Castlereagh and Bismarck) and concluded that he was their disciple, perhaps even an heir. The fact that Kissinger expressed serious reservations about the policies of these statesmen was ignored. The failure closely to examine Kissinger's writings on American foreign policy contributed to the perpetuation of the view that foreign policy is dependent on the will of individual leaders, a view that Kissinger did not share. He knew how much an individual statesman could (and must) do, but – more importantly – Kissinger constantly stressed what a statesman could not do given the structural constraints of the contemporary international system and the nature of the issues to be resolved.[25]

The intensity and frequency with which Kissinger invoked the notion of limits and struggled with it have been ignored.[26] The reason for this neglect of the notion of limits is because Kissinger never provided a systematic analysis of it; in most studies, however, the recognition is evident that Kissinger saw nuclear weapons as a conservative force since they impose limits on statesmen and thus necessitate self-restraint. Yet none of the studies examined how the linkage of sovereignty with nuclear weapons was applied by Kissinger in his analysis of the US–Allied relationship, which led him to conclude that the structural limitations this linkage produced precluded the resolution of the dilemmas of the Alliance in the foreseeable future. Intellectually, for Kissinger, the acceptance of limits was the touchstone of his conservatism,[27] and emanated from the cool calculation of power.[28] The notion of limits was the central theme of Kissinger's political philosophy, and US–Soviet detente and US–West European relations rested on it.

A more meticulous examination of Kissinger's writings would have revealed the following propositions which influenced his policies toward Western Europe:

1. Kissinger believed that the insoluble problems of the Atlantic Alliance were caused by structural constraints and the nature of the issues to be resolved – i.e., political multipolarity and the nature of nuclear weapons – and not by President de Gaulle's intransigence which had severely strained Allied relationships.
2. Kissinger concluded that no final solution of the dilemmas of the

Alliance was possible as long as the North Atlantic Treaty
Organization (NATO) remained composed of sovereign states,
and that it was unlikely that NATO would become a single
political entity in the foreseeable future.
3. He maintained that the structural constraints and the nature of the
   issues to be resolved impose limits on statesmen, thus making the
   resolution of the dilemmas caused by political multipolarity and
   nuclear weapons unlikely. Therefore the US should try to resolve
   issues caused by acts arising from policy.
4. The establishment of a stable international system was Kissinger's
   ultimate goal since it could prevent a nuclear war.[29] Hence, his
   primary concern was the relationshp between the superpowers
   which possessed the overwhelming military capability that could
   transform the international system, or in an attempt to do so –
   each unilaterally – could destroy the world.[30]
5. Kissinger recognized that his policy toward the Soviet Union
   would lead to discord but he was convinced that it would not split
   the Alliance since in the military sphere Western Europe has more
   to gain from it than the US.[31]

These propositions suggested that Kissinger's conclusion that forging
a common Atlantic policy was the most urgent task confronting
American foreign policy, and the recognition that 'there is a price to
be paid', did not necessarily indicate that he would have devoted his
energies to forge such a policy. This conclusion is self-evident. Why
would Kissinger devote his energies to the dilemmas of NATO when
he never failed to stress that the real issues of the Alliance could not
be resolved in the foreseeable future?

In the late 1960s Kissinger believed a better chance existed for the
establishment of a stable international system, his ultimate goal.[32] In
an attempt to achieve this goal, Kissinger was prepared to subordinate the long-standing relationship with the Allies to America's
strategic interest in preserving its global position. In *Nuclear
Weapons and Foreign Policy*, Kissinger had argued that the highest
obligation was not the Alliance or the preservation of Western values
but American security interests, and ultimately national survival. In
his words:

> We should never give up our principles nor ask other nations to
> surrender theirs. But we must also realize that neither we nor our
> allies nor the uncommitted can realize any principles unless we
> survive. We cannot permit the balance of power to be overturned

for the sake of allied unity or the approbation of the uncommitted
... We must beware not to subordinate the requirements of the
over-all strategic balance to our policy of alliances or our effort to
win over the uncommitted.[33]

The cohesion of the Alliance was an essential prerequisite to
Kissinger's global strategy. Kissinger seemed convinced however,
that damage to US–West European relationship by US–Soviet
detente could be controlled since Western Europe has more to gain
from NATO than the US.

The concern here is the linkage of separate policy areas – i.e.,
Kissinger's Soviet policy and Alliance policy – and their linkage with
the conceptions Kissinger advanced in his writings. It is the
elucidation of these linkage relationships that represents the main
contribution of the present study. Specifically, what this study aspires
to do is to explain the linkage between Kissinger's conceptions and
his policies toward the Allies. The attempt is to demonstrate that the
primary motivations guiding Kissinger's policies toward the Allies
can be traced to the views he advanced in his writings about the
Alliance and Western Europe. American policy toward the Allies
had been an important (if not the major) focus of Kissinger's writings
in the 1950s and 1960s. Yet few studies have examined in depth the
linkage between the conclusions he drew in those studies and his
policies toward Western Europe.

Realistically, no analysis of the motivational background of any
policy can ignore the essentially multicausative nature of political
actions. This study is not asserting that Kissinger's academic
conceptions constituted the only factors determining the policies he
pursued. Influences from other sources are not ignored. In the
chapters that follow, every effort is made to highlight those other
determinants of American foreign policy which, apart from Kissinger's conceptions, influenced the course of his policies. In the final
analysis the focus of this study is the linkage between Kissinger's
conceptions and his policies, more specifically the linkage between
his perception of the contemporary international system and his
policies toward Western Europe. In this way, a more comprehensive
understanding than has yet been attempted of Kissinger's policies
toward the Allies during this period will be established.

The principal concern is with conceptions which guided Kissinger's
policies. The interest is the 'why' of policy decisions rather than the
how. This is not a study of the decisionmaking process, nor is it

particularly concerned with uncovering the rivalries in the Nixon
Administrations. Elements of the decisionmaking process and the
bureaucratic struggles are unavoidable in any comprehensive treatment of foreign policy decisionmaking (especially during this period),
and they should not be ignored. The main thrust of the analysis,
however, is to establish a broader understanding of the linkage
between Kissinger's conceptions and his policy toward the Allies. By
carefully examining Kissinger's academic works, his policy statements, and memoirs while in office, and other participants' policy
statements and memoirs, and by focusing on the context in which the
policies were formulated and implemented, this study will show that
Kissinger's policies toward the Allies were consistent with the views
he advanced in his academic writings.

KISSINGER IN PERSPECTIVE

It has to be pointed out from the outset that this review by no means
pretends to be exhaustive. Only those studies which deal directly with
Kissinger and/or his policies toward Western Europe, have been
singled out for review. The scope of the following survey is, however,
broad enough to include the most important works pertinent to this
study; it should also be added that nearly all of the works to be
considered here have been of enormous value in shaping it. Hence,
their generally outstanding merit is not diminished by pointing out
their deviation from the approach adopted here.

In some form or other most studies about Kissinger examine the
linkage between the concepts advanced in his writings and his
policies. In this sense, the approach of this study is similar to ones
adopted there. Few of those studies however, examined in depth (if
at all) the linkage between Kissinger's conceptions and/or his
critiques of the preceding Administrations' policies toward the Allies,
and his West European policies, although most of his writings during
the 1950s and 1960s were devoted to Western Europe and to NATO.

In *Kissinger: Portrait of a Mind*, historian Stephen R. Graubard
argues that most Kissinger experts have focused on what Kissinger
did *after* he joined the Nixon Administration, and gave little attention
to what he proposed before 1969. Graubard is especially critical of
those in the media who presented Kissinger's ideas, feeling they did it
in an inaccurate fashion. In his view this was unjustified since all of
Kissinger's writings are part of public record. Graubard's study is

based on the simple proposition that there is a link between what Kissinger wrote in the 1950s and 1960s and what he did upon joining the Nixon Administration. Graubard concludes his exhaustive review of Kissinger's writings by stating, 'the evidence is irrefutable: the foreign policy strategies and statements of the Nixon administration replicate or approximate procedures and policies recommended by Kissinger in all his published writings'.[34] This study is based on the same proposition. But unlike this study, Graubard does not examine Kissinger's policies; he does not present the reader with the irrefutable evidence.

In his biographical study *Kissinger and the Meaning of History*, political analyst Peter W. Dickson examines the linkage between Kissinger's philosophical perspective on history and his role in the formulation and execution of American foreign policy. Dickson challenges the prevalent beliefs about the origins and the nature of Kissinger's world view. He argues that Metternich was not a model statesman for Kissinger, and disagrees with those who try to associate Kissinger with either Clausewitz or Spengler. Dickson maintains that Immanuel Kant (whose political and ethical writings were the focus of Kissinger's undergraduate thesis, *The Meaning of History*) was most influential in shaping Kissinger's perspective on history and politics.

The central theme of Dickson's study is Kissinger's identification with the philosophical form of Protestanism, especially the Protestant notion of 'spiritual inwardness' which pervades Kant's writings on ethics. This sets the stage for an analysis of Kissinger's political philosophy and an evaluation of his foreign policy. The basic question Dickson attempts to answer is: Why, given this cultural orientation, did Kissinger identify with Bismarck and adopt *Realpolitik* as a guide to policy?

Dickson discovers a linkage between Kant's philosophy of history and Kissinger's policy toward the USSR. In his view, Kissinger believed in the relevance of Kant's political philosophy for the nuclear age. The most significant aspect of Kissinger's reflections on the need to establish a stable international system is the fact that his emphasis on the need for mankind to recognize the 'inherent limitations' concerning the use of nuclear weapons is linked to Kant's concept of 'unsocial sociability'.[35] Kissinger, like Kant, believes that history is not totally chaotic. There is a certain degree of order which reflects two basic realities: (a) the cool calculation of power which reveals to men the inherent 'limits' or finite nature of power; and (b) that in any historical period there is a certain pattern or 'structure' to international relations. The notion there is a limit and structure to power, according to Dickson, gave Kissinger an intellectual framework that enabled him to deal rationally with the inherently formless and irrational process called history.[36] Kissinger used these two fundamental concepts to give coherence to American foreign policy.

The doctrine of limits in Dickson's view is 'the central theme of Kissinger's political philosophy', and US–Soviet detente rested on it. Kissinger maintained that the recognition of the limits of power is in a fundamental sense a moral act, but he never provided a systematic presentation of his doctrine of limits. It was this doctrine, Dickson argues, that accounts for Kissinger's high estimation of Bismarck, who 'believed that a correct evaluation of power would yield a doctrine of self-limitation'.[37]

Dickson concludes that Kissinger's policies do conform closely to his political philosophy of moderation. The harmony between theory and practice, he argues, would have been complete only if it had included the articulation of policy. Dickson maintains that criticism by Brzezinski and others, stating that Kissinger was an acrobat rather than an architect, is unjust because, as Secretary of State, Kissinger made strenuous efforts to educate the public about the thrust and objectives of his policies. Dickson also claims that when Kissinger's policy records are taken as a whole his accomplishments seem to far outweigh his mistakes. According to Dickson, Kissinger was seen as a failure because his egotistical personality and authoritarian style undermined his public credibility, and in turn, his aspiration to be an educator.[38]

Psycho-historian Bruce Mazlish in his study *Kissinger: The European Mind in American Policy*, attempts to describe and analyse the basic elements of Kissinger's personality, behaviour patterns, and his world view. The approach is interpretive. To achieve his objective Mazlish goes back to Kissinger's early years in Germany and traces how Kissinger came to terms with his experience in pre-Nazi and Nazi Germany, and how he entered into the mainstream of American life through the Army, Harvard, and the foreign policy establishment. What Mazlish finds atypical is that Kissinger's Americanization took place primarily through his military experience in the Second World War, and that Kissinger developed a 'conservative worldview', which intrinsically requires activism irrespective of the given historical period.

In analysing Kissinger's 'conservative worldview' Mazlish focuses on what he calls Kissinger's 'compulsive' attention to such themes as holocaust, tragedy, limits, goodwill, and will. Kissinger's working style, negotiating skills, his understanding of the meaning of power, and the Kissinger–Nixon 'special relationship' are all examined. Mazlish concludes by stating that 'I "know" Kissinger better now than does any single friend of his or person whom I interviewed, and perhaps better than Kissinger knows himself'. He argues if Kissinger contributed to the 'Europeanization' of American foreign policy, it is only because Kissinger himself was Americanized. In short, Kissinger's major characteristic is his ability to change and grow.[39]

Mazlish, like Dickson, finds it important to examine Kissinger's notion of 'limits'. According to Mazlish, 'Kissinger was, and is, obsessed with the notion of "limits"', which 'manifests itself most succinctly in Kissinger's basic conservative interpretation of history'. What is special in Kissinger's notion of 'limits' is the intensity and frequency with which he invokes the term and wrestles with the problem. For Kissinger, nuclear weapons impose limits on statesmen, therefore nuclear weapons are a conservative force and statesmen are under the necessity of self-restraint. Mazlish maintained, 'intellectually, acceptance of limits became for Kissinger the touchstone of his conservatism'. But he points out that Kissinger preached an 'active recognition of limits'. Hence neither Bismarck nor Metternich, taken alone, can be said to have served as Kissinger's historical model. It was necessary to fuse the limiting spirit of the one and the will of the other to make the right combination.[40]

The examination of the linkage between Kissinger's personality, concepts, and policies manifests that Kissinger's desired purpose for the power he secured was to help establish a stable international order and definitely not to achieve revolutionary aims. The policies Mazlish examines are those concerning SALT, the Soviet Union, the PRC, and the Middle East. He does not examine Kissinger's policies toward Western Europe which are the focus of this study. Mazlish concludes that 'there is no question that [Kissinger] has a coherent, consistent concept behind his various policies; the difficulty is in locating it in summarized form'. Mazlish maintains, however, there is a definite gap between what Kissinger-the-academic wrote and what Kissinger-the-policymaker did, though he acknowledges that while most of Kissinger's writings were on Europe, most of his policies were on non-European areas.[41]

Kissinger's personal traits, according to Mazlish, play an extremely important role in the formulation and execution of his policies. But these underlying traits must be seen as subordinate to his intellectualization. Finally, Mazlish finds Kissinger's long-range historical and strategic understanding has been faulty. It has been flawed by a conservative world view. On the short range (and on a tactical level), Kissinger's skills are excellent.

Warren G. Nutter's study, *Kissinger's Grand Design*, is an attempt to answer the question: Is there a grand design to Kissinger's foreign policy? Nutter briefly examined Kissinger's outlook as a scholar and his outlook as a policymaker, and he provided an extensive appendix of excerpts from Kissinger's writings on the issues examined to support his critique.

The examination of Kissinger's scholarly outlook focuses on his concepts of peace, power, stable world order and revolutionary power, and his views on the issues of Atlantic unity, European unity, the German problem, arms control, limited war, and diplomacy. Nutter's analysis indicates the vision of Kissinger-the-scholar was one of the West in decline. It also reveals that Kissinger, far from believing in historical determinism, conceived a critical role for human will and imagination in shaping the course of events within the constraints set by the contemporary international system. For Kissinger the embodiment of human will and imagination was the statesman who could mould order out of seeming chaos.[42]

Nutter's examination of Kissinger's outlook as a policymaker focuses on documents issued since the Fall of 1973 when Kissinger became Secretary of State. Nutter notes that at that time a noticeable change occurred in the tone and content of Kissinger's public statements. This examination, indicates Nutter, argues that some profound changes took place in Kissinger's conceptual framework, changes embodied in the policy of detente. Kissinger-the-policymaker implicitly renounced his earlier conviction that only the use of power could check Soviet expansion, and that detente would only demoralize the West and through default lead to Soviet hegemony. As a policymaker, Kissinger viewed detente as an imperative, whereas Kissinger-the-scholar had stressed that diplomacy (and especially summitry) played only a symbolic role in the revolutionary age, Kissinger-the-policymaker argued that negotiations with the Soviets would result in great substantive agreements. The only consistency Nutter finds is Kissinger's insistence on strong conventional forces to defend Western Europe, and his position that the internal transformation of the USSR, if it takes place, would be the result of a slow evolutionary process essentially beyond the influence of outside pressure. Kissinger opposed the Mansfield resolutions and did not demand the liberalization of Soviet emigration as a precondition for improved economic relations. For Nutter the most severe critic of Secretary Kissinger would be Kissinger-the-scholar.

Nutter concludes 'there [was] a grand design to Kissinger's detente', but argues that 'fault can be found with the very conceptual foundation of Kissinger's grand design: his paradigm of a stable world order'. In Nutter's view, the missing element from Kissinger's paradigm is 'the ethic of a peaceful order' which involves more than agreement on the rules of international conduct. He accuses Kissinger of never facing the issue of how agreement is to be reached, and at what cost in terms of other values. Nutter explains that Kissinger never faced the issue because he feared being cast as an ideologue if he revealed his vision of the good society by spelling out the ethical substance he attributes to it.[43]

The West has been resisting Soviet expansion, according to Nutter, not just to preserve the legitimacy of the international system, but to save Western civilization which is threatened by the USSR. The dilemma is how to find a strategy that preserves Western civilization while avoiding catastrophic war. He argues that 'Kissinger's grand design, by ignoring this moral dilemma, cannot provide a relevant solution to the problem'.[44] In my view his conclusion stems from the fact that Nutter's ultimate goal is the preservation of Western civilization, while Kissinger's ultimate goal is survival because Kissinger stated that no principles can be realized unless we survive. Nutter is very critical of Kissinger's grand design, equating it with detente, because it swayed Western psychology toward downgrading the Soviet threat, cutting defence budgets, and disrupting alliances. The result was a further tipping of the balance of power in favour of the USSR. He claims that Kissinger weakened his grand design by posing choices in terms of mutually exclusive alternatives – i.e., either negotiation or confrontation, either detente or disaster, or either status-quo power or revolutionary power. On this point I would argue that Nutter is mistaken because Kissinger, while negotiating with the Soviets, used power to stop their expansion.

Richard A. Falk's study, *What's Wrong with Henry Kissinger's Foreign Policy*, criticizes the performance of the state system in the latter part of the twentieth century by examining the conceptions and policies of Kissinger because, in his view, Kissinger embodies the strengths and weakness of the existing international system. Falk claims he is 'not out to shatter [the] Kissinger myth'.[45] But in the process of outlining what he is not going to emphasize, he points out the weakness of Kissinger's personality and policies. One of the topics Falk does not examine is what he calls the weakening of the more durable alliances with Western Europe and Japan, the focus of this study.

Falk's main criticism is that Kissinger's foreign policy, despite its success in moderating tensions among the superpowers and settling dangerous international conflicts, 'does not sufficiently address the central task of our time – namely, the need to evolve a new system of world order based on principles of peace and justice'.[46] The topic is Kissinger's foreign policy but Falk credits Nixon with the opening to the PRC and US–Soviet detente. He argues that Nixon and Kissinger had a similar view of the state system but that Kissinger did not always agree with Nixon's tactical judgements. In Falk's view, 'Kissinger's diplomatic flair has probably added a measure, perhaps a decisive measure, of effectiveness to what Nixon might have achieved with "ordinary" as distinct from "exemplary" execution of policies'.[47]

The examination of Kissinger's academic writings indicates, Falk argues, that Kissinger believes that there is no place for morality in foreign policy beyond the overarching morality of securing stability – i.e., Kissinger's main concern. It also indicates that in Kissinger's view the threat to international stability comes from the USSR, and that this threat can be met only by military strength and determination to fight throughout the world where and when it is necessary rather than dependence on deterrence alone. Kissinger did not believe that the Soviet challenge would be eliminated by internal evolution of the Soviet system. But he was convinced that, due to the mutual fear of an all-out nuclear war, the prospects for stability would be improved if the West gained in purpose and cohesion, and negotiated with the Soviets to reduce the arms race.

According to Falk, Kissinger's analysis shifted in emphasis from the revolutionary actor to the revolutionary situation. Kissinger saw the contemporary international system as revolutionary due to the spread of Communism, the emergence of new nations, and the proliferation of nuclear weapons.[48] Nevertheless, Kissinger never intended his admiration for Metternich to be understood as tantamount to proposing Metternichian solutions for comparable contemporary problems. He knew many of the elements of stability which characterized the international system in the nineteenth century could not be recreated today. According to Falk, what Kissinger admired was Metternich's understanding of the revolutionary character of the Napoleonic challenge, not Metternich.

Falk argued that 'the Nixon–Kissinger "structure of peace" [was] based on the conviction that no substantial revolutionary threat is at work in world affairs.'[49] Hence, international disputes could be settled by negotiations among the great powers, especially if they did not threaten each other's spheres of influence. This structure did not promise to eliminate violence from international relations, especially not in the marginal sectors of the world (i.e., the entire Third World). Kissinger's success resulted from his understanding and acceptance of the logic of the state. He accepted balance of power mechanisms and political pluralism, and he was willing to use diplomacy if possible but force, if necessary, to settle international conflicts. Falk claimed, despite his protestations, that Kissinger belonged to the Machiavellian tradition of statesman. Therefore, Kissinger's influence cannot be understood by reference to some new set of ideas about the means or goals of foreign policy.

In Falk's view, Kissinger had a coherent view of the state system which permitted policymakers to pursue their interests without fear of moral encumbrance or judgement. Falk argued that Kissinger's approach to international relations resembled his predecessors', but that it was less ideological in two respects. First, Kissinger had been more willing to regard the cold war as a phase rather than a condition in international affairs. And, secondly, Kissinger's indifference to domestic conditions in foreign societies permitted him to forego judgements about the indecencies or inequities of other national systems, as long as repressive governments renounced their revolutionary aims. In short, part of Kissinger's success resulted from his very unconcern with human rights and from the extent to which this unconcern was a shared premise of mainstream statecraft. Kissinger's Machiavellian posture was a welcomed relief to foreign statesmen who had developed a distaste for (and suspicion of) the self-righteous pretensions of American diplomacy.

Falk maintained that Kissinger was effective wherever the game of nations was pursued without ideological or moral imperatives. But he was ineffective elsewhere, especially in relation to overcoming the more extreme patterns of injustice in the Third World or nations in which the American influence was strong. According to Falk, Kissinger was not alone among the world leaders in ignoring injustices in many countries, but 'he [was] part of a conspiracy of silence that [was] directed by the rich and powerful with regard to the deprivations of the poor'. Nevertheless, Falk criticized Kissinger because he not only remained silent about the abuses but supported the covert and indirect moves of American diplomacy used to maintain or create such injustices. Falk attributed Kissinger's behaviour to the hegemonial dimension of the state system, and saw it as important evidence for our appraisal of the system's adequacy to meet human needs. Kissinger's outlook presupposes that it is possible to manage international relations mainly by moderating conflictual relations among governments in the Northern Hemisphere. This conviction, Falk claimed, is the underlying conceptual flaw in Kissinger's approach to global reform, and argued that without an ethic of global concern, the attempt to merely smooth out relations among great powers is a recipe for disaster.

In *Uncertain Greatness*, Roger Morris presented Kissinger's formidable intellectual powers, bureaucratic shrewdness, consummate political skills, and his historic relationship with President Nixon. The elements that made the Nixon–Kissinger relationship special were examined – i.e., their cynicism, their contempt toward the establishment and the foreign policy bureaucracy, their need for secrecy, their insistence on controlling foreign policy from the White House, and their 'intolerance, almost contempt, for democracy'.[50] Morris discussed the establishment of the NSC and the personalities of the individuals in it, as well as the relationship of these individuals with Kissinger. He also analysed the functions of the NSC by examining some of the policies that passed through it. Morris's brief examination of US policies toward Japan, Biafra, the racial conflict in southern Africa, chemical–biological weapons, the PRC and the USSR, manifests why the NSC system failed.

Morris offered insightful yet critical accounts of Kissinger's diplomacy in the final stages of the Vietnam war, his role in the Yom Kippur war, his shuttle diplomacy in the Middle East, and his role in the policy debacles in Bangladesh, Chile, Burundi, Cyprus, Angola, and the Mayaguez episode. The claim was that these policy debacles resulted not only from Kissinger's unchallenged biases and control of the policymaking process, but also from the quiet acquiescence of so many junior men in the State Department. Morris argued that Kissinger succeeded in becoming the sole executor of US foreign policy – a 'de facto President of the United States' – due to the weaknesses of the people he faced, and his ability to seduce, manipulate, and dominate Congress and the Press, both by technique and by doing (at least on the surface) so much of what both institutions conventionally wanted of American foreign policy. According to Morris, Congress and the Press should share the blame for the failure of US foreign policy.

Morris claimed that the criticisms which pounded Kissinger because of detente – most notable, on the Soviet wheat deal of 1972–3 and on human rights in the USSR – were shallow and twisted. Detente was not the cause of the disarray of the domestic food market and the skyrocketing grocery prices. Advocacy by the Department of Agriculture for high prices, bureaucratic inertia, and the actions of the huge American grain companies precipitated those same disastrous consequences as the imagined Soviet grain conspiracy of 1972. Morris felt that the debate over human rights in the USSR exposed the ignorance or acquiesence of the critics who remained silent when Kissinger and Nixon overlooked the genocide in Burundi, the ethnic slaughters in Iraq, Ethiopia, and Uganda, torture in Chile, Indonesia and South Vietnam, and several other cases. Morris maintained that the visible strains caused by detente lay not in the principle of negotiations or the relaxation of tensions but deep in the structure of American foreign policy. The fault lay with uncontrolled, unreformed institutions in American society – i.e., the military–industrial complex with its interest in large defence budgets, public fear and apathy, ignorant, cowed politicians, the cartel of corporate giants which ran the domestic food market with government complicity, and the foreign policy bureaucracies whose status and survival (and isolation from democracy) bred a cynical disregard of ideals and human rights in international relations. In Morris's view, 'Nixon and Kissinger had simply manipulated that system; they were part of it'.[51]

Morris concluded that 'the most telling criticism of Kissinger's achievement will not be that it was often inhumane and devious, but rather that it was too largely irrelevant'.[52] Kissinger's strategy and diplomacy was able to settle the more traditional disputes between nations, but it had little capacity to affect the crises embedded within nations, nor to solve the undiplomatic crises of resource scarcities, and technological and cultural change. Morris asserted that 'Kissinger's dictatorship in foreign policy has been cruel, repressive and wasteful'.[53] Yet Morris seemed convinced that Kissinger's achievements in Peking and Moscow would endure, and would likely be continued and expanded by the next administration.

In *Kissinger: The Uses of Power*, David Landau attempted to expose the shortcomings of Kissinger's worldview and of the Nixon–Kissinger policy by examining US policy in Vietnam during the first Nixon term. Landau viewed Vietnam as 'the core and essence of Kissinger's approach to foreign, policy',[54] and argued that it was in his handling of policy toward Vietnam that Kissinger's view of global stability may best be grasped. But before exposing the shortcomings of Kissinger's worldview, Landau examined its development, and the evolution of the concepts on which it was based. He also examined Kissinger's relationship with the men who influenced his views and promoted his pre-White House career, as well as his relationship with Nixon, and the outlines of the policy they formulated and implemented.

Landau's examination of Kissinger's worldview revealed that the central issue in Kissinger's political life had been the establishment of a stable international order. This issue underlies all of Kissinger's policies. Landau emphasized Kissinger's belief that international stability was possible only if individual nations conducted their relations on strictly non-ideological grounds. Kissinger, he argued, did not see Washington's legitimate goal as the export of Western-style democracy or a capitalist economy to all corners of the globe. This intellectual restraint, according to Landau, sets Kissinger apart from all other American policymakers of our time. Kissinger's opposition to wars of national liberation did not spring from a desire to suppress movements for national independence, but from an intractable fear that if such wars appear to succeed, other greater powers with less noble intentions would be spurred toward ideological quests. Kissinger's belief in diplomacy as the primary instrument of international relations, his desire to maintain total and constant global credibility, and his opposition to bureaucratic involvement in foreign policy were stressed by Landau. But Landau asserted that the most dangerous flaw in Kissinger's line of thinking was his belief that domestic opinion should pose no obstacles to the conduct of foreign policy. In his analysis of US policy in Vietnam, Landau attempted to show that Kissinger's intellectual biases inhibited an early settlement of the war.

The examination of the Nixon–Kissinger policy, which Landau many times called the Kissinger policy, indicated the policy had 'an exquisite internal harmony, a self-contained consistency in it that [bore] the unmistakable stamp of its creator [Kissinger]'.[55] Landau maintained that the policy derived 'from assumptions which Kissinger had nurtured throughout his intellectual life'.[56] Landau, however, criticized the Kissinger policy because, despite its internal consistency, it was 'often ... at odds with the realities of the world outside it'.[57] In Landau's view, the greatest failure of the policy – the continuation of the Vietnam war – was a direct outgrowth of the obsession to be consistent, and credible. Kissinger and Nixon were credited for the fact that, unlike their predecessors, they recognized and took advantage of the conditions that permitted the development of US–PRC rapprochement and US–Soviet detente. Nevertheless, Landau criticized Kissinger for assuming that ideology had disappeared once and for all from Moscow's and Peking's approach to world affairs, and thus conducted US foreign policy on non-ideological bases.

Through exposing the shortcomings of the Nixon–Kissinger policy, Landau criticized the Nixon Doctrine and the concept of linkage, the two main elements of the policy. Nixon and Kissinger, he felt, wanted to avoid nuclear war, but the doctrine of reducing America's military presence while maintaining excessive political commitments made nuclear war more likely. The probability of nuclear war was increased by basing US policy on the concept of linkage which Landau saw as 'a policy of risk'. In his view, 'the linkage theory [was] little more than unreconstructed Cold Warriorism'.[58] Landau maintained that the linkage approach did not lead to a serious conflict because 'the Soviets showed occasional good sense' and did not adopt it, despite the fact they were sometimes 'provoked outright' to do so by Washington's actions.[59]

In the discussion of the concept of linkage Landau devoted a few pages to US policy toward Western Europe. He reported there was a disturbing tendency in the linkage approach to postulate an overall decline in US–Soviet tensions before the conclusion of any specific agreements. Therefore, if it had not been for Willy Brandt's *Ostpolitik* the German issue and the problem of Berlin would have waited for the conclusion of the more fundamental agreements on arms control and European security arrangements. Landau admitted, however, that linkage of the ratification of the German treaties to other issues was an important factor in inducing the Soviets to host President Nixon in Moscow, despite the mining of Haiphong harbour. Nevertheless, he criticized Kissinger for his obsession with manipulating allies, and for demanding that they shape all of their foreign policy actions according to Washington's judgements. In Landau's view, this simplistic approach blurred Kissinger's vision about what was possible in concrete foreign policy situations, and strained America's allied relationships as well.

In *Henry Kissinger: The Anguish of Power*, political scientist John G. Stoessinger examined Kissinger's general philosophy of foreign policy and the connection between Kissinger-the-scholar and Kissinger-the-statesman. Stoessinger's brief examination of Kissinger's philosophy revealed that the pursuit of stable international order was Kissinger's ultimate goal. Kissinger viewed peace as a necessary by-product of a stable world order and feared that, by making peace the ultimate goal, statesmen placed their nations at the mercy of ruthless revolutionaries. Hence, being a prerequisite for peace, a stable international order was the highest good. Kissinger was convinced that to assure the survival of a stable international order the use of force against the revolutionary state was necessary and justified. Stoessinger maintained Kissinger was prepared to live with injustice and order rather than justice and disorder.

The examination also indicated that Kissinger's belief in diplomacy and his willingness to use force led him to advocate the use of tactical nuclear weapons in order to resolve the dilemma created by the advent of nuclear weapons – i.e., nuclear destruction versus total paralysis. But Stoessinger pointed out that Kissinger retracted his belief in tactical nuclear war in *The Necessity for Choice*. Stoessinger argued that Kissinger's recognition of the constraints imposed on statesmen by domestic and international factors did not lead him to a submission to historical determinism, rather he insisted on the power of the individual to affect his destiny. Stoessinger concluded his examination of Kissinger's philosophy by stating 'what can be proved ... is that the intellectual convictions that Kissinger developed a quarter of a century ago survived almost unchanged and were applied by him in a conscious and deliberate effort to pursue his vision of a stable world order'.[60]

The main body of Stoessinger's study dealt with Kissinger's major foreign policy initiatives. Despite some minor criticisms of some of Kissinger's policies, the conclusion was that Kissinger had been consistent, he never wavered in his efforts to establish a stable international order. In Stoessinger's view, however, Kissinger's approach to Vietnam was flawed. Kissinger tried to transplant the lessons of Metternich and Castlereagh, believing that the right combination of diplomacy and force had yielded a negotiated settlement without victory or defeat – the Paris accords of January 1973. Kissinger failed to recognize, according to Stoessinger, that

North Vietnam was a revolutionary state as he had defined it. Unlike Kissinger, Stoessinger believed that the American credibility rose, rather than declined, with the end of the war. Nevertheless Stoessinger saw Kissinger's search for compromise as sincere.

Stoessinger viewed Kissinger's conception of US–Soviet detente as the 'synthesis of all that he had learned from his study of nineteenth century history'.[61] He pointed out that objective factors in the global power constellation (and in particular the rise of China) provided the initial impetus to detente. But 'in addition to elements of luck and timing, it was Kissinger's design and courage that made detente possible at all'.[62] Stoessinger rejected the arguments of the critics and stated that Kissinger was right when he declared the overriding reason for detente was the avoidance of nuclear war. Stoessinger added, 'I believe that if such world cataclysm has become less likely, this is in no small measure to be credited to Kissinger'.[63] Moreover Stoessinger stressed that when detente was tested in the peripheral areas, the evidence suggested that the combination of diplomacy and force worked quite successfully, particularly when combined with linkage.

Kissinger's triangular policy was based, according to Stoessinger, 'on one fundamental assumption that was absolutely essential for its success: the permanent hostility between China and the Soviet Union'.[64] By ending the Vietnam war Kissinger removed the major policy issue on which Peking and Moscow agreed. Both traditional nationalism and Communist ideology were destabilizing factors in the Sino–Soviet relationship. Kissinger believed the future pattern of Sino–Soviet relations to be a kind of Cold War. Therefore by remaining equidistant from both countries, the United States could benefit. Rapprochement with China, Stoessinger argued, became a reality due to the determined action by Kissinger and Chou En-lai and made the Soviet Union more receptive to detente.

The examination of US–West European relations dealt with the Cyprus crisis, the leftist revolution in Portugal, and the 'historic compromise' reached by the Communist parties of Italy and France in 1975. These cases are beyond the scope of the present study, but Stoessinger's conclusions are worth noting. Stoessinger stated that 'Kissinger made policy decisions with regard to Cyprus almost absentmindedly'. Kissinger was distracted by Watergate, nevertheless 'there was . . . the calculus of balance and stability'. He perceived Turkey as a more important asset to NATO than Greece. The fact that Greece was a democracy did not change Kissinger's position. He was forced to choose, and 'stability, not justice, remained the goal of his policy'.[65]

Kissinger's pursuit of stability led him to oppose the expansion of Communist influence in Western Europe. Stoessinger observed that Kissinger's position on Portugal and the 'historic compromise' was not inconsistent with his position on Communism in the peripheral areas. Kissinger had always taken a harder line with Communists in the peripheral areas than with the USSR. He believed these areas had the potential for cumulatively destabilizing, the global balance of power. But no decisive change in the balance of power, short of nuclear war, can take place in the direct relationship between the superpowers. Stoessinger argued that Kissinger's indiscriminate opposition to all forms of Communism might force breakaway groups closer to Moscow and thus bring about the very developments he was trying so hard to prevent. In addition, he argued that Kissinger's outbursts of exasperation in moments of frustration were taken seriously by the Europeans and therefore damaged US–Allied relations.

The examination of Kissinger's role in the Middle East indicated he had managed to narrow differences between Israel and the Arabs more than the preceding mediators. Stoessinger, however, did not dismiss the assertion of the critics of the step-by-step approach that Kissinger had avoided the heart of the conflict by refusing to address the Palestinian problem. Stoessinger revealed Kissinger was neither pro-Israeli nor pro-Arab but pro-equilibrium, and thus consistent with his search for stability and, in turn, peace. Kissinger believed a decisive Israeli victory would have led to another war, therefore only a war without victory (or a total defeat) would have led to stability that would produce peace.

Kissinger's overall approach to Third World problems applied the same mixture of diplomacy and power that was used with the USSR. The new nations were seen as expendable pawns on the global chessboard. Kissinger turned his attention to them after he was forced to do so by the Arab oil embargo and the demands for a new international economic order. He responded by urging the West to unite and to negotiate with the organization of Petroleum Exporting Countries (OPEC) from a position of strength, and attempted to adjust the old economic order to make it more responsive to the demands of the Third World. But Kissinger was not yet ready to abandon the old order.

In 'Scholar Versus Statesman: The Record of Henry Kissinger;

The United States and Western Europe', Jeffry R. Bendel examined the divergence between Kissinger's ideas as a scholar and his policies as a statesman. The examination dealt with Kissinger's policies toward Western Europe from 1969–76. Bendel's brief analysis of Kissinger's perspectives on international relations indicated Kissinger's penchant for secrecy, his opposition to conducting foreign policy bureaucratically, and his beliefs in diplomacy, stability, and morality – i.e., the avoidance of nuclear war. It also revealed Kissinger's preoccupation with the Vietnam war (which Bendel saw as 'his gravest error'), the PRC, and the USSR. Bendel argued that in 1969 a perceptive observer acquainted with Kissinger's world view might have predicted some of his policies. He stated that 'all these views and policies are entirely consistent with Kissinger's world view'. Bendel declared, however, 'I agree – with qualifications – with those who contend that [Kissinger] wrote one thing and did another', and continued by quoting Mazlish. But unlike Mazlish, Bendel did not recognize that while most of Kissinger's writings were about Europe, most of his foreign policy actions were in non-European areas.[66]

Bendel assumed the conclusions drawn from the examination of Kissinger's policies toward non-European areas were applicable to US–West European relations. Therefore his thesis reveals in Kissinger's policy toward Western Europe there was divergence between the ideas of the scholar and the actions of the statesman. Bendel implied if Western Europe had not been of secondary concern to Kissinger, he could have resolved the dilemmas of NATO. What Bendel misunderstood, like most observers of Kissinger, is that in Kissinger's writings the emphasis was on why the dilemmas of NATO could not be resolved in the foreseeable future regardless of who governed in Washington or in the West European capitals. Sovereignty and nuclear weapons imposed constraints on statesmen that even Kissinger could not overcome even if Europe had been his primary concern. In short, Bendel blamed Kissinger for the strains in the Alliance in the 1970s, as others before him had blamed de Gaulle. A more careful reading of Kissinger's writings would have revealed to Bendel why Kissinger did not blame de Gaulle for the 1960s' strains in the US–Allied relationship.

Bendel agreed with de Tocqueville that democracy, and US democracy in particular, lacks the qualities necessary for the successful conduct of foreign policy – i.e., consistency of purpose, secrecy, and manoeuvrability. Yet he argued that Kissinger exacerbated serious strains in the Alliance by using these necessary qualities.

In Bendel's view, most problems of NATO could be resolved only mutually, and Kissinger would have agreed with him. But unlike Kissinger, he did not recognize there might be an 'indivisible interest' in the defence of Europe, but not in other areas of the world. Bendel observed that all members of NATO realize the wisdom of cooperation to defend Western Europe against the Soviet threat. He did not realize that the controversy stemmed from disagreements on how to defend it – i.e., massive retaliation or flexible response, with conventional forces or tactical nuclear weapons.

Kissinger was accused by Bendel of doing nothing to garner the necessary political support to alleviate the increasing imbalance between NATO's conventional defence strategy and the deployment of its forces, nor to resolve the role of tactical nuclear weapons. Bendel failed to explain that the Allies have continuously refused to move beyond anything symbolic in the field of conventional defence. He argued the one positive step taken was the European Defence Improvement Programme (EDIP), but did not point out that the Allies adopted it in order to help the Administration defeat the Mansfield Amendments, and not to increase NATO's dependence on conventional forces. The same weakness appears in Bendel's charge that Kissinger refused to tackle the issue of the role of tactical nuclear weapons. Bendel did not realize that the allies were not ready to reopen the question of command and control of nuclear weapons that had been the primary cause of the strains in the Alliance in the 1960s. Kissinger simply acquiesced in the symbolic action taken by the Nuclear Planning Group. If Kissinger had taken the initiative in the issue as Bendel suggested, the Allies would have probably accused him of pressuring them or of making unilateral decisions, as the preceding Administrations were accused of doing when they sought Allied support for flexible response. Kissinger was also held responsible for Secretary Schlesinger's overt threat in 1973 to move American military equipment out of Germany because the Germans deserted the US in an hour of need. Bendel did not point out that Schlesinger was not one to follow Kissinger's advice.

In the examination of NATO doctrine and strategy, Bendel observed that Kissinger criticized the strategy of flexible response but there was no discussion of Kissinger's conclusions drawn from his analysis of the strategy. He also did not deal with Kissinger's views with respect to the British and French nuclear forces which were at the centre of the controversy over NATO strategy. Instead Bendel focused on Kissinger's proposals for temporary solutions – i.e., the

Executive Committee of the NATO Council. Bendel observed Kissinger's argument that the Alliance should move beyond the nation-state, and was critical for his not moving it in that direction. What was not grasped, however, was that Kissinger did not believe that NATO's dilemmas could be resolved in the foreseeable future. Therefore he was prepared to maintain the hegemonial position of the US which was essential to negotiations with the USSR.

The analysis of US–EEC relations indicated, according to Bendel, Kissinger's conviction that as European unity increased so would the EEC differences with the US. European unity was not a cure-all for lessening the burdens of America's global role, yet Bendel argued that one should have expected Kissinger to allow the EEC to assume increased responsibility (but he did not), and that Kissinger should understand why the EEC could not support his policies in the Middle East. Bendel did not realize, given Kissinger's convictions about the increased divergence of interests, that it was unlikely that decision-making would be shared with the EEC at a time when all initiatives had to be controlled from the White House. Kissinger was also criticized for not doing enough to influence the bureaucracy's traditional belligerency toward the EEC. Bendel conceded, however, that the Allies must bear part of the blame for the deterioration in US–EEC relations.

In the discussions of bilateral relations with Britain, France, and West Germany, Bendel presented some inaccurate findings. He felt cooperation with France was not a very high priority with Kissinger, but most observers (including Ambassador Schaetzel, whom Bendel quotes extensively in his discussion of US–EEC relations) claimed that the neglect of the EEC institutions resulted from Kissinger's preoccupation with France. With respect to Britain, Bendel argued that Kissinger's policies should have been aimed at providing new guidelines for the special relationship and to augment Britain's confidence so that Britain could make a greater contribution. He did not point out that Kissinger had always been sceptical about the special relationship. Bendel criticized Kissinger for using the military ties to Europe to get commercial and economic concessions from the Federal Republic of Germany (FRG), but only in passing did he mention, what he called, the Administration's 'close (or at least adequate) consultation on a few issues (the Berlin Accords, and SALT)'.[67]

Bendel's study cannot be used as a reference source because of its inaccurate and uncritical treatment of his sources. Remarks which cast Kissinger in a sinister light are conveyed with lip-smacking gusto while assessments which do not fit the pattern of divergence are, at best, given cursory treatment. Hopefully, the present study will help to correct this unbalanced account of Kissinger's handling of US–West European relations.

In summary, this review indicates that nearly all prior studies of the linkage between Kissinger's conceptions and his policies reveal consistency to be the major finding. Exceptions were those of Mazlish, Nutter and Bendel, nevertheless, these three studies do find consistency in some important areas. Mazlish's finding of inconsistency is weakened by acknowledgement that while most of Kissinger's writings were about Europe, most of his policies were for non-European areas. Nutter did find consistency in the issues of international stability, West European defence, and the internal transformation of the USSR. As for Bendel, the only inconsistency he found was between Kissinger's specific proposals and his policies with regards to US–Allied relations. The present study examines themes of linkage and consistency, but unlike Bendel's (the only study on the same topic) the time frame will be narrower, and will focus on the linkage between Kissinger's Soviet policy and Alliance policy, as well as their linkage with Kissinger's conceptions of limits which preclude the resolution of the Alliance's dilemmas for the foreseeable future.

LIMITATIONS OF THE STUDY

The primary limitation of this study stems from Kissinger's near-absolute control over crucial documents pertaining to his period in office. This makes it difficult for anyone to determine with precision many of the objectives or motivations underlying his policies. Indeed, Kissinger is probably the only person who knows what American foreign policy was for most of the 1970s, because he systematically excluded others from the decisionmaking process, and even objected to the presence of American interpreters when he negotiated with foreign leaders. As a historian, he was undoubtedly aware that his actions would guarantee that only his memoirs would contain the definitive interpretation of his role in shaping American foreign policy – and, in turn, history.

Having stated the basic aims of this study and its dissimilarity with earlier treatments of Kissinger and his policies, it is important to note that my final evaluation of Kissinger presupposes that ideas play a very important role in his life. In fact, I have tried to understand Kissinger on his own terms, which has not been adequately done so far. This approach runs the risk of taking Kissinger at his own word. Hopefully this critical examination of his conceptions and his policies toward Western Europe will offset any impression that he has been allowed to provide the only definitive interpretation of his role in shaping the US–West European relationship.

ORGANIZATION OF SUBSEQUENT CHAPTERS

Structurally, this study contains eight substantive chapters and a ninth in the form of conclusions. Chapter 2 deals with the intellectual underpinnings of Kissinger's global strategy. Kissinger's models of stable and revolutionary international systems and his perception of the contemporary international system provided the foundations of his policies. Chapter 3 examines Kissinger's global strategy, thus setting the context within which the specific policies toward Western Europe were formulated and executed. Chapter 4 analyses Kissinger's writings about the US–West European relationship; the conclusions drawn from his critiques of American policies toward the Allies in the 1950s and the 1960s revealed the premises on which his West European policies were based. Chapter 5 examines the declaratory policy of the Nixon Administration, more specifically the Nixon Doctrine and its pertinence to Western Europe. The intentions of the Administration and the goals it hoped to achieve in the US–West European relationship are outlined. An analysis of Kissinger's doctrine of strategic sufficiency developed in an attempt to resolve NATO's defence dilemmas while pursuing an arms control policy with the USSR is found in Chapter 6. Also examined is the impact of SALT 1 and the Agreement on the Prevention of Nuclear War on the defence of Western Europe. Chapter 7 is devoted to the Nixon Administration's policies dealing with the issues that could have had an impact on the conventional defence of Western Europe. Chapter 8 discusses the Administration's reaction to issues affecting West European unity. The Administration's reaction to Brandt's *Ostpolitik* is examined in Chapter 9, the examination dealing with the differences in the conceptual frameworks of Kissinger and Brandt, and with Kissinger's endeavours to implement linkage in order to prevent 'differential detente'. Chapter 10 ties everything together by showing the linkage between Kissinger's Soviet policy and Alliance policy, and their linkage with conceptions advanced in his writings.

2 Intellectual Underpinnings of Kissinger's Global Strategy

STABLE AND REVOLUTIONARY INTERNATIONAL SYSTEMS

It is an illusion to believe that leaders gain in profundity while they gain experience. As I have said, the convictions that leaders have formed before reaching high office are the intellectual capital they will consume as long as they continue in office. There is little time for leaders to reflect.

Henry A. Kissinger, *White House Years*.

The intellectual underpinnings of Kissinger's global strategy were best summarized in his doctoral dissertation, *A World Restored* (completed in 1954), where he presented his models for stable and revolutionary international systems. The models were derived from Kissinger's analysis of European diplomatic history during the period between 1812 and 1822. Kissinger explained why he studied that particular period:

The success of physical science depends on the selection of the 'crucial' experiment; that of political science in the field of international affairs, on the selection of the 'crucial' period. I have chosen for my topic the period between 1812 and 1822, partly, I am frank to say, because its problems seem to me analogous to those of our day. But I do not insist on this analogy.[1]

Indeed, as it is evident in Kissinger's subsequent studies, these models did not change although Kissinger discussed some new factors – i.e., the development and deployment of nuclear weapons, and the increase in the number of new nations – which contributed to the revolutionary nature of the contemporary international system. These factors will be examined in the following pages.

Kissinger's world outlook is based on his conception of peace,

31

which he defines as stability based on an equilibrium of forces within a legitimate international order. He stresses that unless a stable-legitimate international order can be achieved, the quest for peace will be self-defeating. He explains why this will be the case:

> Whenever peace – conceived as the avoidance of war – has been the primary objective of a power or a group of powers, the international system has been at the mercy of the most ruthless member of the international community. Whenever the international order has acknowledged that certain principles could not be compromised even for the sake of peace, stability based on an equilibrium of forces was at least conceivable.[2]

Thus, according to Kissinger, the primary objective of nations is not to preserve peace (avoid war), but to achieve stability: 'Stability, then has commonly resulted not from a quest for peace but from a generally accepted legitimacy'.[3]

Kissinger defines legitimacy as 'no more than an international agreement about the nature of workable arrangements and about the permissible aims and methods of foreign policy'.[4] He maintains that legitimacy 'implies the acceptance of the framework of the international order by all major powers at least to the extent that no state is so dissatisfied that ... it expresses its dissatisfaction in a revolutionary foreign policy'.[5] Thus an international order whose structure is accepted by all major powers is stable-legitimate.

A stable international order does not eliminate conflicts among nations but it 'limits their scope'.[6] The limited wars that occur are fought in the name of the existing international structure, and the peace which follows reflects a better expression of the 'legitimate' equilibrium of forces. Diplomacy, which Kissinger defines as 'the adjustment of differences through negotiation',[7] is possible only in a stable international order, since the powers are concerned only with the adjustment of differences. And there is an agreement on what constitutes a permissible difference; conflict within a stable international order thus tends to be limited.

But 'whenever there exists a power which considers the international order or the manner of legitimizing it oppressive, relations between it and the other powers will be revolutionary'.[8] In Kissinger's view a revolutionary power was not one with an objectionable ideology, but one that believed that international relations should be conducted on ideological premises. In this case, it is not the adjustment of differences within the structure which is at issue, but the structure itself. Since the order itself is at issue, diplomacy cannot function even though diplomats can still meet. In a revolutionary order 'diplomacy is replaced either by war or by an armaments race'.[9]

A stable international order 'limits the possible by the just; a revolutionary order identifies the just with the physically possible'.[10] So, while 'adjustments are possible' in a revolutionary order, they are conceived only as 'tactical maneuvers to consolidate positions for the inevitable showdown'[11] that would transform its structure. 'The foundation of a stable order is the relative security – and the relative insecurity – of its members'.[12] But the distinguishing feature of a revolutionary power is its need for absolute security – the neutralization of the opponent – which means absolute insecurity for all the other powers. Therefore absolute security 'is never obtainable as part of a "legitimate" settlement, and can be achieved only through conquest'.[13] Then the quest for absolute security leads to permanent revolution.

The status quo power, however, 'lulled by a period of stability which has seemed permanent ... find[s] it nearly impossible to take at face value the assertion of the revolutionary power that it means to smash the existing framework'.[14] Thus they tend to treat the revolutionary power 'as if it really accepted the existing legitimacy but overstated its case for bargaining purposes; as if it were motivated by specific grievances to be assuaged by limited concessions'.[15] The adoption of an 'appeasement' policy by the status quo powers, according to Kissinger, 'is the result of an inability to come to grips with a policy of unlimited objectives'.[16]

Kissinger maintains that the development of an equilibrium of forces depends not merely on strength but on the resolution to use it. Thus, 'whatever else a revolutionary power may achieve ... it tends to erode, if not the legitimacy of the international order, at least the restraint with which such an order operates'.[17]

According to Kissinger, few periods illustrate the dilemma posed by the appearance of a revolutionary power so well as the period during which Napoleon reigned in France. France, armed with a new philosophy, decided to change the existing international order. Napoleon was not concerned with the adjustment of differences within the accepted framework but with the 'legitimacy' of the framework itself. The political contest had become doctrinal, and an international order based on incompatible philosophies could no longer be accepted. Thus the balance of power lost its flexibility, and the equilibrium of forces was seen by the status quo powers as insufficient protection against France.

In *A World Restored*, Kissinger identified the components of a nation's power and pointed out the relativity of power. At the international level, a statesman's actions are determined by what is considered just, and what is considered possible: 'What is considered just depends on the domestic structure of his state; what is possible depends on its resources, determination and domestic structure of other states'.[18] Therefore a nation's 'foreign policy must be planned on the basis of the other side's capabilities, and not merely of its intentions'.[19] Thus, since 'strength depends on the relative position of states, calculations of absolute power lead to a paralysis of action'.[20]

While Kissinger identifies the components of power, he does not explicitly define the concept of power. He characterizes power as a psychological relationship between those who exercise it and those over whom it is exercised. This is revealed in his discussion of 'diplomacy, the art of restraining the exercise of power',[21] and negotiation:

> In any negotiation it is understood that force is the ultimate recourse. But it is the art of diplomacy to keep this threat potential, to keep its extent indeterminate and to commit it only as a last resort. For once power has been made actual, negotiations in the proper sense cease. A threat to use force which proves unavailing does not return the negotiation to the point before the threat was made. It destroys the bargaining position altogether, for it is a confession not of finite power but of impotence.[22]

Thus the exercise of force does not necessarily enhance a nation's power. 'Napoleon, having failed to establish a principle of obligation to maintain his conquests, would find his power sapped by the constant need for the application of force'.[23]

Kissinger also distinguished limited war from total war and points out that war becomes total 'because the two sides [can] never agree on the precise power relationship'.[24] Total war is conceived as an end in itself, and the rules of war are applied to a peace settlement. 'The logic of peace is proportion and proportion implies limitation but the logic of war is power and power has no inherent limit'.[25] Therefore when the claims of victorious nations are unlimited, they preclude agreement on a new power relationship.

Kissinger's examination of European diplomacy between 1812 and

1822 revealed that the establishment of a stable international order depended on several factors:

1. on the willingness and capability of nations to fight limited wars to achieve limited objectives
2. on the ability of the status quo powers to avoid the outbreak of total war which would threaten the stable international system they tried to preserve, and
3. on the willingness of the status quo powers to negotiate with the revolutionary power while at the same time being prepared to use military force.

Limited war does not demand unconditional surrender since its goal is the achievement of limited national objectives. The defeated powers are not eliminated. They are permitted to re-enter the international system in order to restore the balance of power which is necessary for the achievement of stability. In addition, while agreement by all powers is essential for the establishment of a stable international system, the only powers that could transform it are those with overwhelming military power and the resolution to use it.

The models and concepts – peace, power, limited war, and total war – discussed in the preceding pages were the 'intellectual capital' Kissinger consumed while he was in office. Kissinger refined some of the concepts to reflect more accurately the realities of the contemporary international system, but he did not refine the models for stable and revolutionary international systems since only the superpowers possessed the overwhelming military power that could transform the international system.[26]

KISSINGER'S PERCEPTION OF THE CONTEMPORARY INTERNATIONAL SYSTEM

The contemporary international system is revolutionary according to Kissinger because it contains 'two revolutionary powers, the USSR and the PRC, which pride themselves on their superior understanding of "objective" forces and to which policies unrelated to a plausible possibility of employing force seem either hypocrisy or stupidity'.[27] These powers explicitly reject the notion that harmony between different social systems can exist, and are committed to the transformation of the existing international structure. Thus Kissinger maintains, 'our only possibility for affecting their actions resides in the possession of superior force'.[28]

Kissinger pointed out, however, that a number of new factors have contributed to the revolutionary nature of the contemporary international order. He summed them up 'in three general statements: (a) the number of participants in the international order has increased and their nature has altered; (b) their technical ability to affect each other has vastly grown; and (c) the scope of their purposes has expanded.[29]

The revolutionary character of the contemporary international system is further complicated by the fact that the large number of new nations that emerged from colonial rule injected into their foreign policy the revolutionary fervour that gained them independence. Kissinger calls attention to the fact that 'between the Berlin crisis and the invasion of Czechoslovakia, the principal threats to peace came from the emerging areas'.[30] He explains that this was the result of the following factors:

(a) Domestic weakness encourages foreign intervention. The temptation to deflect domestic dissatisfactions into foreign adventures is ever present
(b) Leaders feel little sense of responsibility to an over-all international equilibrium
(c) The rivalry of the superpowers offers many opportunities for blackmail.[31]

But Kissinger was not primarily concerned with the new nations since they 'weigh[ed] little in the physical balance of power'.[32] What concerned Kissinger was their integration into the international structure which was complicated by the fact that the USSR and the PRC manipulated the hopes and dissatisfactions of new nations in order to prevent the establishment of an equilibrium of forces. Therefore, he saw the new nations only as pawns in a deadly game played by the superpowers, while at the same time he stressed that their integration into the international structure was essential in order to develop an equilibrium of forces.

The most striking feature of the contemporary period, according to Kissinger, is the radical transformation in the nature of power. Kissinger implied a psychological definition of power and introduced an element of uncertainty by stating that 'until power is used, it is . . . what people think it is'.[33] But given the 'nuclear stalemate' the use of military force to achieve national objectives is largely precluded in the case of the superpowers. Superior military power does not guarantee political influence. In addition, no nuclear weapons have ever been used in wartime – except for the two explosions of now obsolete weapons at Hiroshima and Nagasaki – so no experience exists from which to draw the meaning of nuclear power. Thus, 'side by side with the physical balance of power, there exists a psychological balance based on intangibles of values and belief. The presuppositions of the physical equilibrium have changed drastically; those of the psychological balance remain to be discovered'.[34] Consequently statesmen are faced with a dilemma when they attempt to translate power into policy and to conduct negotiations.

The dilemma of relating nuclear power to national objectives is further complicated by the unstable nature of weapons technology – new weapons are developed at five- to ten-year intervals. Terms like 'superiority', 'parity', and 'assured destruction' are not related to operational military strategy, and there is no consensus on their political implications. Nuclear power is, by nature, abstract, intangible, and elusive. Deterrence – the dominant military strategy – depends 'above all on psychological criteria', i.e., on the opponent's calculations of unacceptable risks'.[35] 'For political purposes', Kissinger's primary concern, 'the meaningful measurement of military strength is the assessment of it by the other side. Psychological criteria vie in importance with strategic doctrine'.[36] Consequently, every increment of power is not politically effective. The superpowers' capability to destroy each other cannot be effectively translated into a plausible threat even against nations without the capability to retaliate. Thus, while the margin of superiority of the superpowers over the other states is widening, the other nations have an unprecedented scope for autonomous action. 'In other words, power no longer translates automatically into influence'.[37]

Throughout history a shift in the balance of power was possible only through the acquisition of territory which would increase a nation's population and resources, and in turn, its power. However, nuclear weapons technology makes it possible for nations to shift the balance of power solely through the devlopment and deployment of nuclear weapons within their territory. So in the nuclear era, territorial expansion adds little to effective military power.[38] The result of shifts in the balance of power through developments within the territorial limits of sovereign states is a reduction of wars and an armaments race. Wars between the great powers are reduced, given the risk of nuclear war, but the arms race permits them to maintain

their military superiority, and in turn, their power *vis-à-vis* their
potential opponents.

The reduction of wars does not mean that nations do not attack the
'legitimate' interests of other nations. Attacks have multiplied, but
their forms have changed. Now the legitimate interests of states are
threatened by internal subversion, intervention by 'volunteers', and
by physical and psychological warfare.

Modern technology has multiplied the resources available for the
conduct of foreign affairs and has removed the technical limits from
the exercise of power in foreign policy. This trend has been
compounded by the democratization of politics that enables states to
allocate more resources for competing in the international arena.
Therefore the severity of conflicts among nations could have no
definitive bounds. In addition, given the ideological conflict between
East and West, political loyalties no longer coincide with political
boundaries. 'Conflicts among states merge with divisions within
nations; the dividing line between domestic and foreign policy begins
to disappear'.[39] The result is that some states – Kissinger referred to
the USSR – feel threatened not only by the foreign policy of other
countries but also, and perhaps especially, by domestic
transformations.[40] The tensions produced by ideological conflict are
exacerbated by the reduction in influence of the traditional great
powers. Kissinger concludes that the technical, political, and
ideological revolutions 'have been taking place at a moment when
international relationships have become truly global for the first time;
there are no longer any isolated areas. Any diplomatic or military
move immediately involves world-wide consequences'.[41]

Kissinger was primarily interested in the relationship between military power and diplomacy in stable and revolutionary international
systems, and this was clearly manifested in his discussion of
military bipolarity and political multipolarity. In *American Foreign
Policy*, Kissinger states that the world had become militarily bipolar.
Only the superpowers possess total destructive nuclear military
power. Over the next decade (the 1970s), no other country or group
of countries will be capable of challenging the physical preeminence
of the superpowers. Indeed, he argues, the gap in military strength
between the superpowers and the rest of the world is likely to
increase rather than diminish over that period.[42] But 'military
bipolarity is a source of rigidity in foreign policy' since 'whatever
"balance" there is between the superpowers is regarded as both
precarious and inflexible. A bipolar world loses the perspective for

nuance; a gain for one side appears as an absolute loss for the other. Every issue seems to involve a question of survival'.[43] As a result, according to Kissinger, the policymakers of the superpowers 'have much less confidence' in their ability to restore the equilibrium of forces after a disturbance.[44]

In Kissinger's view, these problems are exacerbated by the fact that

> the smaller countries are torn between a desire for protection and a wish to escape big-power dominance. Each of the superpowers is beset by the desire to maintain its preeminence among its allies, to increase its influence among the uncommitted, and to enhance its security *vis-à-vis* its opponent. The fact that some of these objectives may well prove incompatible adds to the strain on the international system.[45]

Kissinger maintains that 'military bipolarity has not only failed to prevent, it has actually encouraged political multipolarity'.[46] The reasons for this development are obvious:

1. Weaker allies have good reason to believe that their defence is in the overwhelming interest of their senior partner. Hence, they see no need to purchase its support by acquiescence in its policies.
2. The new nations feel protected by the rivalry of the superpowers, and their nationalism leads to ever bolder assertions of self-will.
3. Traditional uses of power have become less feasible, and new forms of pressure have emerged as a result of transnational loyalties and weak domestic structures.[47]

But 'political multipolarity does not necessarily guarantee stability [Kissinger's primary goal]. Rigidity is diminished, but so is manageability'.[48] 'Nationalism may succeed in curbing the preeminence of the superpowers' but it does not necessarily contribute to the stability of the international system. The reason for this is that only the superpowers have the resources to become involved in global issues. Lacking the resources, the other nations gear their diplomacy to domestic politics and are 'more concerned with striking a pose than contributing to international order'.[49]

Kissinger admitted that in the late 1960s 'political multipolarity [made] it impossible to impose an American design'.[50] The challenge for American statesmen would be the development of an international structure based on 'political multipolarity even though overwhelming military strength [would] remain with the two superpowers'.[51] Kissinger was not concerned with the development and deployment of nuclear weapons by Britain and France. In his view, in military matters (and particularly in the nuclear field) the closest cooperation between the Allies and the US is dictated by self-interest, and the Allies have more to gain from it than the US. He pointed out that while the West Europeans feared an American-Soviet condominium 'it [was] almost inconceivable that our allies would prefer to go to war without the support of the United States, given the relatively small nuclear forces in prospect for them'.[52]

Kissinger recognized that in the political and economic fields the temptations for independent action by the Allies are great, and the penalties small. But because of West European dependence on the American nuclear guarantee, he insisted, 'it is hard to visualize a "deal" between the Soviet Union and Europe which would jeopardize our interests without jeopardizing European interests first'.[53] On these points Kissinger is consistent. For him, stability was the ultimate goal and the US held the key to stability. As he explained, 'as long as NATO strategy was nuclear and the United States had no obvious alternative to nuclear retaliation, our Allies were ready to acquiesce in the hegemonial position of the United States. They reasoned that this was the price which had to be paid for an automatic American nuclear response'.[54]

Kissinger suggested that 'cooperation between the United States and Europe must concentrate on issues within the Atlantic area rather than global partnership'.[55] He concluded that while the support of all powers was necessary for the establishment of a stable international system, the only powers that could transform it were the US and the USSR. His main interest was therefore, the relationship between the superpowers.

CONCLUSION

The preceding analysis indicates that Kissinger's models of stable and revolutionary international systems underlie his perception of the contemporary international system. Kissinger did not refine the models, although he acknowledged that the contemporary period was revolutionary because it contained two revolutionary powers, because the number of participants in the international system had increased, and because the radical transformation in the nature of power had made international relations 'truly global for the first time'.

Kissinger sees no need to refine the models since the world is militarily bipolar. Only the US and the USSR possess the over-whelming military power that could transform the international system, or if each unilaterally attempts to do so, they could destroy the world.

Kissinger recognizes that the world is politically multipolar as a result of two factors: (a) the number of participants in the international system has increased; and (b) some of the traditional great powers have regained some of the influence they lost after the First World War. He sees the new nations, however, only as pawns in a deadly game played by the superpowers, and he is not greatly concerned with the European Allies – the traditional great powers – given the relatively small nuclear forces in prospect for them. Nevertheless, Kissinger stresses that the integration of the new nations into the international structure is essential in order to establish an equilibrium of forces, and suggests that cooperation between the US and Western Europe 'must concentrate on issues within the Atlantic area rather than global partnership'.[56]

'In the years ahead', according to Kissinger, 'the most profound challenge to American policy will be philosophical: to develop some concept of order in a world which is bipolar militarily but multipolar politically'.[57] But he realizes that 'a philosophical deepening will not come easily to those brought up in the American tradition of foreign policy'.[58] An international order that could contain the clash of national interests, power rivalries, and ideological antagonisms from engulfing the world in a nuclear holocaust had two structural imperatives according to Kissinger: (a) an equilibrium of military power; and (b) acceptance by the superpowers of certain fundamen-tal principles of legitimate and illegitimate state action in the international system. Kissinger believed that although the structural requirements varied in different historical periods, equilibrium and legitimacy would always be the essential requisites for a stable international system: *neither was sufficient by itself.*

Kissinger's models for stable and revolutionary international systems, and his perception of the contemporary international system, provided the conceptual framework within which he attemp-ted to resolve the fundamental strategic–diplomatic problems of American foreign policy.

Chapter 3 examines Kissinger's global strategy as it manifested itself through particular foreign policies. The analysis will not deal with every policy, but it will focus on those that reflected the fundamental changes in American foreign policy and the congruity of these policies with Kissinger's models for stable and revolutionary international systems.

3 Kissinger's Global Strategy: a Triangular Relationship?

James Reston: When you came to Washington ... it was said that you had a concept of how to achieve order in the world, and yet ... since you have been here, the tendency has been to say that you have not defined your concept, but that actually what you have been doing is negotiating pragmatic problems and not really dealing with the concept or making clear the concept. What is the concept?

Henry Kissinger: We spend the greatest part of our time at the beginning trying to relate it [a problem] to where America and the world ought to go before we ever discuss tactics.[1]

INTRODUCTION

Indeed, Kissinger never explicitly outlined his global strategy – to the delight of his critics – but this did not necessarily indicate that he did not have one. Here it will be argued that Kissinger's policies with respect to major issues – SALT, rapprochement with the PRC, economic detente, and the Vietnam negotiations – did imply some major premises about the emerging international system and about his assumptions concerning how to shape it. These policies (and the implicit assumptions) approximated rather closely to the guidelines for statecraft that Kissinger had articulated in *A World Restored*, as distinct from his writings on military strategy and foreign policy. As Seyom Brown points out, it was 'Kissinger's reluctance to fully share the premises of his actions with his domestic and international audience' that made his policies appear 'more as a brilliantly executed series of improvisations than as a "mosaic" [one of Kissinger's favourite terms] in which each of the parts is integral to the whole conception'.[2] But the best improvisations emanate from a concept underneath the apparent spontaneity, and this was in fact the case with Kissinger's most important policies.[3]

43

When Kissinger assumed office on 20 January 1969, American foreign policy was in crisis. The crisis arose primarily from a collapse of confidence, both at home and abroad, in the US government's capacity to marshal America's capabilities to act purposefully in international affairs. As perceived by Kissinger, the crisis of American foreign policy was in large measure caused by psychological deficiencies rather than material ones. He agreed with the President 'that whatever else a foreign policy might be, it must be strong to be credible – and it must be credible to be successful'.[4]

In Kissinger's view, the restoration of American power required:

(a) an end to the war in Vietnam in a way that would prevent the polarization of American society and maintain the reputation of the US as a nation that sustained its commitments

(b) a realistic definition of America's national security interests in order to avoid depleting the national security resources in the pursuit of idealistic goals, peripheral to the central balance of military and geopolitical power

(c) the development of a concept of international order that, while consistent with the national security interests of the US, would provide a standard of legitimacy acceptable to most nations; and

(d) purposeful and dramatic action on global issues so that American leaders, once again, would reassume their role of pacesetters in the international arena.

In the 1970 annual US Foreign Policy Report to Congress, President Nixon announced that this report 'is more than a record of one year. It is this Administration's statement of a new approach to foreign policy, to match a new era of international relations'.[5] The new approach outlined by the President bore the unmistakable imprint of its principal author, Henry A. Kissinger.[6]

The new power realities that were outlined in the first annual report on US foreign policy were based on Kissinger's perception of the contemporary international system. 'The postwar period in international relations has ended', asserted the President. The ravages of the Second World War had been overcome. 'Western Europe and Japan have recovered their economic strength, their political vitality, and their national self-confidence'. The new nations 'have a spirit and a growing strength of independence', and were not totally dependent on the US. 'Once many feared that they would become simply a battleground of cold-war rivalry and misjudged their pride in their national identities and their determintion to preserve their newly won sovereignty'. In addition, the nature of the Communist world 'has changed – the power of individual Communist nations has grown, but international Communist unity has been shattered ... by the powerful forces of nationalism. The Soviet Union and Communist China ... [have] become bitter adversaries'. Meanwhile 'a revolution in the technology of war has altered the nature of the military balance of power. Both the Soviet Union and the United States have acquired the ability to inflict unacceptable damage on the other, no matter which strikes first. There can be no gain and certainly no victory- for the power that provokes a thermonuclear exchange'.[7]

Kissinger's concepts reappeared only slightly altered in President Nixon's annual reports on US foreign policy. 'American energies were absorbed in coping with a cycle of recurrent crises', the President stated. But 'our opportunity today – and challenge – is to get at the causes of crises, to take a longer view, and to help build the international relationships that will provide the framework of a durable peace'. But 'peace must be far more than the absence of war. Peace must provide a durable structure of international relationships which inhibits or removes the causes of war... We are working toward the day when all nations will have a stake in peace, and will therefore be partners in its maintenance'.[8]

The structure of peace that the Administration was trying to build, according to the President, required a foreign policy that was guided by three basic principles:

(a) 'partnership', a euphemism for the Nixon Doctrine
(b) 'strength', a rationalization of US military capabilities, particularly strategic nuclear forces to preserve a global balance of military power, and regional balances in the context of approaching strategic parity between the US and the USSR, and
(c) 'willingness to negotiate', a vague formulation of what was soon to emerge as the triangular relationship of US–Soviet detente and the US–PRC rapprochement.[9]

However, the conceptual innovation that Kissinger had advocated did not materialize. The first two elements of the structure of peace could hardly be rated as major conceptual innovations, and the third – the promise of a willingness to negotiate – remained little more than a catchy slogan until the surprising demarches toward the PRC and the Soviet Union in 1971 and 1972.

Since Kissinger did not provide an accompanying design or even an outline of the essential characteristics of the structure of peace that was supposed to be produced by the new policies, many unofficial commentators speculated that he wanted to reinstitute the five-sided balance of power that he had written about in *A World Restored*. They found support for this thesis in oblique formulations such as the President's statement to *Time* magazine that 'it would be a safer world and a better world if we have a strong, healthy United States, Europe, Soviet Union, China, Japan; each balancing the other, not playing one against the other, an even balance'.[10]

Kissinger, however, never spoke of this pentagonal arrangement, to which he could not have easily subscribed given his awareness of the degree to which Western Europe and Japan remained militarily dependent on the US.[11] Moreover, Kissinger had always maintained that:

Many of the elements of stability which characterized the international system in the nineteenth century cannot be recreated in the modern age. The stable technology, the multiplicity of major powers, the limited domestic claims, and the frontiers which permitted adjustments are gone forever. A new concept of international order is essential; without it stability will prove elusive.[12]

The fact that Kissinger on several occasions emphasized that his policies toward the USSR and the PRC bore little resemblance to the classical balance of power was ignored. His view on this issue was expressed most clearly in the final annual presidential report to Congress on American foreign policy. According to the report,

We seek a stable structure, not a classical balance of power. Undeniably, national security must rest upon a certain equilibrium between potential adversaries. The United States cannot entrust its destiny entirely, or even largely, to the goodwill of others. Neither can we expect other countries so to mortgage their future. Solid security involves external restraints on potential opponents as well as self-restraint.

Thus a certain balance of power is inherent in any international system and has its place in one we envision. But it is not the overriding concept of our foreign policy. First of all, our approach reflects the realities of the nuclear age. The classical concept of balance of power included continual maneuvering for marginal advantages over others. In the nuclear era this is both unrealistic and dangerous. It is unrealistic because when both sides possess such enormous power, small additional increments cannot be translated into tangible advantage or even usable political strength. And it is dangerous because attempts to seek tactical gains might lead to confrontation which could be catastrophic.[13]

The focus on the traditional balance of power by the press diverted attention from the triangular relationship that by the end of 1969 had emerged as Kissinger's global strategy.[14]

THE UNDERLYING ASSUMPTIONS OF THE TRIANGULAR RELATIONSHIP

It was in Nelson Rockefeller's campaign speeches in 1968 that Kissinger's global strategy for a stable international system first made its appearance in a systematic form. The core of this strategy was revealed by Rockefeller in his first major campaign address. The presidential candidate spoke of the need for closer relations with the two Communist powers and concluded by declaring that 'in a subtle triangle with Communist China and the Soviet Union, we can ultimately improve our relations with each – as we test the will for peace of both'.[15]

The underlying assumption of Kissinger's global strategy was that the USSR and the PRC had not ceased to be revolutionary powers. However, their leaders were no longer comparable to Napoleon since a greater degree of rationality seemed to govern their behaviour.[16] Kissinger's changed perception was based on two factors:

(a) the strategic nuclear balance between the US and the USSR which served as a deterrent against irresponsible behaviour, and
(b) the Sino–Soviet split which had broken the ideological bonds of international Communism, and prompted each power to seek greater participation in the international system in order to gain leverage over the other.

Kissinger did not believe that either the PRC or the USSR would abandon Communism, but given the above factors he was convinced that both were more willing to assist in reducing the risks of nuclear war. Indeed, as developments demonstrated in 1969, Kissinger's reassessments of the USSR and the PRC were warranted.

In Kissinger's view, international stability is possible only if nations conduct their relations and reconcile their conflicts on strictly non-ideological bases. Since a greater degree of rationality seemed to govern the behaviour of the PRC and the USSR, at least with respect to avoiding a nuclear war, Kissinger believed that the US must also moderate her own ideological, moralistic, approach to international relations. The clearest expression of Kissinger's opposition to an ideologically oriented foreign policy was Washington's rapprochement with Peking.[17] The President's report to Congress on US foreign policy stated, 'an international order cannot be secure if one of the major powers remains largely outside it and hostile toward it'.[18] In short, the US was demonstrating that it too was willing to behave in a non-ideological manner in the world arena.

The purpose of the triangular relationship was to convince Moscow that it was fruitless and dangerous to conduct international relations on ideological grounds. In the President's words, 'the fruitfulness of the [US–Soviet] relationship depends significantly upon the degree to which [the USSR's] international behavior does not reflect militant doctrinal considerations'.[19] Kissinger however qualified his receptivity to a non-ideological foreign policy by insisting that negotiations deal with concrete issues on the basis of mutual interest and that negotiating initiatives derive from strength rather than from false hopes for a new era of friendly relations.[20]

The Sino–Soviet split confronted the US with both dangers and opportunities, and Kissinger believed that the US should explore new initiatives *vis-à-vis* both countries. It was essential, however, to convince the Soviet leaders that rapprochement with the PRC was not aimed against the USSR; it was equally important to convince PRC leaders that the US–Soviet detente was not aimed against them. In the first annual report to Congress on US foreign policy the President stated,

> Our desire for improved relations is not a tactical means of exploiting the clash between China and the Soviet Union. We see no benefit to us in the intensification of that conflict, and we have no intention of taking sides. Nor is the United States interested in joining any condominium or hostile coalition of great powers against either of the large Communist countries.[21]

In short, Kissinger believed that by remaining equidistant from both Moscow and Peking and uncommitted in the deepening struggle that separated them, the US could gain leverage over both.

The concept of linkage – the interrelationship of the major issues – was a basic postulate of Kissinger's global strategy. Explaining to Congress the three principles the Administration will observe in approaching negotiations in the 1970s, the President stated,

> The third essential in successful negotiations is an appreciation of the context in which issues are addressed. The central fact here is the inter-relationship of international events. We did not invent the inter-relationship; it is not a negotiating tactic. It is a fact of life. This Administration recognizes that international developments are entwined in many complex ways: political issues relate to strategic questions, political events in one area of the world may have a far-reaching effect on political developments in other parts of the globe. [22]

Kissinger explained, 'We saw linkage ... as synonymous with an overall strategic and geopolitical view. To ignore the interconnection of events was to undermine the coherence of all policy'. [23] Improved relations with the USSR and the PRC would produce dividends in other areas of concern to the US. Indeed, Kissinger believed that the solution of the Vietnam problem lay within the context of improved relations with both the USSR and the PRC. [24] The opening to the PRC would help end the Vietnam war by exerting pressure on Moscow to exert pressure on Hanoi. Kissinger was determined to move on as broad a front as possible so that progress on one issue would affect progress on all. However, his primary objective was the development of a stable international system with all specific policies subordinate to this fundamental objective. [25]

US–PRC RAPPROCHEMENT

The US and the PRC were brought together by a common concern – the USSR. In 1968, the PRC condemned the Soviet invasion of Czechoslovakia and especially the doctrine of 'limited sovereignty' for countries in the Communist camp by which the Soviet Union justified the invasion. This clearly demonstrated that the PRC was challenging not only the ideological preeminence of Moscow, but its geopolitical aspirations as well. Kissinger was not interested in the ideological dispute, because he believed that international stability is possible only if nations reconcile their conflicts on strictly non-ideological grounds.[26] But he shared Peking's concern about the necessity to thwart Moscow's geopolitical ambitions.

In 1969, when the Soviets asked what the US reaction would be to a Soviet attack on the nuclear facilities of the PRC, the issue of whether the US would allow the PRC to be smashed was, according to Kissinger, no longer hypothetical.[27] Now it was essential to support the PRC because, in his view, 'such a demonstration of Soviet ruthlessness and American impotence (or indifference – the result would be the same) would encourage accommodation to other Soviet demands from Japan to Western Europe, not to speak of the many smaller countries on the Soviet periphery'.[28] This geopolitical assessment was made independently by Washington and Peking, and although it did not reflect an agreement between them, it was the basis of the US–PRC rapprochement.[29]

Rapprochement with the PRC was conceived primarily as a means of pressuring the USSR to be more accommodating to the demands of the US, thereby preceding and giving major impetus to US–Soviet detente in the early 1970s.[30] In addition, the recognition of the PRC provided concrete substance to Kissinger's vague concept of an emerging multipolar world. Kissinger continually denied that gaining leverage on the USSR was the central purpose of the US–PRC rapprochement. He believed the leverage would be greater if kept implicit because the Soviet leaders might not have been able to be accommodating toward the US in various issues if it appeared to the international community that they were negotiating under pressure. Nevertheless this geopolitical result of the new triangular relationship was undeniable.

US–SOVIET DETENTE

The US–Soviet relationship was basic to any policy that sought to establish a stable international order because the two superpowers alone possessed the overwhelming military power that could transform the international system.[31] Kissinger was not concerned with the domestic policies of the USSR, since in his view a 'legitimate' state was judged exclusively on the basis of its external goals. As the President stated, 'the internal order of the USSR, as such, is not an object of our policy, although we do not hide our rejection of many of its features. Our relations with the USSR ... are determined by its international behavior'.[32] Kissinger's primary objective was not to

bring about the domestic transformation of the USSR[33] but to adjust
its external goals to the imperatives of a stable international system.
He argued that:

> Detente is not rooted in agreement on values; it becomes above all
> necessary because each side recognizes that the other is a potential
> adversary in a nuclear war. To us detente is a process of managing
> relations with a potentially hostile country in order to preserve
> peace while maintaining our vital interests. In a nuclear age, this is
> in itself an objective not without moral validity – it may indeed be
> the most profound imperative of all.[34]

These views were consistent with Kissinger's writings on foreign
policy, and particularly his conception of a militarily bipolar world.[35]

US–Soviet detente rested on two pillars: on the one hand the
strategic arms limitations talks – SALT; and on the other, economic
cooperation. SALT was facilitated by the following perceptions and
developments:

(a) the mutual recognition by the US and the USSR that parity, or
     some rough equivalence between diverse strategic forces, already
     existed or would soon exist
(b) the recognition by both sides of their mutual vulnerability – that
     neither could avoid its own destruction even if it were to strike
     first
(c) technological advances in the national technical means of
     verification made it impossible to conceal the number and
     location of fixed missile launchers, and
(d) the Soviet leaders were concerned about the impact of a new
     arms race on the Soviet economy, therefore they gave top
     priority to arms limitation.

Economic cooperation rested exclusively on the weakness of the
Soviet economy. In Kissinger's view there was very little the USSR
could do economically for the US. The USSR needed American
trade, technology, and credits. Kissinger hoped that once they
became dependent upon these benefits Soviet leaders might 'become
more conscious of what they would lose by a return to
confrontation'.[36] Kissinger did not believe that trade *per se* would
result in improved political relations, rather he believed that better
political relations would lead to improved trade. As he explained,
'given Soviet needs, expanding trade without a political quid pro quo
was a gift', therefore, 'it did not seem to [him] unreasonable to

require Soviet restraint in such trouble spots as the Middle East, Berlin, and Southeast Asia in return'.[37]

Kissinger's beliefs – that better political relations lead to improved trade and that there was very little the USSR could do economically for the US – precluded any consideration of the fact that interdependence could develop that would permit Moscow to gain leverage *vis-à-vis* Washington. By annulling contracts, the USSR could influence the political–strategic decisions of the US. With respect to trade Kissinger's only concern was to bring 'the United States export control list into line with the somewhat more liberal COCOM list, since otherwise we [the US] merely lost business to our allies without affecting Communist conduct'.[38]

Detente, then, was a relaxation of tensions along a broad front. It was not to be judged piecemeal; a stable international order would emerge from a web of mutual involvements which were part of an indivisible process. Detente or the striving for peace, Kissinger claimed, was both a 'profound moral imperative' and 'historical process' that has no ultimate end or transcendent meaning. Detente as an exercise in moral leadership was primarily the view that Kissinger sought to place before the American public.[39]

THE THREAT OF 'DIFFERENTIAL DETENTE'

While Kissinger was looking to the PRC in order to make the USSR a more manageable adversary, the Soviets were looking to Western Europe, to gain leverage over the US. So the strategic dilemma that Kissinger tried to resolve with the doctrine of strategic sufficiency dovetailed with what Kissinger called 'differential detente'.

The prospect of differential detente emanated from De Gaulle's visit to Moscow in 1966, which opened the door for West European leaders to negotiate bilaterally with the Soviets. The rigid US posture toward the USSR tempted West European leaders to play the role of 'bridge' between East and West, and assured their publics they would not allow American recklessness to start a nuclear war. The Allies had shown interest in mutual force reductions and the long-standing Soviet proposal for a European Security Conference, but in 1969, Chancellor Willy Brandt took initiatives to implement *Ostpolitik* with offers to the Soviet Union and to the German Democratic Republic (GDR) to renounce the use of force and accept the status quo in Central Europe.

In Kissinger's judgement:

> in these circumstances the prospect was real that a 'differential detente' could develop; the Soviet Union could play to these attitudes in Europe while remaining intransigent on global issues of concern to us, thus driving a wedge between us and our allies.[40]

In short, Kissinger reiterated the view he had advanced in his writings.[41] The guiding principle of the Kissinger strategy was that each American decision, every Allied action throughout the globe must be orchestrated into a unified, harmonious gesture toward the USSR.[42] In his mind, no contradiction existed between US–Soviet detente and Allied unity. The former, Kissinger insisted, presupposed the latter.[43]

Kissinger adopted policies that would preclude the development of differential detente because it would have made linkage difficult (if not impossible) to implement, thus reducing his ability to influence the behaviour of the USSR. Policy with respect to Berlin, according to Kissinger, 'became the key to the whole puzzle'.[44] It also demonstrated that his main interest was the US–Soviet relationship, and it countered the thesis that he was trying to establish the nineteenth-century balance of power.

THE STRATEGIC ARMS LIMITATION TALKS – SALT

In 1975, Kissinger was asked what he considered to be his most significant political achievement up to that time. 'SALT', he answered without hesitation, 'without a question, SALT'.[45]

Kissinger's approach to SALT was consistent with his ultimate goal – the establishment of a stable international system – since it would produce one of the two structural imperatives – an equilibrium of military power.[46] A rough equilibrium in strategic nuclear weapons was most desirable in Kissinger's view, since superiority by either side would be destabilizing and exact parity might be impossible to attain, given the differences in American and Soviet strategic weapons systems. In addition, he believed that 'in the years ahead the strategic and political significance of [American] numerical superiority in strategic weapons is certain to diminish'.[47] The concept of sufficiency advanced by Kissinger incorporated both concepts of superiority and parity, and demonstrated his conviction that political will (or the lack of it) were the causes of war, not weapons systems.[48]

In his second annual report to Congress on US Foreign Policy on 25 February 1971, President Nixon stated:

> The concept of sufficiency is . . . in part a political concept, and it involves judgments whether the existing and foreseeable military environment endangers our legitimate interests and aspirations . . . In its broader political sense, sufficiency means the maintenance of forces adequate to prevent us and our allies from being coerced. Thus the relationship between our strategic forces and those of the Soviet Union must be such that our ability and resolve to protect our vital security interests will not be underestimated.[49].

The doctrine of strategic sufficiency as outlined by the President was supposed to accomplish a number of objectives – not all of them compatible.

'In its narrow military sense it means enough force to inflict a level of damage on a potential aggressor sufficient to deter him from attacking.' In this sense, the doctrine of strategic sufficiency incorporated the strategy of assured destruction which was deemed insufficient as a force-planning concept by Kissinger since it was 'limited to the indiscriminate mass destruction of enemy civilians as the sole possible response to challenges'. This increased 'the likelihood of triggering nuclear attacks on our own population', and the greater the force to be used against the Soviet Union, the greater was the reluctance of the US to use it.[50] Kissinger believed that it was essential to develop a flexible range of strategic options because 'our insistence on divorcing force from diplomacy caused our power to lack purpose and our negotiations to lack force'.[51] Assured destruction was an inadequate strategic basis for preventing the USSR from coercing the US and its allies. Now the strategic balance permitted the USSR to neutralize the US ability to deter objectional Soviet behaviour short of direct threats to the US itself.

In *Nuclear Weapons and Foreign Policy* Kissinger had written, 'mastery of the challenges of the nuclear age will depend on our ability to combine physical and psychological factors, to develop weapons systems which do not paralyze our will, and to devise strategies which permit us to shift the risks of counteraction to the other side'. To accomplish this, 'we will have to sacrifice a measure of destructiveness to gain the possibility of fighting wars that will not amount to national catastrophe'.[52] These themes were incorporated in the doctrine of strategic sufficiency.

It was essential, explained President Nixon, that:

Our forces must also be capable of flexible application. A simple 'assured destruction' doctrine does not meet our present requirements for a flexible range of strategic options. No President should be left with only one strategic course of action, particularly that of ordering the mass destruction of enemy civilians and facilities. Given the range of possible political–military situations which could conceivably confront us, our strategic policy should not be based solely on a capability of inflicting urban and industrial damage presumed to be beyond the level an adversary would accept. We must be able to respond at levels appropriate to the situation. This problem will be the subject of continuing study.[53]

Translating these conceptual innovations into operational strategic options proved very difficult and, although the flexible strategic options objective received greater articulation and emphasis during the incumbency of James R. Schlesinger as Secretary of Defence (1973–5), this objective has not yet been achieved.

The flexible strategic options objective could endanger the arms limitation objective of the doctrine of strategic sufficiency, since the deployments on either side should not appear to threaten the other with a disarming attack. But the flexible options objective opened the door to new 'counterforce' weapons and improvements designed to limit the damage Soviet strategic forces could inflict on the US. Consequently, to the extent that the American strategic forces were capable effectively to perform this damage-limited function, they would undermine the USSR'S assured-destruction capability, and thus generate new Soviet force expansion programs. Kissinger however did not share this view because, as the President explained:

Our actions have been designed primarily to guarantee the continuing survivability of our retaliatory forces ... improvements in our existing forces and the development of new programs are not incompatible with negotiations to limit strategic arms. They complement the broad effort of this Administration to guarantee the security of the United States while moving toward a structure of greater international stability and restraint. We have been conscious of the opportunities provided in the Strategic Arms Limitation Talks to add a vital dimension of stability to our competitive relationship with the USSR.[54]

But here was the persistent dilemma: how to relinquish the strategic 'first-strike' option against the USSR, and at the same time keep the

US strategic nuclear umbrella extended over the US allies. The US strategic nuclear umbrella rested on the premise that the US would not allow the USSR to victimize the US allies by threatening a conventional or a nuclear attack, since the US would retaliate with a nuclear strike against the USSR. Such a retaliation would be the first blow in a US–Soviet nuclear war, and by the late 1960s the USSR had attained an intercontinental retaliatory capability that could absorb a first strike and yet still deliver a devastating strike on the US. On this premise rested the strategy of mutual assured destruction (MAD). This development had seriously weakened the credibility of any US threat to initiate a strategic nuclear war between the superpowers – even in response to a Soviet attack on Western Europe. Kissinger feared that if the USSR, but not the US, was capable and willing to resort to force when the secondary interests of the two clashed, the USSR could face down the US in crisis after crisis and ultimately achieve global dominance. However, if the two superpowers were to renounce first-strike capabilities against each other, the credibility of the US nuclear umbrella would collapse and Western Europe would be exposed to Soviet blackmail.

The doctrine of strategic sufficiency permitted the US to continue to deploy strategic nuclear weapons in order to sustain the credibility of its NATO commitments. As the President stated:

> In its broader political sense, sufficiency means the maintenance of forces adequate to prevent us and our allies from being coerced . . .
> But sufficiency also means numbers, characteristics, and deployments of our forces which the Soviet Union cannot reasonably interpret as being intended to threaten a disarming attack. Our purpose, reflected both in our strategic programs and in our SALT proposals, is to maintain a balance, and thereby reduce the likelihood of nuclear war.[55]

Kissinger was less interested in the precise strategic weapons levels agreed upon in SALT than on the psychological benefits that would be derived from it. SALT was conceived as a confidence builder that ultimately would lead to actual disarmament agreements. This conception explains why Kissinger would move at crucial moments to break the deadlock by persuading the President to make numerical concessions without impairing the military balance.

The SALT negotiations, which began in Helsinki on 17 November 1969, culminated in the Moscow agreements – a treaty limiting anti-ballistic missile systems (ABM), and the interim agreement on strategic offensive arms – signed on 26 May 1972 by President Nixon and General Secretary Leonid Brezhnev.[56] The ABM treaty came very close to institutionalizing the doctrine of mutual assured destruction since each party agreed not to deploy ABM systems for the defence of its territory. The treaty limited ABM deployment to two sites in each country, one to protect the capital and the other to protect an ICBM field, and each site was limited to 100 launchers. Clearly the populations of the US and the Soviet Union were to remain unprotected, a result consistent with the doctrine that if a nation's population was exposed to nuclear attack that nation was less likely to start a nuclear war. In Kissinger's judgement, the vulnerability of both superpowers would have a stabilizing effect on the international system.

The interim agreement placed a five-year freeze on strategic offensive launchers with strict limits on numbers and replacement procedures. The Soviet Union was limited to 1618 ICBMs, 950 SLBMs, and 62 submarines, while the US was confined 1054 ICBMs, 710 SLBMs, and 44 submarines. The agreement, however, did not include bombers, landmobile ICBMs, or multiple independent re-entry vehicles (MIRVs). These were to be the subject of the more comprehensive negotiations that were supposed to produce a completed treaty by October 1977. The interim agreement clearly demonstrated that Kissinger was more interested in the psychological benefits that would be derived from it, which would facilitate actual disarmament agreements in the future.

The SALT agreements were Kissinger's major achievements. These were made possible by his ability to cater to the USSR's analogous political needs and to make these even more intense by the acceleration of the US–PRC rapprochement.[57] It was more than coincidental that after President Nixon's 15 July 1971 announcement that he would visit the PRC, that the US–Soviet negotiations produced a number of agreements. On 30 September 1971, agreements were reached on measures to reduce the risk of accidental nuclear war and on procedures to modernize the 'hot line' between Washington, and Moscow.[58] But most significant was the preliminary accord reached on the outlines of a Berlin settlement, and the USSR began to make concessions that produced the outlines of an ABM treaty in early 1972.[59]

On 3 July 1972, less than a week after the Moscow summit had ended, the Final Quadripartite Protocol on the status of Berlin was signed, bringing into force both the Quadripartite and the inner-

German accords. In addition, the final instruments of a peace treaty between the Federal Republic of Germany (FRG) and the USSR were exchanged. These agreements demonstrated that Kissinger's handling of linkage diplomacy had been successful.

BASIC PRINCIPLES OF US–SOVIET RELATIONS

On 29 May 1972, President Nixon and General Secretary Brezhnev signed an agreement of twelve Basic Principles which, according to the President, '[met] some of our fundamental concerns of the postwar period', and 'placed all our other efforts on a broader foundation'. As the President explained, 'A new US–Soviet relationship would require new attitudes and aspirations. It was appropriate that this change be reflected in a formal statement. These principles codify goals that the United States had long advocated.[60]

The agreement stated that the new US–Soviet relationship

> will proceed from the common determination that in the nuclear age there is no alternative to conducting their mutual relations on the basis of peaceful coexistence. Differences in ideology and in the social systems of the United States and the Soviet Union are not obstacles to the bilateral development of normal relations based on the principles sovereignty, equality, non-interference in internal affairs, and mutual advantage.[61]

This general principle that would govern the new US–Soviet relationship clearly demonstrated Kissinger's interest in the external goals of the Soviet Union rather than in its domestic policies.

The agreement also included promises by both superpowers to 'do their utmost to avoid military confrontations and to prevent the outbreak of nuclear war; to always exercise restraint in their mutual relations . . . to negotiate and settle differences by peaceful means', and 'in a spirit of reciprocity, mutual accommodation, and mutual benefit'. In addition, the superpowers agreed to refrain from attempts 'to obtain unilateral advantage at the expense of the other, directly or indirectly', and 'to make no claim for themselves, and not recognize the claims of anyone else, to any special rights or advantages in world affairs'.[62]

In Kissinger's view, the USSR's commitment to these principles was the first step toward the achievement of the second structural imperative of a stable international order – an agreement on what constitutes legitimate state behaviour in the international arena. As the President stated, 'these principles are a guide for future action, not a commentary on the past'. They acknowledge differences, 'but express a code of conduct which, if observed, can only contribute to world peace and to an international system based on mutual respect and self-restraint'.[63] By refusing to recognize the claims of other nations in the international arena, Kissinger hoped that, given the relatively small nuclear forces in prospect for them, they would agree (or at least acquiesce) with the principles agreed upon by the superpowers.

Agreement on what constitutes 'legitimate state behaviour' in the international arena was supplemented by the Agreement on the Prevention of Nuclear War signed on 22 June 1973, in Washington. Article 4 of the agreement committed the superpowers to 'urgent consultation with each other' should a risk of nuclear war result from their bilateral or third-country relations. Kissinger stated:

> The Agreement on the Prevention of Nuclear War reflected our belief that control of arms presupposed restraint in international conduct; that coexistence between the superpowers would ultimately depend on adherence to standards of behavior by which they would learn not to threaten each other's vital interests.[64]

In short, the agreement was an elaboration of the basic Principles of US–Soviet relations signed at the Moscow summit the previous year.[65]

TRADE IN US–SOVIET RELATIONS

Trade was the second vital element in Kissinger's linkage strategy, and in the Fall of 1971 the positive side of linkage was in full swing. The USSR, short of wheat for the coming winter as a result of a bad harvest, was allowed to purchase one billion dollars of American surplus food grains. In February 1972 the USSR informed the US that it was willing to reopen negotiations. These had been suspended for twelve years on the repayment of the outstanding Soviet lend-lease debt from the Second World War. By the spring of 1972 progress on numerous bilateral commercial negotiations between subordinate levels of the governments was sufficiently advanced so that the US–Soviet commercial rapprochement was included as a major item on the summit agenda. The USSR's interest in improving economic relations was probably the reason that Brezhnev did not cancel the summit, although the US bombing raids against North Vietnam and the mining of Haiphong harbour interfered with Soviet shipping.

The agreement on the Basic Principles affirmed that the US and the USSR regarded commercial and economic ties as important and necessary elements in the strengthening of their bilateral relations, and both countries pledged actively to promote the growth of such ties. Both countries also agreed to facilitate cooperation between the relevant organizations and enterprises, and to conclude commercial and economic contracts, both short-term and long-term in nature.

Indeed, 1972 was a record year for US–Soviet trade agreements. In July, an agreement was signed which made it possible for the USSR to purchase $750 million worth of American grain. In August, it was announced that the USSR purchases of American products would exceed the $1 billion mark, and that Occidental Petroleum Company concluded a $3 billion agreement for the exploitation of Siberian natural gas. On 18 October, the lend-lease agreement was signed by the US and the USSR. Moscow agreed to pay back $722 million of its wartime lend-lease debt by the year 2001. This agreement made possible the most significant development of the year in East-West trade, the US–Soviet Trade Agreement, which was signed on the same day.

The terms of the US–Soviet Trade Agreement were negotiated in two sessions of the Joint US–Soviet Commercial Commission, whose creation was agreed upon during the Moscow summit. President Nixon authorized the Export–Import Bank to extend credit and guarantees for the sale of US products to the USSR, agreed to seek congressional extension of 'most-favoured-nations' status, and guaranteed the delivery of 400 million bushels of wheat to Moscow. In addition, provisions were made for the US to set up government-sponsored and commercial offices in Moscow to facilitate the work of American businessmen seeking contracts, with similar provisions being made for the USSR in Washington. To facilitate the delivery of the products, the US and the USSR had signed a Maritime Agreement on 14 October which opened forty ports in each country to the other's shipping.[66]

But the comprehensive US–Soviet Trade Agreement ignited a debate in the US on the entire issue of US–Soviet detente. The debate emanated from the dramatic rise in US food prices (which resulted according to critics from the Soviet grain purchases)[67] and more importantly from the fact the agreement had granted the USSR the 'most-favoured-nation' status. The debate focused on an amendment introduced on 4 October (by Senator Henry M. Jackson and 71 cosponsors), which made the granting of most-favoured-nation status dependent on increased Jewish emigration. Three-quarters of both the House and the Senate endorsed it.

But Kissinger opposed the Jackson amendment because, as he explained:

> the major impact of the continued denial of most-favored-nations status to the Soviet Union would be political, not economic. Most-favored-nations status was withdrawn in 1951, largely as a political act. Our unwillingness to remove this discrimination now would call into question our intent to move toward an improved relationship.[68]

Indeed, he never tired of pointing out that the overriding goal of detente was the avoidance of nuclear war, and that trade could promote political detente only if it was kept politically neutral.

DETENTE TESTED

'Detente' to Kissinger has always been a global proposition. In spite of his focus in the US–Soviet relationship, he was prepared to challenge the USSR's attempts to gain advantage in other parts of the world because stability – Kissinger's prerequisite for peace – would be threatened.

Detente was tested on many occasions in different parts of the world. In 1970 the USSR supported a Syrian drive into Jordan which threatened to upset the delicate balance in the Middle East. At the same time, it attempted to build a nuclear submarine base at Cienfuegos, Cuba. In 1971 it supported India's dismemberment of Pakistan in the Indian–Pakistan war over Bangladesh. In 1973 it threatened unilateral intervention on the side of its Arab allies during the Yom Kippur War, and supplied Hanoi with vital war material. Kissinger used every crisis to demonstrate that the US had both the military power and the will to support its global interests.

On the whole, the evidence suggests that when detente was tested in peripheral areas the combination of diplomacy and force worked successfully, particularly when combined with linkage. Only in Bangladesh does the evidence seem negative.[69] Kissinger's policies during these crises were consistent with his writings – i.e., use of a mixture of diplomacy and force to achieve national objectives and to prevent a revolutionary power from undermining the international system. Unfortunately, it cannot be demonstrated that the actions of the USSR would have been even more aggressive without the restraining fabric of detente, nor can it be demonstrated that more pressure would have produced even greater concessions from Moscow.

The diplomatic achievements of Kissinger with respect to US–PRC rapprochement were less spectacular. But the opening to the PRC was in itself one of Kissinger's major achievements, and it had served its purpose – the USSR had become more accommodating to US demands. In addition the US–PRC rapprochement demonstrated that the bipolar world had ceased and that a triangular power constellation had emerged. But the process was slowed down by the divisive issue of Taiwan.

CONCLUSION

The global strategy which set the context of American foreign policy in the 1970s was conceptualized and executed by Kissinger. The strategy was consistent with Kissinger's models for stable and revolutionary international systems, and his perception of the contemporary international order. The concept of peace – which Kissinger defined as stability based on an equilibrium of forces within a legitimate international order rather than the avoidance of war – underlay his global strategy. Stability-peace had two structural imperatives: (a) an equilibrium of military power, and (b) acceptance by the superpowers of certain fundamental principles of legitimate state action in the international system. Both equilibrium and legitimacy were the essential requisites for a stable international system. *Neither was sufficient by itself*.

In the late 1960s, the establishment of a stable international order was complicated by the fact that the world was militarily bipolar but politically multipolar. Kissinger admits that political multipolarity makes it difficult to impose an American design, and advocates the establishment of an international structure based on political multipolarity and military bipolarity. However, his primary concern was the relationship between the superpowers since they alone possessed the overwhelming military capability that could transform the international system, or in an attempt to do so – each unilaterally – they could destroy the world. The avoidance of a nuclear war was Kissinger's main objective, therefore his global strategy revolved around the US–Soviet relationship. Even America's longstanding relationship with the Allies had to be, in Kissinger's view, subordinated to Washington's strategic interest in preserving its global position. Kissinger was convinced that the highest obligation was neither the Alliance or the preservation of Western values, but American security interests and ultimately survival because unless we survive no principles could be realized. Kissinger's policies with respect to the Soviet Union were based on two factors: (a) the strategic nuclear balance between the US and the USSR which served as a deterrent against irresponsible behaviour; and (b) the Sino–Soviet split which had broken the ideological bonds of international Communism and prompted each power to seek greater participation in the international system to gain leverage over the other.

The Sino–Soviet split confronted the US with both dangers and opportunities. Kissinger explored new initiatives *vis-à-vis* both powers. He was not interested in the ideological dispute between Moscow and Peking, but shared Peking's concern about the necessity to thwart Moscow's geopolitical ambitions. In his judgement, by remaining equidistant from both the USSR and the PRC and uncommitted in the deepening struggle that separated them, the US could gain leverage over both. Thus the opening to the PRC was conceived as a primary means of pressuring the USSR to be more accommodating to the demands of the US, so it preceded and gave major impetus to US–Soviet detente during the early 1970s. In addition the recognition of the PRC provided concrete substance to Kissinger's vague concept of an emergng multipolar world. By the end of 1969 the triangular relationship of US–PRC rapprochement and US–Soviet detente had emerged as Kissinger's global strategy.

The concept of linkage was a basic postulate of Kissinger's global strategy. He believed improved relations with the USSR and the PRC would produce dividends in other areas of concern to the US, and particularly they would help end the war in Vietnam. When the USSR began to explore bilateral relations with West European nations – in an effort to gain leverage over the US, and especially the FRG – Kissinger adopted policies which precluded the development of 'differential detente' which would have made linkage difficult to implement.

The US–Soviet relationship was basic to any policy that sought to establish a stable international order. Therefore US–Soviet detente was the central element in Kissinger's global strategy, and it rested on two pillars, the strategic arms limitation talks – SALT – on the one hand, and economic cooperation on the other. SALT was facilitated by a number of mutual US–Soviet perceptions and developments while economic cooperation rested exclusively on the weakness of the Soviet economy.

Kissinger's approach to SALT was consistent with his goal – the establishment of a stable international system – since it would produce one of the two structural imperatives, an equilibrium of military power. A rough equilibrium in strategic nuclear weapons was the most desirable in Kissinger's view since superiority by either side would be destabilizing and exact parity might be impossible to attain, given the differences in American and Soviet strategic weapons systems. The concept of sufficiency advanced by Kissinger incorporated both concepts, and demonstrated his conviction that political will or the lack of it – not weapons – were the causes of war.

The SALT agreements – the ABM Treaty and the Interim Agreement on Strategic Offensive Missiles – clearly demonstrated that Kissinger was less interested in the precise strategic weapons levels agreed upon than on the psychological and political benefits that would be derived from them. Indeed, the achievements of SALT made possible the agreement on the Basic Principles which would place the new US–Soviet relationship on a broader foundation. The basic principles were seen by Kissinger as the first step toward the achievement of the second structural imperative for the establishment of a stable international order, namely an agreement between the superpowers on what constitutes legitimate state action in the international arena.

Kissinger considered SALT as his most significant achievement in office because it brought the establishment of a stable international system a step closer. SALT also demonstrated that a triangular relationship could produce dividends in many areas of concern to the US. The opening to the PRC made the USSR more accommodating to US demands and the SALT agreements were in large part a result of US–PRC rapprochement. US–Soviet detente made possible the Quadripartite Agreement on the status of Berlin, thus depriving the Soviet Union of an issue – access to Berlin – on which the only recourse the US had was to threaten nuclear war, an unacceptable strategic option to American policy makers of the late 1960s. These achievements demonstrate that during the first Nixon Administration Kissinger's global strategy gave coherence and purpose to American foreign policy, made possible some fundamental changes in American diplomacy, and brought the establishment of a stable international order a step closer to achievement.

4 The US and Western Europe: a Troubled Partnership

INTRODUCTION

The ultimate goal of Kissinger's global strategy – the establishment of a stable international order – was in Kissinger's view threatened by the political multipolarity of the 1960s. Kissinger recognized that political multipolarity makes impossible the imposition of an American design. Instead, he advocated the establishment of an international system based on political multipolarity and military bipolarity. He was convinced, however, that the threat emanating from political multipolarity could be significantly reduced by resolving some of the apparently insoluble problems which beleaguered NATO. In his perceptive books, *The Necessity for Choice* and *The Troubled Partnership*, Kissinger maintained that the forging of a common Atlantic policy with Western Europe was the most urgent task confronting American foreign policy.[1] Hence his appointment as President Nixon's Assistant for National Security Affairs generated the hope in Western Europe that some of NATO's problems would be resolved.

In that and in other writings Kissinger maintained that no area of policy illustrated more dramatically the tension between political multipolarity and military bipolarity (as well as the integral relationship between diplomacy and strategy) than US policy toward NATO.[2] Kissinger's exhaustive analysis underlined the limits imposed on statesmen by structural conditions, limits with which statesmen must learn to live.[3] Moreover, his criticisms of US policies toward NATO highlighted the false premises on which these policies were based. From Kissinger's point of view, 'American policy has suffered from an unwillingness to recognize that there is a price to be paid,'[4] if the problems confronting NATO are to be resolved. Kissinger rejected the prevailing view that President de Gaulle was the cause of the bitter controversy between the US and Western Europe.

66

De Gaulle's intransigence, Kissinger argued, had severely strained the pattern of Allied relationships which emerged in the late 1940s and early 1950s, but de Gaulle could not have disrupted the Alliance by himself.[5] 'Fundamental changes have been taking place in the relative weights of Europe and the United States, in the nature of Alliances and in the character of strategy'. Hence, '[a]llied relationships would have had to be adapted to new conditions, no matter who governed in Paris – or in Washington'.[6]

This chapter will deal with Kissinger's analysis of the structural problems of NATO and of the nature of the issues that must be resolved. The focus will be on the consistency of Kissinger's conceptions with respect to the limits imposed on statesmen by the contemporary international system and by the nature of nuclear weapons, rather than on the specific proposals he put forth at various times. It is essential to understand the limits Kissinger perceived in order to understand his policies towards Western Europe.[7] Warren Nutter, in his critique of Kissinger's grand design, argued that by posing choices in terms of mutually exclusive alternatives (either political unity or disintegration), Kissinger saw little that could be done to resolve NATO's dilemmas.[8] Nutter, as well as most of Kissinger's critics, focused on specific proposals of Kissinger-the-scholar and his failure as a policymaker to implement them, and failed to recognize that given the limits Kissinger perceived, he was prepared to perpetuate the American hegemony to maintain the cohesion of NATO in the immediate future.

POLITICAL MULTIPOLARITY: THE CHANGED NATURE OF ATLANTIC RELATIONSHIPS

In the late 1940s and early 1950s, when the present pattern of Atlantic relationships was established, American dominance in Western Europe was unchallengeable. Western Europe depended on the US for its economic recovery, domestic cohesion, and defence. This dependence permitted the US to make NATO policy and US–West European cooperation and consultation was limited to the technical implementation of American policies. American policymakers identified the interests of the US with the general interest, and were convinced that any criticism of their policies by the Allies could be overcome by extensive briefings and insistent reiteration. This American attitude was in part encouraged by Western Europeans. The Allies, given their economic weakness, their inability (however temporary) to play an effective role in the international arena, their fear of an imminent Soviet attack, as well as their fear of American withdrawal, adopted a policy of influencing American decisions rather than developing policies of their own. When dissatisfied with NATO policies, Western European leaders delayed the implementation of agreed measures rather than developing realistic alternatives. In fact, they were more concerned with extracting American reassurances than with encouraging a consistent US policy. By the late 1950s, however, Western European leaders began to challenge not only the implementation of American policies but the validity of American conceptions as well.

In Kissinger's view, the period of the unchallengeable 'American hegemony came to an end in the late 1950s and early 1960s under the impact of four events in which United States policy had played a major role: European economic recovery; European integration; decolonization; and the Cuban missile crisis and its aftermath'. Kissinger observed that 'each of these events illustrates that results cannot always be judged by the intentions of those whose policies start a historical process, even less by their pronouncements'. But, more importantly, his analysis of these events manifested what Kissinger considered to be the false premises of US policies toward Western Europe.[9]

The economic recovery of Western Europe began in 1947 with the Greek–Turkish Aid Programme and the Marshall Plan. In April 1948, Congress appropriated over $5 billion to implement the Marshall Plan, and by 1952 – when military aid began to supplant economic assistance – the US had expended nearly $14 billion in promoting Western European recovery. According to Kissinger, the US promoted West European recovery because it saw Western Europe as a potential partner which would share the burdens and responsibilities of world leadership. Official pronouncements of the US purposes revealed the expectation that after its recovery Western Europe 'would continue to pursue parallel, if not identical policies' with the US. But Kissinger asserted that 'this was ... always unlikely'.[10]

With the economic recovery of Western Europe, its traditional political dynamism would return. This development would permit Western European leaders to assert their own view of the world, a view that would reflect the historical perspectives and national interests of their own nations rather than those of the US.[11] The process of Western European economic integration increased the assertiveness of the Allies in defending their interests. The US promoted economic integration because it was viewed as the first step toward political unity. The European Economic Community (EEC) was seen by the US as an 'outwardlooking' institution which meant that it would not discriminate against American interests. But Kissinger considered this highly unlikely because the internal logic of a common market produces its own necessities. 'It is the essence of a common market', he argued, 'that it will maintain some tariff barriers against the outside world and, as internal barriers are lower than external ones, a measure of discrimination will be unavoidable'.[12] The fact that trade barriers can be reduced only as a result of governmental negotiations was bound to increase the disputes between the US and Western Europe, especially when the economic strength of the EEC increased. Moreover, the EEC had created a middle bloc between the US and the USSR, and when the economic interests of the EEC coincided with the political goal of France to assert a more independent role for Western Europe, the result was the exacerbation of tensions in NATO.

But Kissinger recognized that the stability and self-confidence of Western Europe was 'still shaky' despite its economic recovery. This becomes apparent, he argued, when the Allies are examined individually and not collectively, as they often are by American policymakers.[13] Kissinger insisted that the disparity in economic strength between the US and its Allies would continue, but also argued that the tension in NATO generated by economic factors could be reduced if the US policy takes 'account of two contradictory trends: Europe's economic and psychological recovery and the tenuousness of this assertiveness'.[14]

Decolonization was the third event that contributed to Western Europe's political dynamism. After giving up their colonial empires (often under the pressure from the US), the Allies began to develop a specifically European role and ceased to see themselves as world powers. Moreover they were convinced (with the possible exception of Britain and Portugal) that their security was not directly threatened by crisis in other parts of the world. But in the 1960s the principal threat to world peace seemed to lie not in a Soviet attack on Western Europe, but in trouble spots outside the Atlantic region.

In the 1950s, the US refused to support the Allies in Asia and in the Middle East. Now West European leaders justified their unwillingness to support the global commitments of the US by repeating the American argument of the 1950s that the larger interests of the free world are sometimes served by allowing for differing, occasionally even competing, Western approaches to the emerging nations.[15] When Western European leaders have supported the global commitments of the US, their major objective (according to Kissinger) has been to gain a veto over American actions. This is evident in the thrust of their recommendations which stress the necessity to avoid a direct showdown and even the semblance of risk.[16] In other words, the roles of the US and its Allies are precisely reversed. Western Europeans do not consider their vital interests at stake in America's extra-European involvement.

The American conviction that West European economic recovery and political unity would enable the Allies to play a global role misses the whole point. According to Kissinger 'Countries do not assume burdens because it is fair, only because it is necessary'.[17] Kissinger rejected the argument that the Allies should play a more active global role because their resources were adequate for such a task; in his view, the Allies did not possess the resources. Kissinger maintained that even if they did, availability of resources does not guarantee an interest in assuming global responsibilities. This was demonstrated by US policy prior to the Second World War, when the US possessed the resources but not the philosophy for a global role. Hence it did not assume global commitments.

Kissinger maintained that in the postwar period, the US was 'the only member of NATO with worldwide interests, and this produce[d] unavoidable differences in perspective'.[18] He argued that 'partially as the result of decolonization, Europeans are unlikely to conduct a significant global policy whatever their resources or their degree of unity'. Therefore 'cooperation between the United States and Europe must concentrate on issues within the Atlantic area rather than global partnership'.[19] In other words, Western Europe was assigned a regional role by Kissinger despite the fact that France and Britain were seeking to play a global role, even though smaller than that of the US and the USSR.

But 'even within the Atlantic area', Kissinger insisted, 'a more equitable distribution of responsibilities has two prerequisites: There must be some consensus in the analysis of the international situation, at least as it affects Europe; there must be a conviction that the United States cannot or will not carry all the burdens alone'. In Kissinger's view 'neither condition is met today'. American leadership, by precluding any independent Western European initiatives, convinced the Allies that the US would carry all the burdens alone, while consultation could not create the necessary consensus. Kissinger insisted that improved consultation could only alleviate, not remove, the difficulty.[20]

The Cuban missile crisis in October 1962 was the fourth event that contributed to Western Europe's political independence. The outcome of the crisis was a setback for the USSR, and it had a negative impact on the relationship between the US and Western Europe. The crisis ushered the relationships of the superpowers into a new phase; both the US and the USSR were now convinced that the risks of nuclear war were real, and took steps to reduce them. In the summer of 1963 the US and the USSR negotiated and signed the Nuclear Test Ban Treaty which limited the arms race by prohibiting above-ground nuclear testing. In 1968 they signed the Nuclear Non-Proliferation Treaty, each pledging to halt the distribution of nuclear weapons. The USSR had pushed for a non-proliferation agreement and (as it doubtless intended) the Non-Proliferation Treaty intensified strains with NATO. France refused to sign it, and the FRG moved toward approval most reluctantly.

Moreover the Soviet leaders began weapons programmes that would increase the USSR's nuclear power, and thus preclude a similar outcome in another crisis. By the late 1960s the USSR was approaching nuclear parity with the US. This development complicated the strains within NATO by reducing, in the Allies' view, the credibility of the US' nuclear guarantee.

The Allies were not consulted during the Cuban missile crisis although de Gaulle (in his words) was informed.[21] When the US consulted the Allies (as it did with respect to the Non-Proliferation Treaty), consultation was limited to specific provisions. But it was the underlying philosophy which concerned the Allies, especially Italy and the FRG. The result was that bilateral US–Soviet agreements were seen by Western Europeans as the forerunners of a more comprehensive agreement that would affect their vital interest but would be negotiated without them. The American response to the Soviet invasion of Czechoslovakia in August 1968 (and especially the temporary postponement of the SALT negotiations), reinforced that conviction. But while the Allies feared a bilateral agreement between the superpowers, they no longer feared a Soviet attack, and the urgency for Allied cohesion diminished. Meanwhile, the credibility of the US nuclear pledge was increasingly undermined by Soviet

ICBMs. The result was the increase of Western European initiatives toward Moscow.

The Third Force tendencies in Western Europe were bound to increase as detente progressed.[22] Kissinger saw little that could be done about it within the existing NATO framework. He argued:

> The issue is not whether the United States would make a 'deal' contrary to the interests of its Allies. It is rather that in an alliance of sovereign states each country will think that it is a better judge of its own requirements than any partner, however close. No ally will be prepared to let another negotiate about what it considers its vital interests.[23]

Kissinger believed that Western Europeans opposed bilateral US–Soviet negotiations from which they were excluded not because they disagreed with the underlying philosophy, but because they did not want to establish a precedent for changes in other policies. Moreover, unilateral changes in US strategic doctrine undermined Allied leaders who had staked their prestige on US policies and created a sense of impotence in Western Europe. However, some Allied leaders, unlike de Gaulle, did not fully express their disquiet because they did not want to further undermine the cohesion of NATO on which their national security was thought to be dependent. De Gaulle's policy, Kissinger argued, produced an illusion of West European strength and self-confidence while the acquiescence of other leaders produced the illusion that the present NATO framework was natural. But neither of these reflected the existing reality in Western Europe.

For Kissinger, Western European unity (either on a federal or on a confederal model) is the only alternative for both the US and Western Europe. But he considered this 'a problem primarily for the Europeans' and urged the US not to commit its diplomatic energies to one particular form of unity – that of federalism.[24]

Kissinger insisted that an effective Western Europe could not be built without the full support of Britain, but he rejected the view that British membership in the EEC should be a direct objective of American foreign policy since Britain was ambivalent about its commitment to European unity.[25] He recognized that a united Western Europe would challenge American leadership in NATO and complicate negotiations with the Soviet bloc, since in the political and economic fields the temptations for independent initiatives are great and the penalties small.[26] Kissinger, however, was not concerned, because as he explained, 'it is hard to visualize a "deal" between the USSR and Europe which would jeopardize our interests without jeopardizing European interests first'.[27] This lack of concern stemmed from his conviction that as long as the defence of Western Europe depended on the American nuclear guarantee the Allies would acquiesce in the hegemonial position of the US.[28]

To summarize Kissinger's views, the disputes within the Atlantic Alliance reflected the changes that were taking place in the relative positions of Western Europe and the US. When Western Europe recovered economically from the war and regained its traditional political dynamism, the need for economic and military aid from the US declined. This development, he believed, deprived the US of the instrument that had been used to maintain discipline within the Alliance. Western European leaders were now pursuing policies that reflected the national interests of their own nations. Their assertiveness in defending these interests increased as a result of West European economic integration. These developments shattered the American beliefs that after its recovery Western Europe would continue to pursue parallel if not identical policies with the US, and that the EEC would not discriminate against American interests. Moreover, Kissinger maintained that the economic integration did not lead to political unity as the US hoped it would. Decolonization enhanced Western Europe's political dynamism, but reduced significantly its willingness to share with the US the burden and responsibilities of world leadership. And finally, the Cuban missile crisis and its aftermath convinced the Allies that the threat of a Soviet attack on Western Europe no longer existed. This perception contributed to Western Europe's political independence but raised new fears about the credibility of the American nuclear guarantee.[29]

What made the disputes within the Alliance insoluble was the nature of nuclear power which changed the nature of all alliances and altered the integral relationship between diplomacy and military strategy.

NUCLEAR WEAPONS: THE CHANGED NATURE OF ALLIANCES

According to Kissinger, throughout history alliances have been created for three basic reasons:

1. to provide an accretion of power – and the wider the Alliance the greater its power to resist aggression
2. to leave no doubt about the alignment of forces
3. to transform a tacit interest in mutual assistance into a formal obligation.[30]

Kissinger, however, saw inconsistency among these reasons even before the advent of nuclear weapons. The attempt to combine the maximum number of states for joint action occasionally conflicted with the desire to leave no doubt about the collective motivation. The wider the alliance, the more various were the motives animating its members, and the more intense and direct had to be a threat to produce a united response. In the case of NATO, however, the inconsistency among these reasons has been largely overshadowed by the perceived threat of a Soviet attack and the ever-present fear of West Europeans that the US might withdraw its forces from Europe.[31]

NATO meets three of four requirements Kissinger considers vital to the effectiveness of an Alliance. First, NATO has a common objective – defence against the Soviet military threat. Second, a degree of joint policy sufficient to define the *casus belli* exists (this was explicitly stated in Article 5 of the North Atlantic treaty).[32] Third, the military organization of NATO permits the Allies to take joint action once the political decision is made. But NATO does not meet the fourth requirement, penalties for non-cooperation do not exist, hence American protection is often taken for granted and the mutuality of obligation is in danger of breaking down.

The advent of nuclear weapons compounded the difficulty in maintaining the effectiveness of an alliance. Nuclear war requires tight command and control of all nuclear weapons which in Kissinger's view is inconsistent with an alliance of sovereign states. Moreover the nuclear war risk has a negative impact on the credibility of the traditional pledges of mutual assistance. Kissinger argued that in the past, alliances held together because they believed the 'immediate' risk of war was less than the 'ultimate' danger of facing a preponderant enemy alone.[33] But the deployment of nuclear weapons by the USSR made nuclear war the worst contingency for NATO. This generated uncertainties on both sides of the Atlantic about the course of action Allies would take in a time of crisis. The US fears that West Europeans might accept Soviet domination rather than face national destruction, while West Europeans seriously question whether the US will risk a nuclear war to defend Western Europe. The result of these uncertainties was the development of theories of nuclear control that either turned NATO into a unilateral US' guarantee or called into question the utility of NATO altogether.

The bitter controversy between the US and France clearly manifested how nuclear weapons have affected the credibility of traditional pledges of mutual assistance. The US sought to turn NATO into a unilateral American guarantee, which it is believed to be; American policymakers consistently maintained that the West European contribution to the overall nuclear strength of NATO was negligible. President Kennedy described the French nuclear programme as 'inimical' to NATO, and Secretary of Defense Robert McNamara called the West European nuclear forces 'dangerous', maintaining that they were 'prone to obsolescence' and 'lacking in credibility'.[34] These views emanated from the efforts of the Kennedy and Johnson Administrations to develop the new strategic doctrine of flexible response and to have it accepted as the official NATO doctrine. Flexible response – a strategy for discriminately conducting nuclear war – required a centralized system of command and control, and highly invulnerable strategic forces. Hence the existence of national strategic forces not under American control was inconsistent with these essential requisites. In addition, the French and British nuclear forces were seen as divisive because they implied distrust of the US and diverted resources from the conventional build-up which these administrations were urging the Allies to undertake.[35]

Kissinger did not share these views and argued that 'for their limited objectives, the British and the French nuclear forces are not so ineffective as we sometimes insist'.[36] Kissinger seemed to share the British and French view that several centres of decision would complicate the USSR's calculations, and thus enhance deterrence. The American opposition stemmed from the conviction that the British and the French nuclear forces were a possible replacement to US nuclear forces. But Kissinger viewed them as a complement to US strategic power, and not as an alternative.

Kissinger argued the fact that the British and French nuclear forces could not deal with all nuclear threats would not lead to the dissolution of NATO as their opponents often alleged. Rather, a partnership in planning between Europe and the US would develop. The purpose of the British and the French nuclear forces, Kissinger maintained, should be to deal with problems of special concern to the Allies. In particular, they could allay the fear that emphasis on local defence would enable the USSR to devastate Europe while it spared the US. Kissinger suggested that a constructive policy would be not to obstruct the French nuclear programme but to assist in its development – if only by aiding the development of delivery vehicles. He insisted, however, that American assistance to France and Britain in the nuclear and related fields should be made dependent on fulfilling their commitments to strengthen their conventional forces, and not to spread nuclear weapons to other countries without the consent of the US.[37]

In the American view, according to Kissinger, the Allies are necessary, not because they increase the overall military strength of NATO, but because they permit the US to resist Soviet aggression by means less cataclysmic than nuclear war. Because of this view, the US has been treating NATO as if it were a single political unit and that, Kissinger insisted, runs counter to the fact that NATO is composed of sovereign states which will not acquiesce to any strategic doctrine which appears to threaten their national existence.[38]

The US made various proposals for sharing the control of nuclear weapons, such as the Multilateral Force (MLF), the double-veto system, and 'earmarking' and 'assignment' of nuclear weapons to NATO. But Kissinger cut through the sophisticated elaboration of these proposals to point out that they were designed to make American nuclear weapons control more bearable, not to alter it. The central feature of these proposals has been the retention of ultimate American control over nuclear weapons because in spite of nuclear sharing the US would retain its veto over the use of nuclear weapons. The issue of nuclear control was the fundamental problem confronting NATO in the early 1960s, but Kissinger saw no prospect for resolving it, 'because the issue of nuclear control was inherently divisive'.[39] In his view, the risk of nuclear war could not be reliably combined with the key attribute of sovereignty, the unilateral right of a sovereign state to alter its strategic or political views.[40]

French strategic doctrine was based on the premise that alliances had lost their utility altogether. General Pierre M. Gallois argued that nuclear weapons have made alliances obsolete because, faced with the risk of total destruction, no nation will jeopardize its survival for another. Each nation then must acquire its own nuclear forces to defend itself against direct attack. Kissinger accepted Gallois's argument that the threat of nuclear retaliation had lost some of its credibility, but feared that (if accepted) it would put an end to NATO and would lead to international chaos, given the proliferation of nuclear forces. Moreover Kissinger maintained that the Gallois theory would 'transform a degree of uncertainty into a guarantee that the United States would not come to the assistance of its Allies', thus greatly simplifying the calculations of the Soviet Union. [41]

But a degree of uncertainty is essential to deterrence, and Kissinger stressed that it must be maintained. If not, it would facilitate the implementation of 'the Soviet strategy of ambiguity which seeks to upset the strategic balance by small degrees and combines political, psychological, and military pressures to induce the greatest degree of uncertainty and hesitation in the minds of the opponent'. The threat of all-out war is more credible as a deterrent to a direct threat to a nation's survival than to a challenge to an ally. Hence Kissinger argued:

> If the Soviet bloc can present its challenges in less than all-out form it may gain a crucial advantage. Every move on its part will then pose the appalling dilemma of whether we are willing to commit suicide to prevent encroachments, not one of which seems to threaten our existence directly but which may be a step on the road to our ultimate destruction. [42]

Kissinger indeed believed that the USSR presented its challenges in less than all-out form, and opposed the withdrawal of forces from Europe.

Kissinger stressed:

> It is high time to end the threat that our commitment to the defense of Europe is conditional on one particular organization of nuclear forces. The fact is that we cannot withdraw from Europe even if we do not obtain our preferred strategic arrangements. To threaten to do so is both dangerous and empty. It is dangerous because it indicates that our commitment is not firm; and it is empty because we can no more withdraw from Europe than from Hawaii. [43]

Kissinger feared that if the threat was taken seriously by West Europeans, it would lead to neutralism. This development would alter the existing balance of power in favour of the USSR, and thus threaten the existing international stability.

The range of nuclear weapons poses another dilemma for NATO. Traditionally a distant ally could help only if it were able to bring its military strength to bear in the area of conflict. If not, the threatened ally could either resist or surrender. If it resisted in the face of overwhelming military power, it had to be psychologically prepared to accept physical destruction. In NATO, the European Allies strive for deterrence by adding the military power of the US to their own. At the same time, they seek to reduce damage of themselves to a minimum, should deterrence fail. Intercontinental ballistic missiles have made it possible to combine these two objectives. Hence part of the strategic debate involves jockeying to determine which geographic area will be the theatre of war if deterrence fails. But, as Kissinger pointed out, 'this obviously cannot be made explicit'.[44]

Related to this part of the strategic debate is the question as to the type of war to be fought in case of Soviet attack. A conventional war (or a limited nuclear war confined to Europe) is a less damaging strategy to Americans than a direct nuclear exchange with the USSR. A direct nuclear exchange between the superpowers is the strategy promoted by the Allies, which argue that the threat of nuclear retaliation is a more effective deterrent. In Kissinger's view, this dispute is not likely to be resolved because:

> the choice between nuclear and conventional war is no longer entirely up to the West. Whatever its preference, NATO will have to prepare for the introduction of nuclear weapons by the opponent. Any war will be nuclear, whether or not nuclear weapons are used in a sense that deployment – even of conventional forces – will have to take place in a nuclear environment.[45]

The role of conventional forces is inextricably related to this debate. NATO doctrine prior to 1962 described conventional forces as the 'shield', and nuclear weapons as the 'sword' of the Alliance. Conventional forces were to be a 'tripwire' that would unleash the strategic nuclear forces of the US. When the strategic balance began to change, the US increased its pressure on West Europeans to strengthen their conventional forces. But the Allies seemed convinced that an increase in their forces would raise doubts about the US nuclear guarantee, thus making Soviet aggression more likely. Moreover some of the objections of the Allies to strengthening their conventional forces are based on fiscal considerations similar to those that prompted some Americans to advocate the reduction of US forces in Europe. The actual increases in conventional forces made by the Allies have been only large enough to induce the US to keep its troops in Europe, but not so high as to provide a real alternative to the strategy of massive retaliation.

In December 1962, however, the Nassau Agreement reversed the traditional NATO concepts of 'shield' and 'sword'. This decision was made bilaterally by the US and Britain: nuclear weapons were now described as the 'shield' and conventional forces as the 'sword' of NATO – implying a preference for a largely conventional defence of Western Europe. The Kennedy Administration (by placing a heavier emphasis on conventional defence) generated great concern among the Allies, who believed that massive retaliation would be automatic. The Administration's efforts to develop a strategic doctrine – flexible response – with a maximum number of options coincided with de Gaulle's policy to assert a more independent role for France, thus adding urgency to the debate over the role of conventional forces.

From Kissinger's standpoint, the controversy was inevitable and not likely to be resolved because the US saw the conventional forces in military terms while West Europeans saw them in symbolic terms – i.e., a means to obtain American nuclear protection. Kissinger was greatly concerned with the growing support in both London and Washington for reduction of conventional forces, and advised against such a step because it would have a negative impact on NATO, especially since the US had been pressuring West Europeans to increase their forces.[46]

The debate over nuclear or conventional defence also involves the problem concerning the role and control of tactical nuclear weapons, an issue which in Kissinger's view required urgent attention, but had been 'swept under the rug'. Tactical nuclear weapons were introduced into the NATO arsenal in the mid-1950s to offset the permanent numerical superiority of Soviet conventional forces. They included almost everything from artillery pieces with ranges of about fifteen miles to Pershing missiles with ranges up to 700 miles (in the improved version). These weapons were 'tactical' in the sense that they were stationed in Europe and under the control of the Supreme Allied Commander, Europe (SACEUR), since some of the longer-range weapons were indistinguishable from those controlled by the Strategic Air Command (SAC). Moreover, tactical nuclear weapons were under the double-veto system which required the consent of both the US and the host country before they could be used. To some Allies, these weapons became a touchstone of the American commitment to the defence of Western Europe and a guarantee of an automatic nuclear response, once war reached a certain scale.

Kissinger argued that tactical nuclear weapons present particular difficulties of command and control but insisted that their 'mission ... should not be considered in isolation from the other, primarily

strategic operations which will be taking place'.[47] By confining the
use of tactical nuclear weapons to the combat zone, a strategy would
guarantee the devastation of Europe, but would not deter the USSR
since Soviet territory would be spared. Such a strategy Kissinger
maintained, 'even if it succeeded in stopping the attack, would
eliminate Europe as a factor in international politics; it would
guarantee that any other threatened area would surrender'.[48]
Moreover, Kissinger feared that such a strategy would stimulate
neutralist tendencies in Western Europe and destroy the psychological basis of any common Allied effort.

Kissinger summed up the debate over nuclear or conventional
defence as follows:

> Exclusive United States control of nuclear strategy is politically
> and psychologically difficult to reconcile with a strategy of multiple
> choices or flexible response. The European refusal to assign a
> meaningful military mission to conventional forces in Europe is
> incompatible with the indefinite retention of large United States
> forces there. If the United States places a high enough value on
> conventional defense, it will have to concede Europe a measure of
> autonomy in nuclear control. Or else it will have to move to an
> effective sharing of political sovereignty. If the Europeans want to
> insist on an automatic nuclear response, a reconsideration of our
> conventional deployment on the Continent will become inevitable.
> Refusal to face these facts will guarantee a perpetuation of present
> disputes and increasing disarray within NATO.[49]

In other words, Kissinger maintained – and still does maintain – that
as long as NATO is composed of sovereign states there is no prospect
for resolving any of its problems. An ideal solution would be political
integration of the entire Atlantic community, because then the
control of nuclear weapons and the deployment of NATO forces
would become technical issues.[50] But Kissinger recognized that it
was highly unlikely that NATO would become a single political unit
in the foreseeable future.[51] In his view, the next best solution would
be West European political unity – perhaps a federation –
accompanied by a European nuclear force.[52]

Military bipolarity has encouraged political multipolarity, thus
contributing to the change in the nature of alliances in yet another
(rather negative) way. In a bipolar world, the balance between the
superpowers is regarded as both precarious and inflexible. A gain for
one side appears as an absolute loss for the other. Neither the US nor

the USSR can permit a major advance by the other, whether the area in which it occurs is formally protected by an Alliance or not. This inevitably leads to the weakening of Allied cohesion. The Allies believed that their defence is in the overwhelming interest of the US, hence they see no need to purchase its support by acquiescence in US policies.

The weakening of Allied cohesion produces polycentrism which in Kissinger's view reflects not the emergence of new centres of physical power but the attempt by the Allies to establish new centres of decision.[53] France is the most evident example of polycentrism. De Gaulle recognized that his independent policies could not fundamentally affect the circumstances in which the US might be prepared to use its nuclear weapons. The widening gap in military strength between the US and Western Europe is not likely to discourage polycentrism as long as the world remains bipolar with respect to nuclear weapons. On the one hand, the risk of nuclear war calls into question the American commitment to the defence of Western Europe. On the other, the issue – a Soviet attack on Western Europe – with respect to which the threat of massive retaliation is credible is so clear-cut that it requires no formal reinforcement.[54]

The US assertion – that in the nuclear age an isolated strategy is no longer possible – misses the central point according to Kissinger. '[P]recisely because an isolated strategy is indeed impossible, allies have unprecedented scope for the pursuit of their own objectives'.[55] Kissinger was convinced that the more detente proceeded (real or imaginary) the more West Europeans would pursue independent policies to achieve their national objectives, even at the expense of the US and NATO unity.

The preceding examination reveals that NATO's strategic dilemma has developed because there is an increasing inconsistency between the technical requirements of military strategy and the political imperatives of the nation-state. In Kissinger's view, three factors have produced this dilemma:

1. the need for central command and control of nuclear weapons
2. the desire of each major ally to have substantial influence on NATO decisions in defining the *casus belli* (especially during a crisis), and in the planning of the controlled military operations foreseen by the doctrine of flexible response
3. and the need of the major Allies to share in the prestige and the political power which control of nuclear weapons confers.

What perpetuates NATO's strategic dilemma is the fact that 'there is no scheme which can reconcile these objectives perfectly as long as the Atlantic Alliance remains composed of sovereign states'. The unwillingness of both the US and the Allies 'to admit that the genuine conflict of interests exists' only exacerbates and perpetuates the bitter disputes in NATO.[56]

From Kissinger's point of view, the only political solution that could resolve NATO's dilemmas – a supranational political and defence community – was unattainable within the foreseeable future. But the question was: what could be done in the immediate future to maintain the cohesion of NATO and its effectiveness as an instrument for defence in an atmosphere of detente?

NATO STRATEGY: THE SECURITY DILEMMA OF WESTERN EUROPE

In Kissinger's view, almost all of the outstanding issues in Western Europe depended upon the resolution of one basic issue – the significance of all-out nuclear war for the defence of Western Europe.[57] The declining credibility of the threat of massive retaliation was at the centre of the dispute between the US and its European Allies. Kissinger summed up the security problem of Western Europe as follows:

> (a) The Soviet Union can threaten all of Europe from its own territories. Consequently, alliances are not essential for its safety. (b) No European country alone is capable of withstanding Soviet pressure. Security is therefore inseparable from unity. (c) The threat of all-out war is losing its credibility and its strategic meaning. (d) The defense of Europe, therefore, cannot be conducted solely from North America, because the aggressor can pose threats which will not seem to warrant total retaliation and because, however firm allied unity may be, a nation cannot be counted on to commit suicide in defense of a foreign territory.[58]

This problem could have been resolved if NATO had developed a common strategy which had not forced the US to choose between massive retaliation and inaction in the defence of Western Europe. With respect to nuclear weapons, whether strategic or tactical (theatre), Kissinger saw no prospect of developing a common NATO strategy and maintained that 'the doctrine of massive retaliation [would] remain valid'.[59] But he insisted that the strengthening of NATO's conventional forces was essential if the US was to escape from the dilemma of either defending Western Europe with nuclear weapons or not defending her at all. A strong conventional force capable of withstanding a wide range of challenges would enable NATO to resist Soviet blackmail. The stronger the local forces, the less the likelihood that certain kinds of threats would be made at all. The ability of the Atlantic Alliance to resist Soviet encroachments would be increased if a strong conventional force maximized the number of military alternatives between surrender and total war. For Kissinger, a strong conventional force was the only way to make the available power relevant to objectives likely to be in dispute.

Deterrence would be enhanced if NATO developed a conventional force that posed a risk to the USSR out of proportion to the objectives to be obtained. Kissinger maintained that a strong conventional force in Western Europe would perform a vital function even if it could not withstand every scale of Soviet attack. At the very least, such a force would drive the USSR into a scale of military effort which would remove any doubt about its ultimate intention, and thus make the Western threat of massive retaliation more convincing. According to Kissinger, 'the most favorable situation would exist if the military establishment in Europe could not be overcome locally. Then the risk of initiating all-out war would be shifted to the Soviet Union'. This generates 'a very crucial psychological obstacle' to a full-scale attack on Western Europe since it raises the risk of all-out war to an intolerable level for the USSR.[60]

A strong conventional force backed by a credible strategic and tactical nuclear capability was in Kissinger's view the best means for deterring the spectrum of alternative strategies open to the USSR – i.e., nibbling tactics, nuclear blackmail, and nuclear war. Kissinger argued that '[if] the impotence of NATO [were] to be demonstrated, all other areas would fall to the Soviet Union almost by default'.[61] However if Western Europe proved capable of resisting Soviet pressure, and if US support appeared suited to the nature of the Soviet threat, then it would be possible to challenge any demonstrations of Soviet power.

Present NATO forces, Kissinger argued, combined the worst features of massive retaliation and local defence. The forces are larger than required for a 'trip-wire', yet too weak to resist a major Soviet attack. The existing forces tend to tempt Soviet pressure and fuel West European irresolution in the face of pressure. Kissinger feared that the Western European resistance toward increases in conventional forces would make American disengagement inevitable and would deter the US from seeking Soviet concessions in negotiating for it. He opposed the reduction of US forces in Europe and stressed that 'if the United States understands its own interests, it will not pursue so irresponsible a course'.[62]

Kissinger did not believe that the replacement of US forces by West European divisions would solve the basic dilemma and insisted that it was vital that the defence of Western Europe involve American forces from the outset. This strengthened deterrence, since the risk to the USSR was raised. Even a limited war in Western Europe involving the US represented an intolerably high risk of all-out nuclear war, if only because Soviet leaders could not be confident that either superpower knew how to keep the war from escalating. If deterrence failed, only American involvement could keep the war localized since the US was the only NATO member with an adequate retaliatory capability. Kissinger maintained that 'an effort by either Europe or the United States to leave the defence of Europe entirely in European hands would prove disastrous to all partners'.[63]

Kissinger, therefore, was not prepared to leave the defence of Western Europe to the Allies. This became clear when he stated:

> While our allies have a right to insist on American participation in their defence and must be able to count on it, they should not be permitted to prescribe a course of action which involves the most catastrophic risks, the more so if this strategy reduces the willingness of *all* partners to resist the most likely challenge. A local deterrent in Europe is required to increase the range of our options and to bring the deterrent policy of NATO into line with the strategy it is prepared to implement. A strategy of local defense is essential not as a device to save the alliance, though it will serve this purpose. Rather, the alliance alone offers the possibility of a strategy which does not inevitably involve catastrophe.[64]

The strengthening of conventional forces in Europe was also seen by Kissinger as an essential prerequisite to effective arms control negotiations. He argued that '[to] undertake a major program of controlling nuclear weapons without restoring the balance of conventional forces [was] sheer irresponsibility'.[65] The reasons were obvious, The inadequacies of the current NATO forces provided no incentive for the USSR to agree to any meaningful arms control schemes. The Soviets probably believed that they could gain no additional security from arms control proposals. Alternatively, given the growing support in the US for force reduction in Europe, they could achieve the objectives of arms control through unilateral NATO reductions. Without the strengthening of NATO's conventional forces, the USSR might not even have taken NATO proposals seriously because it already felt protected by its local preponderance.[66]

An ideal scheme for European security, Kissinger insisted, 'must take care not to wreck NATO', because without NATO each West European nation would face the USSR alone. It must retain the capability for local defence, lest West Europeans become demoralized by the threat of Soviet conventional and tactical nuclear strength. And it must also give assurances to the USSR against attack from NATO territory. In Kissinger's view, 'the question then becomes whether it is possible to conceive of two military establishments on the Continent capable of defensive action but deprived through appropriate control measures of offensive power. Can these objectives be reconciled?'[67] The likelihood that they could be seemed remote to Kissinger.

For arms control to be effective in Central Europe, Kissinger argued that it must accompany a political settlement, because 'as long as Germany remains divided the danger of an explosion exists, whatever the wishes of the chief protagonists'. Hence the two problems of German unity and arms control in Central Europe are closely related. A united Germany without arms control would frighten all the states surrounding Germany, while arms control without a united Germany would be either a palliative or would magnify conflicts in Central Europe.[68] Kissinger, however, saw no prospects for German unification within the discernible future.[69]

THE PROBLEM OF GERMANY

European defence, Kissinger argued, was inconceivable without the full participation of Germany, politically and militarily. From his standpoint:

> The ideal situation would be a Germany strong enough to defend itself but not strong enough to attack, united so that its frustrations do not erupt into conflict and its divisions do not encourage the rivalry of its neighbors, but not so centralized that its discipline and

capacity for rapid action evoke countermeasures in self-defence. Such a Germany has existed only at rare periods. To help establish it must be a major task of Western policy.[70]

Germany has held the key to the stability of Europe for at least three centuries. In the twentieth century Germany twice violated European (and, in turn, world) stability. In the postwar period Germany emerged as the balance wheel of NATO. Hence, in Kissinger's view, the cohesiveness of the Alliance would be tested more severely by the problem of German unity than by the issue of nuclear control.[71]

The problem of Germany was according to Kissinger complicated by three factors:

(1) NATO is an alliance of status quo countries; yet one of its principal members [FRG] seeks a basic change in the status quo. (2) None of Germany's allies shares her national aspirations [desire for unification] with equal intensity. (3) Germany's past has left a legacy of distrust that creates special obstacles to its international role.[72]

Even if NATO cohesiveness was enhanced, Kissinger argued, it would be very difficult to reconcile these divergences. But what compounded the difficulty was the rivalry between France and the US in that each tried to gain the support of the FRG for its policies by holding out vague hopes for the achievement of Germany's national goals.

In an atmosphere of detente the potential for conflict between the FRG and the other NATO members was increased. Detente in Kissinger's view implied tacit acceptance of the status quo by most members of NATO. But to Germany, it implied a sacrifice of basic national aspirations since detente would enhance the consolidation of the East German regime. Kissinger criticized American policy-makers for hinting that the FRG should be more flexible toward the East, and insisted that 'while the Federal Republic should not be urged into bilateral dealings with the East, it should be given every encouragement to make a major contribution to the formulation of an Allied position on Germany'.[73]

Kissinger maintained however, that 'any policy on Germany must deal with three problems: (1) relations with the Soviet Union. . ., (2) relations with the East German satellite regime and (3) relations with the East European governments.' Kissinger argued that in all three the interests of Germany and the other NATO members were potentially divergent; hence a common Allied policy was precluded. Nevertheless, at the very least, the interests of the Western Allies must be synchronized.[74]

Moreover according to Kissinger, any policy for Germany's future must reconcile three incompatible factors: '(1) the German desire for self-determination, (2) the East European concern for security and (3) the Soviet concern lest a unified Germany impair its own security and shake its international position.'[75] These factors can be partly reconciled by Germany's acceptance of its eastern border. This is essential, Kissinger argued, otherwise German unification 'is impossible so long as it is considered an inevitable prelude to a new set of pressures in Eastern Europe'.[76]

The division of Germany, according to Kissinger, would persist whatever the policy of the Alliance. The issue however is not whether unification could be achieved, but what attitude the Allies should take toward this fact. 'The division of Germany may be unavoidable; but the cohesion of the Atlantic Alliance requires that there is no ambiguity about the reason for it'.[77] In other words, the onus for perpetuating the division of Germany must be placed on the USSR, otherwise the FRG could not be expected to place full reliance on the Alliance as the best means for achieving its national interests. It would instead deal separately with the USSR, thus initiating a race for accommodation on the part of other NATO members, and thereby splitting NATO. The collapse of NATO from Kissinger's standpoint would lead to acquiescence in Soviet power elsewhere, thus the transformation of the international system would be achieved by default.

There was no doubt in Kissinger's mind that 'the long term hope for German unity . . . resides in the unity of Europe'.[78] And the unity of Europe required a stern refusal to recognize East Germany in its present form. Recognition, he insisted, must be linked to the prerequisite of self-determination. Progress toward German unification on any other basis would be self-contradictory. The outcome would be Soviet hegemony over all of Germany. The policy of NATO should then be to isolate East Germany, not to expand relations with it.

Similarly NATO should not negotiate away the independence of West Berlin, or legitimize the status of East Berlin under the illusion that any permanent agreement on the status of Berlin is better than no agreement at all. For Kissinger, the issue is not whether Berlin is worth a war (as is often asserted), rather it is the issue of credibility (one of his primary concerns). Because Berlin has become the touchstone of NATO's European policy, a defeat in Berlin would illustrate to the free world that the protection of the US is illusory. Acceding to the Soviet position on Berlin and East Germany was, in Kissinger's view, the beginning of the end.[79]

CONCLUSION

Kissinger's analysis of the structural problems of NATO and of the nature of the issues that must be resolved led him to conclude that no final solution is possible as long as NATO remains composed of sovereign states. Furthermore, he felt it would be unlikely that NATO would become a single political entity in the foreseeable future. Kissinger's analysis also revealed the premises on which his policies toward Western Europe were based.

In Kissinger's view, West European stability and self-confidence was precarious despite Western Europe's economic and psychological recovery. Kissinger agreed that Western Europe could and should make a greater contribution to NATO, but he opposed any attempts to pressure the Allies on this issue. The psychological impact would be rather negative, thus impeding progress in the political field. Unlike most Americans, Kissinger maintained that a united Western Europe would not be prepared to share world-wide burdens and responsibilities which a Western Europe composed of independent states was reluctant to assume. Moreover he insisted that West European unity would not resolve most Atlantic disputes. Rather it would magnify the economic, military and political differences between the US and Western Europe. The reason is obvious, the stronger the economic or political unit the more formidable is its bargaining power.

Kissinger accepted the fact that no matter what structure emerges in Western Europe, a difference in perspective with the US is probable, particularly about policies outside of Europe. In the present NATO framework, a wise policy can only mitigate the impact of this difference, it will not remove it. The recognition of this fact led Kissinger to conclude that cooperation between US and Western Europe must centre on issues within the Atlantic area rather than global partnership. From his point of view, American acceptance of West European autonomy also implied West European acceptance of American autonomy with respect to areas in which West European interest has lessened.

The issues that threatened the unity of NATO in the late 1950s and in the early 1960s – strategic doctrine, nuclear control, and West European unity – were likely to reappear. But although Kissinger saw no prospect for resolving them, he did not fear they would split NATO for the simple reason that in the military sphere Western Europe has more to gain from NATO than the US.

5 The Nixon Doctrine and Western Europe: a 'Genuine Partnership'?

Genuine *partnership* must increasingly characterize our alliance. For if we cannot maintain and develop further such a relationship with our North Atlantic allies, the prospects for achieving it with our other friends and allies around the world are slim indeed.
President Nixon, 18 February 1970.

INTRODUCTION

President Nixon's criticism of US foreign policy towards Western Europe during the Kennedy and Johnson Administrations, and the appointment of Kissinger as Assistant for National Security Affairs, generated hope in Western Europe that the US would focus on some of the apparently insoluble issues which permeated the US–West European relationship. This hope lay to a large extent in Kissinger's conviction that the forging of a common Atlantic policy with Western Europe was the most urgent task confronting American foreign policy.[1]

During the first Nixon Administration, however, Kissinger devoted his diplomatic energies to detente with the USSR, rapprochement with the PRC and the war in Vietnam; hence, he paid little attention to Western Europe. The Atlantic Alliance, which had been the focus of his academic writings, had virtually disappeared from his set of priorities. But Kissinger was aware of the serious strains in the US–West European relationship, and often criticized the new economic competitiveness and the growing nationalism of the Allies. He perceived West European leaders as weak and ineffectual, and when they pursued independent policies as de Gaulle had done (despite his admiration for the General), they appeared opposed to the US.[2]

Allied leaders in turn became concerned with the administration's preoccupation with the USSR, the PRC and Vietnam, and accused Kissinger of placing US–Soviet detente before the interests of the Atlantic Alliance – which he had done.[3] Moreover, West European

90

leaders resented Kissinger's high-handed tactics. By 1973 – The Year of Europe – it became apparent that the US–West European relationship was drifting from respect and friendship into mutual resentment and hostility. Kissinger's concentration on the Atlantic Alliance in the spring of 1973 was short-lived; the Yom Kippur War in October and Watergate absorbed most of his diplomatic efforts. Thus, once again, Western Europe was relegated to the periphery of Kissinger's (and in turn, US) attention.

This chapter will examine the Nixon Doctrine which provided the focus for US foreign policy toward its allies in the context of US–Soviet detente and US–PRC rapprochement. This analysis will focus on the consistency between the Doctrine, Kissinger's perceptions of the contemporary international system, and the changed nature of the Atlantic relationship. An examination of the Doctrine (as outlined by President Nixon in his annual foreign policy reports to Congress) provides the basis for answering the following questions: Did the Doctrine, as elaborated by the President following his informal remarks in Guam, reflect Kissinger's views? How would the Doctrine influence US–West European relations in the 'era of negotiations'? Would the implementation of the Doctrine produce drastic changes in the Atlantic relationship, or would it maintain American predominance?

KISSINGER'S PERCEPTIONS AND THE DESIGN OF THE NIXON DOCTRINE

'Doctrine' in foreign policy is not an American invention; nevertheless in the postwar period, it has become a prized American institution.[4] Although the doctrines in American foreign policy have never been satisfactorily defined, in their broadest form doctrines are systematic statements on foreign policy that provide some guiding principles for the Administrations that formulate them. Doctrines, William Safire notes, are 'policies that have hardened with acceptance', and he observes that 'when the word is applied in retrospect it usually sticks; when it is announced as a policy, it usually fades'.[5] This observation seems to be applicable to all postwar doctrines in US foreign policy. The Truman Doctrine, under which the US entered the postwar international system, merged with the Containment Doctrine which was followed by the Doctrine of Massive Retaliation, the Eisenhower Doctrine, The Doctrine of Flexible

Response, the Johnson Doctrine, and finally the Nixon Doctrine. Whether these doctrines will remain fixed in the pattern of the Monroe Doctrine is open to question. But with respect to the US–West European relationship, the Nixon Doctrine might in the long run play as vital a role in the evolution of American foreign policy as did the Truman Doctrine.[6]

The role of doctrine in US foreign policy reflects the dynamics of the American political process. 'It is in the nature of that process', observes Walter F. Hahn, 'with its provision for regular and orderly changes of political power and its emphasis on "discontinuity within continuity", that each succeeding president feels impelled to place upon his tenure the distinct imprint of his political philosophy and programs'.[7] A doctrine, then, reflects presidential philosophy, predilections, and political needs. But it also signals the adjustment of American foreign policy to profound changes in the international system. In this respect, the Nixon Doctrine may in the long run prove to be as momentous a departure in American foreign policy as was the Truman Doctrine. It can be argued, however, that in the postwar period each successive presidential doctrine represented changes in the American approach and emphasis rather than in the basic substance of foreign policy. Does this observation apply to the Nixon Doctrine?

The Nixon Doctrine had its genesis in President Nixon's informal remarks in Guam of 25 July 1969, but some time passed before the Administration decided that its rationalization for disengagement from Vietnam was a doctrine.[8] Like its predecessors, the Nixon Doctrine was not a blueprint of policy. Rather, it consisted of a set of broad principles initially applied to the US policy toward Southeast Asia, around which a more comprehensive global conception began to take shape. Inevitably, Western Europe would be touched by this development.

The Doctrine was outlined by President Nixon in his first annual foreign policy report to Congress on 18 February 1970. In the President's words:

> Its central thesis is that the United States will participate in the defense and development of allies and friends, but that America cannot, and will not, conceive *all* the plans, design *all* the programs, execute *all* the decisions and undertake *all* the defense of the free nations of the world. We will help where it makes a real difference and is considered in our interest.[9]

The Nixon Doctrine redefined containment. Under the Doctrine, the US would retreat from the apparently limitless support for anti-Communist regimes everywhere. American policymakers would identify priorities, recognizing that some regions of the world are more important than others. The President emphatically stated, 'Our interests must shape our commitments, rather than the other way around'.[10] The administration was convinced that 'this is the approach which will best encourage other nations to do their part, and will most genuinely enlist the support of the American people'.[11] This was essential for the success of its foreign policy given the lack of bipartisan foreign policy consensus.

The President stressed, however, that the US would not withdraw from world affairs because 'peace in the world will continue to require us to maintain our commitments – and we will'.[12] The US 'will keep all of its treaty commitments ... both because of their intrinsic merit, and because of the impact of sudden shifts on regional or world stability', which would cause disruption and invite aggression thus making the establishment of a stable international order impossible.[13] In the Administration's view, failure to maintain the integrity of US commitments would threaten the credibility of the US – and, in turn, the success of its foreign policy. President Nixon and Kissinger agreed that 'whatever else a foreign policy might be, it must be strong to be credible – and it must be credible to be successful'.[14] The President did not rule out new commitments, but he indicated that his Administration would apply a more rigorous criteria before assuming them.

Kissinger's intellectual imprint on the features of the Nixon Doctrine is prominent.[15] In 1968, in 'Central Issues of American Foreign Policy', Kissinger provided what seems to be an early definition of the Doctrine. He argued:

> To act consistently abroad we must be able to generate coalitions of shared purposes. Regional groupings supported by the United States will have to take over major responsibility for their immediate areas with the United States being concerned more with the overall framework of order than with the management of every regional enterprise.[16]

This was essential according to Kissinger since 'political multipolarity makes it impossible to impose an American design'.[17] The validity of this statement was demonstrated in Vietnam. The concept of Vietnamization, which Kissinger advanced in 'The Vietnam Negotiations' in *Foreign Affairs* in January 1969, was deliberately integrated into the Nixon Doctrine.[18] Southeast Asia was viewed by Kissinger as a region of lesser priority; thus disengagement was possible. The Vietnamese would have to defend themselves, though with the continued blessing and material support of the US.

The Nixon Administration, however, set Western Europe apart from all other commitments. This fact was made evident by the President's trip to Europe starting on 23 February 1969, only a month after his inauguration. The trip pleased the West European leaders, who viewed it as an indicator that President Nixon was going to attach more importance to relations with Western Europe than his predecessors. What they did not grasp was the fact that behind the acceptable aspects of his policy he was contemplating some adjustments in US–West European relations. The main features of the Administration's policy toward Western Europe were outlined by the President in his annual foreign policy report to Congress.

In his first report to Congress President Nixon distinguished Western Europe from all other commitments. He emphatically stated, 'The peace of Europe is crucial to the peace of the world . . . For the foreseeable future, Europe must be the cornerstone of the structure of a durable peace'.[19] This message was reiterated in every foreign policy report to Congress.

The President also stressed that the purpose of his first visit abroad was to reaffirm America's commitment to partnership with Europe. In his words:

> A reaffirmation was sorely needed. We had to reestablish the principle and practice of consultation. For too long in the past, the United States has led without listening, talked *to* our allies instead of *with* them, and informed them of new departures instead of deciding with them.[20]

This statement of intent was consistent with the perceptions of both President Nixon and Kissinger. Presidential candidate Nixon had lashed out at President Johnson in 1968 for ignoring NATO, particularly for President Johnson's failure to mention NATO in the 1968 'State of the Union Message'.[21] Kissinger had a long record of interest in the issues confronting the US–West European relationship and his perceptions with respect to the Atlantic relationship were incorporated *only slightly altered* in the elaboration of the Nixon Doctrine and its application to Europe.

In explaining the impact of the Doctrine in the different regions of the world, the President stated: 'In Europe, our policies embody precisely the three principles of a durable peace: partnership, continued strength to defend our common interests when challenged, and willingness to negotiate differences with adversaries'.[22] In other words, broadly construed, the Nixon Doctrine implied a restructuring of the Atlantic relationship around the three elements of the structure of peace: partnership, strength, and willingness to negotiate.

The elaboration of each element, however, contains both the opportunities and, more importantly, the *limitations* that Kissinger perceived in his analysis of the Atlantic relationship. Most studies of the Administration's policies toward Western Europe have focused on Kissinger's failure to exploit the perceived opportunities in implementing some of the proposals advanced in his writings. But it will be argued here that the limitations Kissinger perceived were a better guide to the Administration's policies toward Western Europe.

PARTNERSHIP

'Genuine *partnership*', stressed President Nixon, 'must increasingly characterize' the Atlantic relationship. The pattern of American pre-dominance, appropriate in the 1950s and early 1960s, 'must change' to match the political multipolarity of the present international system. This was essential because of Western Europe's economic recovery, the return of its traditional political dynamism, and its economic integration which had changed the region's position in the international system, and therefore its role in the Western Alliance. But while acknowledging that a more genuine partnership is 'in America's interest', the President stressed that as this partnership developed, 'the balance of burdens and responsibilities must gradual-ly be adjusted to reflect the economic and political realities of European progress'. The West European allies 'deserve a voice in the Alliance and its decisions commensurate with their growing power and contributions'. The President sought to reassure the Allies that greater contributions on their part, and the move from dominance to 'genuine partnership' was not a step toward disengagement. In his words, 'we cannot more disengage from Europe than from Alaska'.[23]

But can such statements reassure the Allies? As Kissinger had pointed out in *The Troubled Partnership*, 'It is not enough to say that the United States will take the defence of Europe as seriously as that of Alaska. Precisely because Alaska is not sovereign, it can be defended by a strategy which might prove unacceptable to our European allies'.[24]

In the Administration's view, it was essential to reassure the Allies because, despite their criticism of American dominance and assertions of autonomy, they feared American disengagement. For this reason, the Allies had opposed pressures by previous Administrations to make a greater contribution to NATO. A greater contribution would eventually reduce their dependence on the US and in their view lead to US withdrawal. The fear of American disengagement had intensified by 1969, given Senatorial pressures for unilateral troop withdrawals and talk of US–Soviet detente. If the Allies were not reassured, they would refuse to assume burdens and responsibilities that reflected their economic and political vitality, or they would make their own diplomatic initiatives toward Moscow (or both), thus threatening the Administration's strategy.

In *The Troubled Partnership*, Kissinger asserted that the forging of a common Atlantic policy with Western Europe was the most urgent task confronting American foreign policy. This assertion reappeared only slightly altered in the President's foreign policy report to Congress on 25 February 1971. According to President Nixon, 'To link together the foreign and defence policies of a uniting Europe and the United States will be another test of our sense of community and of our ability to perceive and pursue our common interest'.[25] In the near future however, 'the tangible expression of the new partnership is' in the view of the Administration, 'in greater material contributions' by the Allies.[26]

But 'burden-sharing' was a controversial issue within the Alliance, and Kissinger had argued that 'countries do not assume burdens because it is fair, only because it is necessary'.[27] This idea reappeared in the President's foreign policy report to Congress. The US, stressed the President:

> will look to others for a greater share in the definition of policy as well as in bearing the costs of programs. This psychological reorientation is more fundamental than the material redistribution; when countries feel responsible for the formulation of plans they are more apt to furnish the assets needed to make them work.[28]

The concept of burden-sharing under previous Administrations stressed that Allies should share the American burden. The Nixon

Administration, however, redefined the concept in the hope that the Allies would respond positively. According to the President, the Allies should not share the US burden:

the thrust of the Nixon Doctrine is that their primary task is to shoulder their own. The emphasis is no longer on their sharing the cost of America's military commitment to Europe – although financial arrangements may play a part – but on their providing the national forces needed in conjunction with ours in support of an effective common strategy.[29]

Kissinger had criticized American policymakers for acting as if their role was primarily one of drawing up and selling American designs. This approach had encouraged West European leaders to try to influence US decisions rather than develop their own strategies and approaches. Moreover, when dissatisfied with NATO policies they delayed the implementation of agreed measures rather than develop their own realistic alternatives. This had led to a negativism characterized by a greater awareness of risks than of opportunities, and by a general fear of any departure from the status quo.[30] In the Administration's view in the 1970s, 'there is no "status quo" – the only constant is the inevitability of change'.[31] Hence, the President was indicating that his Administration '[would] concentrate more on getting other countries engaged with us in the formulation of policies; they will be less involved in trying to influence American decisions and more involved in devising their own approaches'. This was essential because 'there [could not] be a structure of peace unless other nations help fashion it', and accept it.[32] This agrument was consistent with Kissinger's view that only 'the acceptance of the framework of the international order by all major powers' could guarantee stability–peace.[33]

The President acknowledged, however, that on some major issues – Berlin, Mutual and Balanced Force Reductions, the Conference on Security and Cooperation in Europe, the 'German question', and US–Soviet detente – the US and its European Allies 'do not have identical national concerns and cannot be expected to agree automatically on priorities or solutions'. Nevertheless, the Administration's 'principal objective should be to harmonize our policies and insure that our efforts for detente are complementary' because 'a differentiated detente, limited to the USSR and certain Western allies but not others would be illusory'.[34] The Administration seemed convinced that its objective would be achieved since

'European and American interests in defence and East–West diplomacy are fundamentally parallel and give sufficient incentive for coordinating independent policies'.[35]

West European unity was another controversial issue confronting the US and its Allies. The President, in explaining his Administration's position on the issue, reiterated the arguments advanced in Kissinger's writings. He criticized the preceding Administrations for turning into an ardent advocate of federalism as the only road to European unity and thus harming, rather than helping, progress toward this goal. The President stressed that 'the structure of Western Europe itself – the organization of its unity – is fundamentally the concern of the Europeans'. He expressed the Administration's support for the strengthening and broadening of the European Community, while acknowledging that American interests 'will necessarily be affected by Europe's evolution', and that the US 'may have to make sacrifices in the common interest'. In the Administration's view, 'the possible economic price of a truly unified Europe is outweighed by the gain in the political vitality of the West as a whole'.[36]

The preceding discussion indicates that the ideal new partnership under the Nixon Doctrine was a relationship among 'equals'. It meant a retreat by the US from the heavy-handedness and arrogance that had often characterized its relations with Western Europe in the past. 'This Administration', the President stated, 'does not view our allies as pieces in an American Grand Design'. But it also required greater cohesion on the part of the Allies and their assumption of a more equitable share of the common Alliance burden.[37]

STRENGTH

In the shifting environment of superpower strategic parity in the 1970s, 'strength' in the US–West European context meant essentially maintaining the credibility of the NATO deterrent against aggression on Western Europe. In the President's words:

> we shall provide a shield if a nuclear power threatens the freedom of a nation allied with us or of a nation whose survival we consider vital to our security. Nuclear power is the element of security that our friends either cannot provide or could provide only with great and disruptive efforts... Their concern would be magnified if we

were to leave them defenseless against nuclear blackmail, or conventional aggression backed by nuclear power.[38]

The Administration was trying to reassure West Europeans who doubted the credibility of the American nuclear guarantee. At the same time, it expressed its concern about nuclear proliferation which would threaten the implementation of its global strategy. 'The spread of nuclear capabilities', in the President's words, 'would be inherently destabilizing, multiplying the chances that conflicts could escalate into catastrophic exchanges'.[39] For this reason the Administration encouraged other nations to sign the Non-Proliferation Treaty.

But providing the 'nuclear shield' required the 'preservation by the United States of a sufficient strategic nuclear capability', stressed the Secretary of Defense, Melvin R. Laird, in his defense report before the House Armed Services Committee.[40] To achieve this objective the President, despite Congressional pressures, announced his commitment to maintain existing strategic forces with relatively little change. The Administration opposed sharp cutbacks on strategic programmes because they would prevent the deployment of forces essential for 'strategic sufficiency' given the continuing growth of Soviet forces, and would eliminate any Soviet incentives for an agreement to limit strategic arms. They would also raise serious concerns among West Europeans, who viewed the US commitment to deter Soviet aggression as being based mainly on US strategic forces. At the same time, the Administration opposed sharp increases because those might lead the Soviets to misunderstand US intentions and make new strategic investments, thus damaging the prospects for reaching agreement on arms limitations.[41]

But the Administration's view was that the shift in strategic realities required a greater role for general purpose forces in deterring the use or the threat of force below the level of general nuclear war. Hence, the Administration tried to resolve the dilemma of relating military power to national objectives and, in turn, translating military power into policy that would enhance its position in conducting negotiations. Kissinger had criticized the failure of the US to harmonize doctrine and capability, and his views were evident in the President's discussion of US military posture.[42]

The stated basis of US conventional posture in the 1960s was the '2½ War' principle which the Administration rejected because the necessary force levels were never reached.[43] In an effort to harmonize doctrine and capability, it chose the '1½ War' strategy.

Under it, the US would maintain peacetime general purpose forces adequate to deter (or, if necessary, defend) against a major threat or an attack on the interests of the US and its allies in Europe or Asia, and simultaneously cope with a minor contingency elsewhere.[44] But the President emphatically stated that US forces 'will be developed and deployed to the extent possible on the basis of a common strategy with our allies and a common sharing of the defence burden'.[45] In other words, for the element of 'strength' to be effective a greater contribution was required from Western Europe. Furthermore, the Administration's view of 'strength' related to the continued economic and political growth and consolidation of the Western World.[46]

NEGOTIATIONS

The third element of the structure of durable peace, 'negotiation', to be successful required both the cohesion and strength of the Atlantic Alliance. As the President stated in his first foreign policy report to Congress, 'in partnership with our allies, secure in our own strength, we will seek those areas in which we can agree among ourselves and with others to accommodate conflicts and overcome rivalries'.[47]

But as Kissinger had argued, there was a lack of consensus within the Alliance in the analysis of the international situation as it affects Europe. Hence, during periods of detente each ally makes its own approach to Eastern Europe or the USSR without attempting to further a coherent Western strategy. During periods of crisis, there is Allied pressure for American reassurance, but not for a clearly defined common philosophy. The lack of a common Western strategy made consultation within the Alliance especially difficult (and often irrelevant) because the issues solved were peripheral while the central issues were inadequately articulated.[48] In Kissinger's view, 'Consultation . . . is least effective when it is most needed: when there exist basic differences of assessment or of interest. It works best in *implementing* a consensus rather than in *creating it*'. Nevertheless, Kissinger argued that 'an improvement in the consultative process should be one of the primary objectives of the alliance'.[49]

These views reappeared in the foreign policy reports to Congress. President Nixon, in articulating the American negotiating posture, stated:

When we conduct bilateral negotiations with the USSR, as in SALT, partnership involves close consultation with our allies both to protect their interests and solicit their views. In turn, partnership requires our allies, in their negotiations, to pursue their course within a framework of common objectives.[50]

In the Administration's view, consultation was not a right of the Allies. The US must be consulted with respect to Allied initiatives towards the East. Could this be a subtle message to the Allies that they should not follow the FRG's policy toward the East?

Consultation, however, could not solve the fundamental problem of divergent national interests. Kissinger had argued that if Americans 'face the fact that the interests of Europe and the United States are not identical everywhere, it may be possible to agree on a permissible range of divergence'. Thus, each partner retains a measure of flexibility.[51] But the question is: Who decides what the 'common' strategy should be when agreement is not reached?

Kissinger's answer was clear in his writings. The *US* should decide what the Alliance strategy should be because 'close coordination between Europe and the United States in the military sphere is dictated by self-interest, and Europe has more to gain from it than the United States'. The West European dependence on the American nuclear guarantee permitted the US to set the agenda in the political sphere as well. In Kissinger's view, 'disagreements on peripheral issues may be the price for unity on issues that really matter', namely defence against Communist aggression. But, more importantly, he argued that 'third-force' dangers 'have been overdrawn. It is hard to visualize a "deal" between the Soviet Union and Europe which would jeopardize our interests without jeopardizing European interests first'.[52] In short, Kissinger's criterion for judging correct Allied behaviour was simply the willingness of the Allies to shape their foreign policy actions according to American judgements.[53]

The elaboration of the Nixon Doctrine in its application to Western Europe implied a restructuring of the Atlantic relationship around the three elements of the structure of peace: partnership, strength, and negotiations. To facilitate the process, the Nixon Administration redefined the US position on a number of controversial issues such as European unity, burden-sharing, and conventional strategy, and reiterated the US commitment to defend Western Europe with nuclear weapons. The Administration indicated, however, that it expected the Allies to assume a more equitable share of the common Alliance burden. The Administration also expressed the desire to consult with the Allies when it negotiated with the USSR, but indicated that it expected the Allies to consider the interests of the US when they conducted bilateral negotiations with the East. But while redefining the US position on the controversial issues confronting the Alliance, and expressing the desire to resolve them, the Administration failed publicly to acknowledge the limitations imposed by structural conditions. These limitations (in Kissinger's view) prevented the resolution of the structural problems of the Alliance, thus making the *continuation of American primacy* essential in the near future.

THE DILEMMA OF IMPLEMENTATION

The successful implementation of Kissinger's global strategy had three basic components. The first component was US–Soviet detente which consisted of the strategic arms limitation agreements (SALT), the progressive meshing of the two superpowers in a network of specific economic and functional agreements and the declaratory policy of joint conflict management (Basic Principles). The second component, relating directly to US–Allied relations, was continued and undiminished primacy – described by Kissinger as 'control' or 'hegemony' – of the US in relationship with its principal Allies in Western Europe (and Japan). As George Liska argued, 'The cohesion of the American alliance system was seen as the necessary prerequisite to a viable détente system and any future negotiations implementing détente (such as negotiations about European security and mutual force reduction)'.[54] The third, but less important component, was the need to prevent Third World vacuums created by US disengagement from being filled by the USSR, the PRC, a regional middle power, or any other force other than the one sanctioned or tolerated by the US.

The underlying thesis of the Nixon Doctrine, according to Liska, is to be found in Kissinger's global strategy which 'had one central object: to reduce the scope of any devolution from the previously held American (imperial) positions to the benefit of either major allies, major adversaries, or of Third-World middle powers, while reducing the costs of upholding essential American interests'.[55] This goal would ideally be achieved by diplomatic means that:

1. fitted the emerging tripolar – and ultimately still bipolar – structure of the international system as well as the domestic

consensus in the United States for economic development and at least on apparent retrenchment, and

2. would indefinitely postpone any more substantial restructuring of US positions until stabilized relations between the United States and the Soviet Union have minimized the twin dangers of transitional instability and temporary power vacuums.[56]

Liska's interpretation of Kissinger's global strategy is shared by Stanley Hoffmann, who argues that:

[the strategy] showed that primacy remained an American goal ... to be maintained by a combination of greater subtlety and greater toughness, two ways of restoring flexibility... On balance, America's grip was tightened, and the gain in flexibility the Allies made were strictly subordinated to those of the United States.[57]

Hoffmann maintains that 'insofar as the old goals of containment and primacy persisted, there could be no loosening of America's hold on its allies'. He seems to doubt that the Nixon Doctrine was a new policy on behalf of the old Alliance ties but argues that, if it was, 'it amounted to a multiple demotion of the Alliances' partly due to the new ordering of priorities – the top priorities being the search for a stable international structure and the new triangular relationship. Moreover, the return to an 'American national interest' approach after years of an 'interest of the free world' approach sharpened the demotion. This new nationalistic style pervaded the Doctrine – a unilateral decision not to reduce America's commitments but to differentiate the way in which they would be carried out according to a new hierarchy of US interests.[58]

Neo-isolationism is a charge that cannot plausibly be levelled at the Nixon Doctrine. Although it defers to American as well as global realities, the Doctrine is not a subterfuge for an American withdrawal from the international system. The President emphatically stated, 'this is not a way for America to withdraw from its indispensable role in the world'.[59] Indeed, reverberating in the Nixon Doctrine are the positive strains of a new American role in world affairs. Its implicit message is that not only must global change be recognized and accommodated, but the US is in the unique position to take the lead in establishing a new international structure. However, criticism regarding the Doctrine attaches less to design and more to implementation.[60]

The Nixon Doctrine presented the Administration with a dilemma which became evident as soon as the Administration had begun to implement its global strategy. The dilemma related to the problem of reconciling the 'era of negotiations' with the demands of partnership. Could the US and its Allies maintain and strengthen the old ties while moving toward new relationships with adversaries? President Nixon acknowledged the dilemma. Referring to the initiatives towards Peking and Moscow and the concern they generated in Japan and Western Europe that Allied interests were being sacrificed, the President said:

> our relations with our allies appeared for a period of several months to be somewhat out of phase with the innovations taken in our relations with our adversaries... By the end of the year [1971], however, it was clear that our initiatives toward both our friends and our adversaries were in basic harmony.[61]

But, is there such a 'basic harmony'? As Walter F. Hahn argues, this dilemma transcends the requirements of polite consultation with the Allies – of keeping them informed of American initiatives toward Moscow or Peking: 'Much more fundamentally at issue in the period of transition heralded by the Nixon Doctrine is the meaning of "partnership" and its prerequisites'.[62]

The Nixon Doctrine called for a strong and united Western Europe, 'a single entity making policy for Western Europe in all fields, including diplomacy and defence'. A united Western Europe capable of playing a greater role in the international system 'would add flexibility to Western diplomacy'.[63] Could Western Europe be transformed into a unified centre of power simply because the Nixon Doctrine called for it? There has been some progress in the harmonization of national policies in Western Europe, especially in economic integration, but similar progress has not been made in the political and military spheres. The obstacle lies in the traditional political difficulty of several states of roughly equal power and status subordinating their divergent interests and their national independence to the requirements of a unified defence force, and the special difficulties of creating a joint nuclear force that includes some kind of participation by the FRG.

The prospect of greater political cohesion becomes all the more elusive in the era of detente. Once the cement of fear crumbles, from where will come the new incentives for European unification, greater defence efforts, and a more equitable sharing of the common defence burden between the US and Western Europe?

Many Americans, impatient with what they believed to be the continuing 'free ride' by Western Europe, supported a substantial troop withdrawal from Europe.[64] Could a substantial troop withdrawal supply the galvanizing impulse to Western Europe? It might, but there was a greater risk recognized by the Administration. Too rapid a withdrawal would spur the forces of fear, disparity and perhaps, closer ties between Western Europe and the USSR, rather than the impulse of unification and greater US–West European cooperation. Largely in response to that perceived danger, the Administration opposed Senatorial pressures for unilateral force reductions in Europe.[65]

However, if Western Europe became a single entity it would threaten Kissinger's triangular diplomacy because, as he explained, regardless of what structure emerges in Western Europe 'a difference in perspective with the United States is probable, particularly about policies outside Europe'.[66] In short, 'a united Europe is likely to insist on a specifically European view of world affairs – which is another way of saying that it will challenge American hegemony in Atlantic policy'.[67] Hence, despite Kissinger's acceptance of a single West European entity in the abstract, and an apparent willingness to pay the price, *there seemingly was incongruity* between the Administration's advocacy for a united Europe and the prerequisites of tringular diplomacy.

Western Europe still needs US assistance, Kissinger stressed in *The Troubled Partnership*. This is especially true in the development of an independent nuclear force, which is essential if Western Europe is to become a unified centre of power, since the credentials of power in the late twentieth century are inescapably nuclear.[68] Will the US provide the necessary assistance to its European partners to develop a credible nuclear deterrent? The emphasis of the Nixon Doctrine on partnership appears irreconcilable with the past, almost obsessive, American objective to achieve central command and control over the nuclear weapons of the Alliance within the present framework of NATO. This objective was shared by the Nixon Administration which sought to assure nations signing the Non-Proliferation Treaty that they would not be subject to nuclear blackmail or nuclear aggression.[69] To be sure, the Administration viewed with equanimity the emergence of a European defence community even if such a community were to construct a European nuclear force around an Anglo-French nucleus. But it did not encourage this development, which for all practical purposes remained hypothetical.[70]

Moreover, the development of a credible European nuclear force requires the participation of the Federal Republic of Germany. But the problems generated by the issue of German participation are acute because influence in the control and command of the nuclear force is likely to be proportional to a nation's financial contribution. The Federal Republic, given its resources, is likely to be dominant. In *The Troubled Partnership* Kissinger addressed the problems generated by the fear of German domination of a European nuclear force, emphatically stating:

> Such a prospect is not in the interest of NATO, of European cohesion, of the Federal Republic or of international stability. It would push the most exposed ally into the forefront of every dispute. It would make the Federal Republic, which already has the largest conventional army, the most significant nuclear power in Europe as well. This would again raise fears that a decade and a half of far-sighted German policy have only begun to erase. It might fuse anti-American, anti-German and anti-nuclear feelings into a dangerous wave of neutralism.[71]

In other words, the participation of the Federal Republic would prevent both European unification and the development of a nuclear force because it would awaken latent distrust all over Europe and in the USSR which might attempt to prevent the development of a European nuclear force by unleashing a series of crises. And no European country is likely to run major risks so that the FRG can have control of nuclear weapons. Kissinger also argued that if the US aided the development of a European nuclear force, the risk existed – due to the fear of German domination – that Britain and France would in time move away from the Alliance that threatened to turn into a German–American arrangement.[72]

There is *incongruity* between the Administration's call for greater self-reliance on the part of the Allies, and its opposition to military independence for the only Allies that could substantially provide for their own security. Apart from the new nationalistic style and national pride – that of being a superpower – the Nixon Administration was moved by two familiar and compelling reasons to perpetuate the American hegemony in the military field and especially the nuclear field. First, only the US had the requisite experience and capability to control the global military equilibrium. Secondly, the emergence of independent military forces would eventually lead to independent nuclear forces which would undermine international order and endanger peace. A third, less compelling, reason at the height of the Cold War was added: the emergence of one or more new major centres of military decisionmaking which would endanger the 'era of negotiation'. An independent West European nuclear force would upset the military equilibrium and the whole set of stabilized bilateral relationships that underlay detente. The USSR and the PRC would view a new military power as contravening the conditions of the new era of diplomatic accommodation and manoeuvre within mutual restraints among adversaries. 'They would not be alone in this view', argues Robert E. Osgood.[73]

This consideration is particularly pertinent to the logic of retrenchment. The Administration's ability to reduce America's burden of involvement without undermining its global commitments and influence or the confidence of its Allies critically depends upon reducing the level of international tensions and the expectation of war with adversaries. Kissinger's global strategy sought to foster the international conditions under which this objective may be attained.[74]

The Nixon Doctrine envisions the maintenance of America's dominant role in containing the USSR, but at a lower level of effort, of a diminished prospect of armed intervention, and with greater material assistance from Allies. The major West European Allies (and Japan), by a policy of more active projection of their political influence and economic power and through their increased contributions to their own defence, will impose additional constraints upon Communist ambitions and influence. However, the basic structure of their relationship to the US and the Communist powers is not expected to change. The Allies will assume greater responsibilities, but within the existing security framework. They will assert their own policies and realistic options more actively, but they will remain America's faithful and cooperative Allies. They will carry more of the burden of their defence, but not seek military independence from the US. As Hoffmann observed, 'The United States ... could use the Alliances as stilts on which to tower over its communist rivals or over other blocs that might challenge the United States, such as the Organization of Petroleum Exporting Countries (OPEC) or the Group of 77 Third-World nations'.[75]

Kissinger was convinced that despite the growing differences between the US and its Allies on economic and monetary matters, the Allies would continue to accept American hegemony in the security field since it is in their interest.[76] Since the US manages the military equilibrium *vis-à-vis* the USSR, it should determine not only the military posture of the Alliance but also – to a large extent – the diplomatic strategy towards the East. This was essential given the Administration's dependence on linkage and the need to manipulate the incentives that would bring the USSR into the process. Kissinger frowned upon Chancellor Brandt's *Ostpolitik* because he feared that Bonn might make concessions to Moscow which would weaken the Alliance, and that Bonn might offer economic rewards that would make Washington far less attractive to Moscow.[77] He kept the Allies from interfering in the Administration's management of the triangular relationship by reminding them of the importance of the security function that tied them to the US, namely the residual hostility of the USSR and the PRC.[78]

The Administration recognized the risk that if it pressed its military, economic, and diplomatic policies upon the Allies – as one expects the leader of the Alliance to do – while trying to induce them to increase their share of the common defence burden, the Allies could decide that the benefits of the US nuclear guarantee are not worth the costs. They could then decide, individually or collectively, to seek their own accommodations with the USSR whether or not they tried to back their diplomatic independence with their own military force. Two factors tend to increase this risk:

1. in the era of detente, the apparent decline of the Soviet military threat reduces the incentives of West European leaders to defer to American decisions about the policy requirements of their own interests and the interests of the Alliance, and

2. the Administration's concession of strategic parity to the USSR through the SALT agreements combined with its military retrenchment, while the Soviet global military presence and political reach increase tend to undermine West European confidence in the credibilty of the American nuclear guarantee.

Kissinger, however, was convinced that as long as the US maintains a credible military presence in Europe and informs and consults West European leaders about its bilateral dealings with the USSR and the PRC, there are strong practical incentives for the Allies to cooperate with his global strategy. The existing time-tested security framework provided by US troops and nuclear weapons relieves West Europeans of the material and political burdens they would have to assume – burdens they considered onerous and inadequate to meet their goals. This framework underwrites the detente atmosphere that enables them to pursue independent economic and political policies without being too concerned about security considerations. Kissinger's conviction was strengthened by his belief that West Europeans could not overcome the formidable political obstacles inherent in 'undiluted sovereignty' that would permit the development of an independent military force.[79] Therefore the Allies should regard the preponderant American role as a good bargain.

CONCLUSION

The analysis of the Nixon Doctrine in its application to Western Europe indicates that it is *consistent* with Kissinger's perceptions of the contemporary international system as manifested in the Administration's preoccupation with the triangular relationship, and with his analysis of the structural problems of NATO and the nature of the issues that must be resolved. However, the elaboration of the three elements of the structure of peace indicate that the Administration tried to solve those problems caused by acts of policy, such as European unity and burden-sharing, rather than the problems produced by structural conditions due to the advent of nuclear weapons and undiluted national sovereignty. But even with respect to the problems that the Administration sought to solve, it failed to consider, in its elaboration of the Doctrine, the dilemmas that Kissinger had discussed in his writings.

The fact that the Doctrine did not deal with the problems of the Alliance caused by structural conditions also reveals Kissinger's influence. His analysis of the structural problems (discussed in Chapter 4) led him to conclude that no final solution was possible as long as NATO remained composed of sovereign states, and that it was unlikely that NATO would become a single political entity in the foreseeable future. His criticisms of the previous Administrations' failure to resolve the issues confronting NATO focused not so much on their failure to deal with its structural problems, but on their propensity to raise issues that could not be resolved due to structural conditions. Kissinger's conviction that the structural problems could not be resolved in the near future was probably the reason for the Administration's unwillingness to deal with them, even in the abstract design of the Doctrine.

The conclusion that the structural problems of the Alliance could not be resolved in the foreseeable future convinced Kissinger that the incentives for West Europeans to work within the existing structure of the Alliance clearly outweighed the incentives to supplant the American military dominance despite US–West European differences over economic and monetary matters. Indeed, the fear that the US may lack the will and lose the means of protecting them, or that its preoccupation with the tripolar relationship may jeopardize their interests, only moved West Euopëans to make more strenuous efforts to keep the US engaged in their behalf.[80] Aware of the structural conditions and the limitations they imposed on the Allies, as well as the fears of West Europeans, Kissinger exploited these conditions and fears to the *sole* benefit of American primacy in the Atlantic relationship. And, given the prerequisites of the triangular relationship, this was *absolutely* essential.

The elaboration of the Nixon Doctrine indicates that in the Administration's view the only developments that were likely to alter the present distribution of power within the Atlantic Alliance were a resurgence of the Allies' will to become a 'superpower', and America's withdrawal of the nuclear guarantee. There were no signs of the first development, but the second development seemed more likely. If the US abandons Western Europe, however, it will probably be by neglect rather than design, and will result in the transformation of the international system. This is exactly what Kissinger's global strategy sought to prevent.

The issues that the Administration attempted to resolve were those caused by acts of policy, and it is to those that I now turn.

6 The Dilemmas of Common Defence: US Initiatives, Allied Reactions

INTRODUCTION

In 1969, US–West European discussions with respect to common defence were dominated by five issues. The first issue concerned the credibility of the doctrine of flexible response which had been officially adopted by NATO in 1967 under American pressure. The second was SALT and its effect on the defence of Western Europe. The third was the levels of US troops in Europe and the growing Senate pressure to reduce them unilaterally. Fourth was the perennial issue of burden-sharing, and the fifth issue was Mutual and Balanced Force Reductions (MBFR).

The Nixon Administration recognized that in the late 1960s the basic relationship of power and interests between the US and its major West European Allies (Britain, France, the FRG, and Italy) remained remarkably stable despite the resurgence of the economic power and political assertiveness of the Allies. This recognition was evident in Kissinger's memorandum to the President in March 1970. Responding to President Nixon's question as to whether American leadership in Atlantic affairs was still needed in light of the progress in European integration, Kissinger stated: 'American leadership remained central'.[1] He added:

> I had to stretch no conviction to render this verdict; it was the core of my own beliefs. American weight and leadership were still needed ... because for all their economic progress the Europeans plainly had not developed the cohesion, the internal stability, or the will to match the power of the Soviet Union.[2]

In short, Kissinger reiterated the implicit message of *The Troubled Partnership*, namely, the maintenance of US hegemony in the Alliance was still essential.[3]

In its efforts to resolve these issues, the Administration sought to preserve the underlying structure of power and interests within the Alliance (and Japan) as the basis for elaborating a more comprehensive *modus vivendi* with the USSR (and the PRC).[4] Kissinger and the President agreed that no peaceful international development (next to US–Soviet detente and US–PRC rapprochement) would affect American foreign policy more than a change in the basic configuration of power and interests between the US and its major European Allies (and Japan).[5]

The greatest change in the US–West European relationship would be a shift from the Allies' military dependence upon the US to substantial military autonomy. The Administration regarded any movement by the Allies toward greater military and political independence as threatening to the global diplomatic equilibrium. Hence, in the name of creating a 'genuine partnership' with the Allies, the Administration indirectly discouraged greater independence by combining concessions to Allied independence with new bonds of consultation. The efforts by the Administration to resolve the issues confronting the Alliance demonstrated that while the US–West European relationship was subordinate to US–Soviet detente and US–PRC rapprochement, the objectives sought were consistent with Kissinger's global strategy and the Nixon Doctrine.

This chapter examines the efforts of the Nixon Administration to resolve three issues of the common defence confronting the US–West European relationship: (i) the US strategic doctrine; (ii) SALT; and (iii) the Agreement on the Prevention of Nuclear War. The analysis focuses on: (a) the consistency between the actual resolution of these issues and Kissinger's views, as manifested in his writings and in the elaboration of the Nixon Doctrine,[6] and (b) the consistency between the Administration's stand on these issues and Kissinger's global strategy.

THE STRATEGIC ISSUES: THE DOCTRINE OF STRATEGIC SUFFICIENCY

In Chapter 3 it was pointed out that Kissinger's examination of the strategic debate in NATO had led him to conclude that the issues were insoluble in the foreseeable future, given the increasing inconsistency between the technical requirements of military strategy and the political imperatives of the nation-state.[7] His criticism of the previous Administrations' policies focused not on their inability to resolve the strategic issues (Kissinger believed that the nuclear issues could not be resolved),[8] but on the propensity of these Administrations to change nuclear strategy unilaterally and then pressure the Allies to accept it as the official NATO strategy. Therefore, it was highly unlikely that Kissinger would support a change in NATO strategy that would only intensify the strategic debate in NATO at a time when its cohesion was vital to the successful implementation of his global strategy. Europe's nuclear dilemmas were not at the top of Kissinger's agenda – nor, for that matter, the agenda of the West Europeans.

In 1969, however, the Nixon Administration decided to redefine the strategy for general nuclear war. Kissinger recognized the need for the reexamination of the US military doctrine because, as he stated, 'I was . . . concerned that as strategic equivalence between the United States and the Soviet Union approached, strategic forces might be used in less than an all-out attack'.[9] He urged the President to request the Pentagon to devise options to meet contingencies other than all-out nuclear war (which was done), while he and his staff with the President's support undertook a reexamination of the military doctrine.[10]

This review was essential for three reasons: (a) to adjust US nuclear strategy to new realities, given the approaching strategic equivalence between the US and the USSR; (b) to enable the Administration to plan and defend its military programmes in Congress; and (c) to control the public debate with respect to ABM and MIRV systems and lead it away from emotionalism. The result of the reexamination was the doctrine of 'strategic sufficiency' which related US strategic planning to the destruction not only of civilians (as the doctrine of assured destruction did), but to military targets as well.

Kissinger was primarily interested in the relationship between military power and diplomacy and argued that strategic sufficiency gave the US at least the theoretical capability to use forces for objectives other than the mass destruction of populations.[11] He recognized, however, that translating these doctrinal innovations into operational plans would prove far more difficult.[12]

In Western Europe, this unilateral change of US strategy did not ignite a debate as the doctrine of flexible response had done. A number of factors can help account for the muted reaction of the Allies.

1. Under the sufficiency doctrine the US retained the strategic first-strike option against the USSR, thus keeping the US strategic umbrella extended over the Allies.
2. West Europeans were 'consulted' with respect to the SALT talks and SALT did not deal with the issues that most directly concerned West Europeans – the British and French nuclear forces, and the forward-based systems (FBS).
3. The Administration was not opposed to the nuclear forces of Britain and France and permitted the French to acquire some of the military sensitive information and equipment that the US used to withhold.[13] The French *force de frappe* ceased to be a point of political contention and leverage.
4. The Administration was willing to consider the views of the Allies on issues that directly affected their security – i.e., forward-based systems, Mutual Force Reductions (MFR), and the Conference on Security and Cooperation in Europe (CSCE).
5. The Administration avoided what Kissinger called one of the 'real issues' – i.e., the role of tactical nuclear weapons in the defence of Western Europe.
6. The Administration opposed the Mansfield Resolution calling for the unilateral reduction of US troops in Europe.

In the President's words, the doctrine of strategic sufficiency required 'the maintenance of forces adequate to prevent [the US] and our Allies from being coerced'.[14] Therefore the Administration opposed sharp cutbacks in strategic programmes because such cutbacks would not permit the US to satisfy the sufficiency criteria. In addition, the Administration supported programmes that improved the survivability of nuclear forces – i.e., increasing the hardness of Minuteman silos (thereby reducing their vulnerability to nuclear attack), and adding MIRVs to some of the strategic missiles to ensure a credible retaliatory capability.[15]

By incorporating the themes of superiority and parity, the concept of sufficiency advanced by Kissinger permitted the US to continue to deploy strategic nuclear weapons in order to sustain the credibility of its NATO commitments while negotiating strategic arms limitations with the USSR. The ambiguity of the doctrine was purposefully designed to obscure the inherent cross-purposes of strategic arms control (SALT) and the continued reliance on strategic weapons to defend Western Europe. In short, it permitted the US to maintain the strategic first-strike option against the USSR thus keeping the US strategic umbrella extended over the Allies.[16] In Kissinger's view, this was essential because as he had argued, 'as long as Nato strategy was nuclear and the United States had no obvious alternative to nuclear retaliation our Allies were ready to acquiesce in the hegemonial position of the United States'.[17] The concept of sufficiency allowed Kissinger to maintain the hegemonial position of the US and the acquiescence of the Allies which were essential to the success of his policy toward the USSR.

Under Secretary Laird, the Department of Defense seized upon the ambiguity of the concept, and established elastic definitions of what would constitute an adequate military balance *vis-à-vis* the USSR. The military planning objectives were broadened to ensure that:

(a) the strategic forces of the USSR could not inflict more damage in the US than the US forces could inflict on the USSR

(b) each leg of the strategic triad (bombers, land-based ICBMs, and sea-based SLBMs) would be independently capable of surviving a surprise Soviet attack and striking back with an unacceptable level of damage, and

(c) the number of weapons deployed on each side should not appear to give the USSR an advantage.[18]

It appears that the ambiguity of Kissinger's concept of sufficiency and the deployment of new weapons systems justified by it fulfilled the West European need for reassurance. If the US and the USSR were explicitly to renounce first-strike capabilities against each other in order to resolve the arms control dilemma, the central element of the NATO strategic umbrella would have collapsed and Western Europe would have been exposed to nuclear blackmail by the USSR. Kissinger was determined to prevent this development, and with the concept of sufficiency he could maintain the cohesion of NATO under US leadership.

West Europeans were not prepared to examine the inherent cross-purposes of the sufficiency doctrine – i.e., strategic arms control – and continued reliance on new strategic weapons to defend Western Europe. The European reluctance to question the new doctrine was evident in Chancellor Brandt's remarks during his visit to Washington in April 1970. He stated: 'I referred to the dictum that America could no more detach itself from Europe than it could from Alaska. Europe, I said, would no more be able to detach itself from America than it could from itself'.[19]

A more careful reading of *The Troubled Partnership* by the Chancellor would have revealed that Alaska, in Kissinger's judgement, not being sovereign, could be defended by a strategy which might prove unacceptable to the Federal Republic and the other European Allies. But the Chancellor (like most West Europeans) shared Kissinger's view that NATO's nuclear dilemma could not be resolved in the foreseeable future. Therefore even if the Chancellor was aware of the distinction that Kissinger drew between Alaska and Western Europe (and he probably was), he was not about to draw attention to it. By pointing out the difference between Alaska and Western Europe, the Chancellor would have raised issues that were put to rest in 1967 when NATO, under American pressure, officially adopted the doctrine of flexible response.

By reiterating Kissinger's conviction, the second statement in the Chancellor's remarks revealed why West Europeans were not about to question the sufficiency doctrine. Kissinger believed that incentives for West Europeans to work within the existing structure of NATO clearly outweighed incentives to supplant the American military dominance, despite differences over economic and monetary matters.

The approaching strategic parity between the US and the USSR and the Soviet numerical superiority in conventional forces should have raised the 'real' issue according to Kissinger – that is, the role of tactical nuclear weapons in the defence of Western Europe. Kissinger had criticized American policymakers for '[sweeping] under the rug' an issue requiring urgent attention.[20] Yet once in office he did nothing to resolve it, other than heed its existence in the President's annual foreign policy reports to Congress.[21]

The Administration accepted a temporary compromise on the issue that emerged from the discussions initiated by the Europeans in the NATO Nuclear Planning Group (NPG) in 1968.[22] The Administration's decision was consistent with Kissinger's view that the issue of tactical nuclear weapons could not be resolved as long as NATO was composed of sovereign states.[23] Moreover, the Administration was not likely to tackle an issue that since 1968 had produced serious differences of opinion in the discussions of the Nuclear Planning Group.[24]

Both sides of the Alliance concur in giving tactical nuclear weapons a crucial role in deterrence by flexible response. But the US and its European Allies arrived at this agreement from different perspectives. For the US tactical nuclear weapons are devices to implement the nuclear guarantee while postponing the decision for strategic nuclear war. This prompts a search for options to use tactical nuclear weapons without crossing the strategic threshold. Conversely, the Allies (for whom any substantial tactical nuclear engagement would be a disaster) prefer to regard tactical nuclear weapons as a delicate trigger on the strategic forces of the US. It is not that West Europeans would welcome a strategic nuclear war; it is simply that any large-scale war in Europe (conventional or nuclear) would be annihilation for the Allies. West Europeans therefore, favour a strategy of forward defence to protect their territory from becoming a battlefield, and a policy of nuclear deterrence to prevent the strategy from being tested.

Denis Healey, the British Minister of Defence, explained the British position on the role of tactical nuclear weapons when President Nixon visited London in February 1969. Healey argued that NATO's conventional forces would be able to resist a Soviet attack for only a few days, hence early use of nuclear weapons would be essential. He stressed that it would be crucial to let the USSR understand that the West was determined to escalate to a strategic nuclear exchange rather than surrender. NATO, however, should seek to reduce destruction to a minimum. The British solution (supported by the FRG) was to use a very small number of tactical weapons as a warning to the Soviets that the West was ready to escalate to a strategic nuclear exchange. This 'solution' was adopted by the NPG. The 'demonstrative use' of nuclear weapons meant setting off a nuclear weapon in some remote location – i.e., in the air above the Mediterranean – which did not involve many casualties as a signal of Western willingness to escalate to a strategic exchange if the warning failed.[25]

West Europeans supported the demonstrative use of tactical nuclear weapons because it would spare their countries from devastation early in the conflict while it guaranteed a US nuclear response. Kissinger acquiesced but did not vigorously support this solution because, as he stated:

I never had much use for this concept. I believed that the Soviet Union would not attack Western Europe without anticipating a nuclear response. A reaction that was designed to be of no military relevance would show more hesitation than determination; it would thus be more likely to spur the attack than defer it. If nuclear weapons were to be used, we needed a concept by which they could stop an attack on the ground. A hesitant or ineffective response ran the risk of leaving us with no choices other than surrender or holocaust.[26]

In short, for Kissinger the NPG decision manifested the West's lack of political will. Kissinger was however, determined to demonstrate that the West had both the capability as well as the will to challenge the USSR's attempts to expand its influence. The nuclear alert during the Yom Kippur War was the best example of Kissinger's efforts to demonstrate that the West did have the political will to contain the USSR.[27]

In the 1972 foreign policy report to Congress, the President spoke favourably of NPG for making important progress in its review of key questions concerning nuclear doctrine. He acknowledged that the issues were difficult, and that there were divergences of view, but tried to reassure the Allies by stating, 'we will not impose our view'.[28] In other words, the Nixon Administration would not follow the pressure tactics of its predecessors in an attempt to change NATO doctrine unilaterally.

The 1973 military alert caused alarm in Western Europe because the US made the decision without consulting or notifying the Allies in advance. Although West European leaders did not publicly challenge the action itself, their isolation from the decision which could have affected the security of Western Europe only increased their sense of impotence in the crisis.[29] Allied concern concentrated on the fact that there had been no prior consultation over an alert that involved US troops stationed in Western Europe.

Kissinger admitted that 'abstractly, our allies were justified in their complaints', but justified his actions on the basis of time limitations and the need for secrecy.[30] Britain, the only ally to be informed of the military alert before it was implemented, did nothing to stem the tide of criticism from the other Allies in order not to draw attention to the fact that she still enjoyed preferential status in Washington.[31]

Kissinger's position on nuclear strategy while in office was consistent with his views in *The Troubled Partnership*. American military planners shared Kissinger's view that the nuclear dilemma could not be resolved to the complete satisfaction of both the US and its European Allies. According to Kissinger, Secretary Laird was correct when he reported to the President: 'The longer term problem of divergence between American and European views on strategy remains'.[32]

The West European nuclear forces (and especially the French *force de frappe*) were other issues that had generated conflict within NATO. In the 1960s, American efforts to control all nuclear weapons in the Alliance were evident in the opposition to the nuclear programmes of Britain and France. These efforts were interpreted by West Europeans as an attempt by the US to reserve the right to define what constituted the vital interests of the Alliance as a whole. In short, the US was trying to ensure that it could 'decouple' its defence from that of Western Europe. This was what the Allies sought to prevent by opposing the unilateral change of US strategic doctrine. After his retirement in 1969, President de Gaulle expressed the West European fear with respect to such changes. In a conversation with Andre Malraux, de Gaulle said; 'Despite its power, I don't believe the United States has a long-term policy. Its desire, and it will satisfy it one day, is to desert Europe. You will see'.[33]

Conscious of the negative psychological impact that such views could have on the cohesion of NATO, Kissinger attempted to dispel them. President Nixon, in his foreign policy reports to Congress, acknowledged the contribution the British and the French nuclear forces make to the deterrent posture of the West. In the President's words: 'The nuclear forces of the United States, supplemented by the nuclear forces of our allies, remain the backbone of our deterrent'.[34] This ackowledgement reflected Kissinger's view that the nuclear forces of the Allies should be seen as a complement (and not as an alternative) to US strategic forces.[35] Indeed, the French *force de frappe* ceased to be a point of political leverage or contention within the Alliance. The French military in many ways quietly coordinated its plans and exercises with NATO's. The Administration was well disposed to explore the possibilities of military cooperation with France and, according to Kissinger, 'not even the possibility of limited cooperation in the nuclear field was excluded'.[36] In fact, the Administration permitted France to acquire some of the military sensitive information and equipment that the US used to withhold.[37]

In summary, while in office Kissinger's handling of the strategic dilemmas of NATO was consistent with the views he advocated before he became Assistant to the President for National Affairs. His analysis of the structural problems of NATO and of the nature of the issues that had to be resolved had led him to conclude that no final solution was possible as long as NATO remained composed of sovereign states. Therefore he made no real effort to deal with these dilemmas. Nevertheless, as strategic equivalence between the US and

the USSR approached, a reexamination of the strategic doctrine
became necessary. Kissinger and his staff undertook the task and
developed the new doctrine of strategic sufficiency. But the new
doctrine's purposefully designed ambiguity did not ignite a debate in
the Alliance. West Europeans seemed satisfied with the doctrine
which permitted the US to deploy nuclear weapons which sustained
the credibility of the US strategic umbrella. Strategic parity and
Soviet numerical superiority in conventional military forces, however, revived the 'real' issue – namely, the role of tactical nuclear
weapons in the defence of Western Europe. But Kissinger main
tained a low profile and acquiesced in the NPG solution. By pressing
the issue, he could only have exposed the illogicalities and differences
within the Alliance, something West Europeans sought to avoid.

SALT I AND THE DEFENCE OF WESTERN EUROPE

In the 1960s, West Europeans saw no quantitative or qualitative
developments in the strategic arsenals of the superpowers that would
threaten their security. The emphasis had always been on nuclear
deterrence. West Europeans had rarely (if ever) been willing to
devote serious attention to the role of conventional and tactical
nuclear forces needed to support the doctrine of flexible response. As
far as SALT was concerned, the emphasis on deterring a Soviet
attack by threat of massive retaliation had made West Europeans
highly sensitive to the political credibility of strategic deterrence but
relatively insensitive to the technical and quantitative relationship
between American and Soviet strategic forces.[38]

In their view, the political credibility of deterrence would not be
affected by SALT if the US retained: (a) the capability to inflict an
unacceptable level of damage to the USSR, and (b) the credibility of
its commitment to inflict such damage in response to a Soviet attack
on Western Europe. By those standards – and not by any criteria of
quantitative superiority or parity – they assessed developments in the
strategic arms race between the superpowers.

West European attitudes towards the deployment of the American
'Safeguard' ABM system and the rapid growth after 1967 of Soviet
ICBM strength clearly illustrated this point. As Ian Smart reported,
in the case of the ABM debate in the US, one persistent element in
the West European public reaction was 'a type of anxious irritation –
not with reference to America's predicament but with reference to

America's preoccupation'.[39] Outside technically sophisticated governmental circles, the military arguments for and against the ABM deployment fell on deaf ears. What was more generally recognized was the implication (justified or otherwise) that the US might be about to insulate itself from its European Allies, practically and emotionally, by deploying a new defence system in its own territory. The spectre of 'Fortress America' seemed, however illogical, to draw nearer.[40]

In contrast, Smart reported, the growth of Soviet ICBM strength between 1967 and 1971 left West Europeans almost totally unmoved. Part of their complacency rested on the belief that the US would never permit the USSR to achieve the level of superiority which would make possible a totally disarming first-strike. Part of it, however, was more rational. West Europeans recalled the state of mutual nuclear deterrence which was already asserted to exist between the superpowers in the early 1960s. The strategic forces of the USSR and the US were far smaller then, and potential Soviet second-strike capability was only a fraction of the present US capability. With that in mind, West Europeans were – and are – strongly conservative in estimating the level of potential damage which in fact either superpower must threaten in order to deter the other. The belief that 100 or 200 thermonuclear weapons would survive to strike Soviet territory has generally seemed to be enough to deter any rational leadership in Moscow.[41]

During the President's visit to Western Europe in 1969, he was urged by its leaders to start the SALT negotiations as rapidly as possible and to consult them as they progressed. President de Gaulle and the British Foreign Secretary Michael Stewart strongly urged President Nixon to pursue SALT. When Walter Scheel (the leader of the Free Democratic Party, and later foreign minister) visited Washington, he argued that West Europeans no longer feared a US–Soviet condominium. When the Administration delayed the talks to review options and link SALT to other issues, many West European leaders stressed its urgency.[42] Those in the US who were urging strategic arms limitation argued that the Allies desired it. Under Kissinger's concept of strategic sufficiency, the US continued to deploy new weapons systems in order to shore up the credibility of its commitment to NATO. Therefore, West Europeans viewed SALT as an attempt by the superpowers to limit strategic arms to some rational level. In addition, SALT was seen in Western Europe as consonant with efforts to secure a more general relaxation of East–

West tensions. By late 1969, those efforts were gathering their own momentum in Western Europe.[43] Chancellor Brandt's *Ostpolitik* was a manifestation of that momentum.

The dominant reaction in Western Europe to the announcement that the SALT negotiations would begin in Helsinki was positive with numerous political and editorial voices greeting the US–Soviet agreement with approval and relief. Most West Europeans believed that the US–Soviet strategic arms competition had long passed the level of appropriate rationality. Within official circles however, those who had urged the President to start the SALT negotiations as soon as possible began to grasp the implications of strategic parity that would be ratified by SALT.[44] Some feared that American negotiators focusing on the technical objectives would be outmanoeuvred by their Soviet colleagues who concentrated on political objectives. Others feared the US might sacrifice some of its capability to protect Allies in order to obtain advantages in terms of the strictly bilateral military balance.[45] The greatest fear (apart from the military implications of SALT), however, was that the Nixon Administration might become so politically intoxicated by the experience of negotiating directly and privately with the Soviet leadership as to diminish the value it placed on political intimacy with the Allies. This fear had been generated during the negotiation of the Non-Proliferation Treaty, when West European governments were purposefully excluded (without consultation) from the discussions between American and Soviet representatives in Geneva and elsewhere.[46]

Aware of the West European reactions, Kissinger summed them up for the President:

> It is a fair estimate that some of the original enthusiasm for SALT is waning. One reason for this is the underlying concern over the effect of a SALT agreement. Some countries apparently fear that an agreement based on parity would leave the Soviet Union with a substantial margin of superiority in conventional forces in Europe, and the net result would be that the overall deterrent against Soviet tanks might be weakened. There is also some concern, mainly German, that the connection between SALT and political matters is no longer to be maintained.[47]

The Nixon Administration, conscious of the fact that Allied unity was essential to its policy towards the USSR, made energetic efforts to calm the fears and doubts which existed within the official West

European circles and satisfy their desire for close consultation. President Nixon had begun the process in February 1969, when he formally pledged full consultation in the North Atlantic Council in Brussels, conditional only upon the content of such discussions being treated with the greatest secrecy. During the latter stages of preparation and the negotiations themselves, American representatives regularly went to Brussels to brief the Council on US positions and on the progress in Helsinki and Vienna.[48] Moreover, the American Ambassador to the European Community (J. Robert Schaetzel), reported that Kissinger – who personally conducted the most sensitive SALT negotiations through the backchannel – would return from Moscow by way of Paris, Bonn, and London for consultations. The discussions were secretive and bilateral and, although he discussed matters of critical concern to NATO, he did not add NATO headquarters to his itinerary.[49]

But not all West European governments were entirely satisfied by this procedure. Some of the Allies discovered that the Administration's eagerness to consult meant little more than a willingness to inform others of decisions already made and executed; most were highly critical of Kissinger. But few should have been surprised, since a more careful reading of Kissinger's writings would have revealed that his behaviour was consistent with his beliefs. First, SALT would affect NATO's nuclear dilemma, which Kissinger believed could not be resolved as long as NATO was composed of sovereign states. Secondly, Kissinger was convinced the NATO bureaucracy (like any bureaucracy) would stifle the creativity necessary to succeed in his negotiations with the Soviets.[50] Thirdly, he viewed consultation within the existing Alliance framework as little more than a palliative. The issues it solves were peripheral, while the central issues were inadequately articulated.[51] And fourthly, Kissinger believed that the Allies' 'passion for consultation meant in practice the desire to limit America's freedom of action' while 'not all ... allies were equally prepared to constrain their own'.[52] Therefore, it was highly unlikely that Kissinger would have attempted to build a consensus on SALT within the Alliance, and in the process deprive himself of the essential secrecy and creativity. As he argued: 'It can never be the task of leadership to solicit a consensus, but to create the conditions which will make a consensus possible'.[53] On the whole, however, the regular briefings succeeded in containing West European nervousness both on technical matters and on the important issue of political intent.

During 1969 and early 1970, it became clear that although SALT was intended to codify and formalize the bilateral relationship of nuclear deterrence between the superpowers, it would touch upon several issues which were of direct concern to West European governments. Two issues raised by SALT were the viability of the British and French nuclear forces and the deployment of intermediate-range and medium-range ballistic missiles (IRBMs/MRBMs) in Western Russia, aimed at West European targets. The British and French governments were fearful because in their absence SALT might impose limitations on their nuclear deterrents. The West German government and others initially believed that SALT might lead to some limitation of Soviet IRBM/MRBM deployment. In contrast, the growth of Soviet ICBMs between 1967 and 1971 left West Europeans almost totally unmoved.[54]

The French and the British nuclear forces were not affected directly by SALT since neither country was a party to the negotiations. SALT, however, could have indirectly affected those forces in a number of ways:

(a) The credibility of the British and French nuclear forces depended on the size and effectiveness of Soviet defences. Therefore, the ABM systems which helped to bring SALT about could have reduced the utility of the British and French deterrents if SALT did not limit the Soviet ABM system.

(b) The British Polaris force was still heavily dependent upon American cooperation, hence a possible US–Soviet agreement to reduce superpower cooperation with third countries concerned the British government.[55]

(c) The British and French nuclear forces are part of the total Western strategic strength, therefore if the USSR obtained American agreement to a limitation of that strength as a whole, the US then might have passed some part of that limitation to Britain and France.[56]

The second issue raised by SALT was the Soviet IRBM/MRBM force in the western part of the USSR.[57] This force aimed at West European targets seemed more threatening than the larger number of Soviet ICBMs and SLBMs targeted on the US. The immediate impulse of some West Europeans (particularly in Bonn) was to call for the limitation or reduction of the Soviet IRBM/MRBM force as an important Western objective in SALT, and (since the initiative

would have to come from Washington) to regard the Administra-
ion's response as a test of its alleged concern for the interests of its
European Allies.[58] This impulse was eventually suppressed; the
reasons why remain concealed by the secrecy which surrounded the
discussion on SALT in the North Atlantic Council and the bilateral
discussions between Kissinger and West European leaders. But it
probably became clear to West Europeans (soon after SALT began)
that the inclusion of Soviet IRBMs/MRBMs would greatly weaken
the effort of the US to resist Soviet attempts to raise what soon
emerged as the most unsettling SALT issue to West European
governments – namely, the issue of forward-based systems (FBS).[59]
The Allies urged the Administration to resist Soviet attempts to
include FBS in the negotiations. This, however, was not necessary
since the Administration was unwilling to discuss the FBS with the
Soviets because the conventional role of American FBS was (and is)
a concern of the US.[60]

West European leaders might have realized that the IRBMs/
MRBMs, being old and inaccurate, were a less important component of the USSR's overall nuclear capability against Western
Europe. Attempts to include these missiles in SALT might have
complicated the negotiations and delayed agreement, thus out-
weighing any advantage which might have come from their ultimate
limitation. Moreover, Bonn saw its own detente diplomacy (*Ostpolitik*) as complementary to the SALT negotiations, and sought to
reduce inter-Allied tension.[61]

West European reactions to the Moscow Agreements of 26 May
1972 were mixed. Within the West European defence ministries and
disarmament sections of the foreign ministries, disappointment and
satisfaction were evident.[62] Disappointment in the limited arms
control effect of the agreements was contrasted with concern about
the quantitative advantages conceded to the USSR in offensive arms.
Yet there was satisfaction because the agreements did not limit the
FBS which directly affected West European security, and because the
ABM Treaty had prolonged the effectiveness of the British and the
French strategic forces. But there was anxiety that the stage might
have been set for future constraint of FBS, and of West European
nuclear forces, or of technical exchanges in the nuclear weapons field
between the US and its European Allies.

The ABM Treaty prolonged the deterrent value of the British and
the French nuclear forces by limiting Soviet ABM systems. This left
many targets of value for West European deterrent forces outside the

ABM-covered area. But even within the Moscow area (which was covered by an ABM system) the small nuclear forces of the Allies could cause damage on soft targets within that area. ABM systems provided a means of reducing the damage caused by a ballistic missile attack, but (unless they were extraordinarily excellent in performance and reliability) they were not likely to prevent all damage to a critical target. Therefore the ABM Treaty increased – or at least did not reduce – the credibility of the offensive forces of non-signatories. At the same time, however, the treaty created an atmosphere of detente which made the British and French nuclear forces appear less necessary to their publics, which were eager to reduce defence spending.[63]

The Administration, to reassure the Allies, asserted that Article IX of the ABM Treaty (which prohibits the transfer of ABM technology to third countries) did not establish a precedent for a parallel prohibition in the case of strategic offensive weapons technology.[64] Additionally, it rejected the Soviet attempt on 17 May 1972 to bring British and French ballistic-missiles submarines within the scope of SALT limitations. These efforts to reassure the Allies did not remove the anxiety. The fact that the issues had arisen encouraged some West Europeans to expect their resurrection in SALT II. Persistent American assurances to the contrary only reinforced the suspicion that the US might eventually be tempted to concede the inclusion of FBS in SALT II. This allowed the possibility for disruptive effects within the Alliance to remain.[65]

Within broader politically informed groups in Western Europe, reactions to the SALT agreements were both less specific and less ambivalent. The agreements were seen as a type of superpower endorsement for the process of East–West detente as a whole; few were interested in their detailed provisions. The important consideration seemed to be what Kissinger emphasized in Kiev on 29 May 1972, when he said: 'To put the central armaments of both sides for the first time under agreed restraint is an event that transcends in importance the technical significance of the individual restrictions that were placed on various weapons systems'.[66]

West European public opinion at large, however, responded to SALT I agreements with a sort of contented apathy. Since the opening of SALT in November 1969, a number of other international issues had climbed to a higher place in the priorities of West Europeans (a collapse of SALT would have been a major event).

THE AGREEMENT ON THE PREVENTION OF NUCLEAR WAR

NATO's defence dilemmas resurfaced in June 1973, when President Nixon and General Secretary Brezhnev concluded The Agreement on the Prevention of Nuclear War. Article 4 of the agreement committed the superpowers to 'urgent consultations with each other' should a risk of nuclear war result from their bilateral or third-country relations. But Article 6 (which was included in the agreement at the continued insistence of Kissinger) stated that 'nothing in this Agreement shall affect or impair: (a) the inherent right of individual or collective self-defence as envisaged by Article 51 of the Charter of the United Nations ... and (c) the obligations undertaken by either Party towards its allies or other countries in treaties, agreements, and other appropriate documents'.[67]

Kissinger believed that Brezhnev's proposals for a treaty between the US and the USSR renouncing the use of nuclear weapons against each other was designed to 'dismantle the military strategy of NATO ... and ... isolate China ... or any other country with nuclear aspirations',[68] whose territorial integrity was essential to the international equilibrium. The Soviet proposals did not preclude the use of nuclear weapons in a war involving NATO and the Warsaw Pact. Their use, however, would have been confined only to the territory of Allies, thereby making the use of nuclear weapons against the territory of the superpowers proscribed.[69] In other words, the proposed Soviet treaty would have protected the superpowers against nuclear destruction even in a European war, while guaranteeing the devastation of each country's Allies. Acceptance of the Soviet draft treaty by the US would have destroyed NATO, since its defence depended on the American nuclear guarantee.[70] Moreover, acceptance of the Soviet draft treaty would have alarmed the PRC, since it would have seen it as a sign of the much dreaded US–Soviet collusion.[71]

But despite formal reassurance (Article 6) that US Alliance commitments remained unaffected, the way the agreement was concluded generated serious concern in Western Europe that availability of US nuclear weapons in a crisis might depend upon the uncertain outcome of US–Soviet negotiations, which might take precedence over Alliance consultations. Chancellor Brandt, President Pompidou, and Prime Minister Heath had been briefed by Kissinger several times about the progress of the negotiations. The

Prime Minister and the Chancellor supported the Administration, but President Pompidou did not. He did not, however, make his reservations public. The three leaders were informed about the conclusion of the agreement 2½ days before it was signed, but they were pledged to secrecy. The concern of the Allies was intensified by the fact that their ambassadors were informed of the agreement only 6½ hours before it was signed, even though it had been a subject of US–Soviet discussion for more than a year. There was therefore, no opportunity for full consideration of the agreement by their respective foreign policy and defence establishments.[72]

When the agreement was brought before the North Atlantic Council in June 1973, it was strongly criticized by the British permanent representative even though it was largely a British draft.[73] The permanent representative of the FRG supported British criticisms. Later, French Foreign Minister Jobert challenged Kissinger to reconcile the requirement for NATO consultation in a nuclear crisis with the US pledge to consult the USSR in similar circumstances.[74]

Ironically, Kissinger had ignored his own earlier warning that 'bilateral dealings with the Soviets, from which our Allies are excluded or about which they are informed only at the last moment, are bound to magnify Third Force tendencies'.[75] But as it has been pointed out, Kissinger was convinced that 'Third-Force dangers ... [had] been overdrawn'. He could not 'visualize a "deal" between the Soviet Union and Europe which would jeopardize [American] interests without jeopardizing European interests first'.[76]

Kissinger's actions were consistent with his views – that secrecy was essential in the conduct of successful negotiations, and that consultation within the existing Alliance framework can be nothing more than a palliative since the issues it 'solves' are peripheral. Moreover, Kissinger's actions reflected his conviction that 'disagreement on peripheral issues may be the price for unity on issues that really matter'.[77]

In this case, the peripheral issue was consultation with the Allies, but the real issues from Kissinger's viewpoint were the prevention of nuclear war and the establishment of a stable international system. On these issues Kissinger maintained the Allies were united. These goals were brought closer to achievement by the agreement since the actors who could transform the international system agreed upon a 'workable' arrangement, and on the permissible aims and methods of foreign policy. These, Kissinger had been arguing, were the essential requisites for peace.[78] In his words:

The Agreement on the Prevention of Nuclear War reflected our belief that control of arms presupposed restraint in international conduct; that coexistence between the superpowers would ultimately depend on adherence to standards of behavior by which they would learn not to threaten each other's vital interests.[79]

In short, the agreement was an elaboration of the Basic Principles of US–Soviet relations signed at the Moscow summit the previous year.[80] The Administration invoked the agreement only once, during the Yom Kippur War, when it warned the Soviets that their unilateral intervention would violate its provisions. But the crisis demonstrated, according to Kissinger, that 'the dangers of nuclear war are repelled not by a document but by strength, resolve and determined diplomacy'.[81] In other words, the Allies (and the PRC)[82] should not view the agreement as proof of a developing US–Soviet condominium.

CONCLUSION

In 1969, the approaching strategic parity between the US and the USSR necessitated the reexamination of the US strategic doctrine and revived a number of insoluble issues of the common defence. But the Nixon Administration recognized the basic relationship of power and interests between the US and its major European Allies (and Japan) remained remarkably stable despite the resurgence of the economic power and political assertiveness of the Allies. In its efforts to resolve some of the issues of the NATO defence, the Administration sought to preserve the underlying structure of power and interests within the Alliance as the basis for pursuing detente with the USSR and rapprochement with the PRC. President Nixon and Kissinger agreed that, next to US–Soviet detente and US–PRC rapprochement, no peaceful international development would affect American foreign policy more than a change in the basic relationship of power and interests between the US and its major European Allies (and Japan). The greatest change in this relationship would have been a shift from Allied military dependence upon the US to substantial military autonomy. Such a shift was regarded by the Administration as a threat to the global diplomatic equilibrium and Kissinger's global strategy.

The reexamination of the US strategic doctrine undertaken by

Kissinger resulted in the doctrine of strategic sufficiency which incorporated the themes of superiority and parity. The doctrine (although being a unilateral change of US strategy) did not spark a debate within the Alliance as the doctrine of flexible response had done. The purposefully designed ambiguity of the doctrine obscured the inherent cross-purposes of strategic arms control (SALT) and the continued reliance on strategic weapons to defend America's Allies. It appears the ambiguity of Kissinger's concept of sufficiency, which permitted the US to maintain the first-strike option against the USSR, kept the American strategic umbrella extended over the Allies, justified the deployment of new weapons systems, and fulfilled the West European need for reassurance. Moreover, the Administration did not pressure the Allies to accept the new doctrine as the official NATO doctrine, nor did it seek changes in the official NATO doctrine of flexible response.

NATO's nuclear dilemmas were not at the top of Kissinger's agenda (nor, for that matter, the agenda of West European leaders, who shared Kissinger's view that these dilemmas could not be resolved in the foreseeable future). This was evident in the Administration's acceptance of the NPG decision supporting the demonstrative use of tactical nuclear weapons in the defence of Western Europe. Kissinger acquiesced, but did not vigorously support the NPG decision which he felt manifested the West's lack of political will. The Administration was not opposed to the nuclear forces of Britain and France. On the contrary, it acknowledged the contribution these forces made to the deterrent posture of the West, a view Kissinger had advanced in his writings.

The muted reaction of the Allies to SALT resulted from the fact that West Europeans were 'consulted' and that SALT did not deal with the British and French nuclear forces and FBS, issues that concerned the Allies directly. In their view, as long as the US retained the capability to inflict an unacceptable level of damage to the USSR and the credibility of its commitment to inflict such damage in response to a Soviet attack on Western Europe, the political credibility of deterrence would not be affected by SALT. From the West European viewpoint, the doctrine of strategic sufficiency guaranteed the credibility of the US nuclear commitment to Europe. In addition, SALT was seen by the Allies as consonant with their efforts to secure a more general relaxation of East–West tensions, and in particular with Chancellor Brandt's *Ostpolitik*.

Allied reactions to the SALT agreements were mixed. Within the

West European defence and foreign ministries, both disappointment and satisfaction were evident. Disappointment in the limited arms control effect of the agreements was contrasted with concern about the quantitative advantages conceded to the USSR in offensive arms. There was satisfaction because the ABM treaty prolonged the deterrent value of the British and French nuclear forces and because the agreements did not limit the FBS. But there was anxiety that the stage might have been set for future constraint of FBS and West European nuclear forces. This anxiety was intensified by the Agreement on the Prevention of Nuclear War which generated serious concern among the Allies that availability of US nuclear weapons in a crisis might depend upon the uncertain outcome of US–Soviet negotiations, which might take precedence over Alliance consultations. But on the whole, the general West European satisfaction with the Administration's policies precluded a movement towards greater military independence.

The criticism of the Allies did not focus on the Administration's policies *per se*, but on the process by which these issues were resolved. Most West Europeans leaders were highly critical of Kissinger, who handled most of the critical negotiations with the USSR. Rather than consulting them in advance, he informed them after decisions had been made and executed. But few should have been surprised. A more careful reading of Kissinger's writings would have revealed that although he stressed the forging of a common Atlantic policy with Western Europe as the most urgent task confronting American foreign policy, his primary goal was the establishment of a stable international system. Hence his main focus was the USSR, the only other power besides the US that could transform the international system.

Kissinger viewed consultation within the existing Alliance framework as a palliative which failed to articulate the 'real' issues, and a means by which the Allies could limit America's freedom of action. Therefore, it was highly unlikely that Kissinger would have attempted to build a consensus within the Alliance on SALT and the Agreement on the Prevention of Nuclear War, and in the process deprive himself of the essential secrecy and creativity. Moreover, Kissinger was convinced that despite their adverse reaction to his tactics, the Allies were really united on the real issues – namely the prevention of nuclear war and the establishment of a stable international system, both of which were brought a step closer to achievement by his policies.

7 US Troops in Europe

The evolution toward US–Soviet strategic parity in the late 1960s had strengthened the need for conventional forces in NATO. Yet there was a growing Senate pressure for a reduction of US troops in Europe. In preparing for the twentieth-anniversary celebration of NATO in Washington, Kissinger in a memorandum urged President Nixon to emphasize the Administration's commitment to maintain strong American forces in Europe, but pointed out that Congressional support required proportionate contributions from the Allies.[1] This recommendation was consistent with Kissinger's conviction that the defence of Western Europe could not be left to the Europeans, regardless of their stand on burden-sharing. But it also reflected his concern that Congress might legislate troop reductions unless the Allies appeared to make the proportionate contributions.

THE MANSFIELD RESOLUTIONS

The Nixon Administration began to study the issue of US troops in Europe in November 1969, following the request for NSSM 84. After several delays in the production of the study, the results were reviewed in the National Security Council (NSC) system during the summer and Fall of 1970, culminating in a Cabinet-level NSC meeting in November.[2] According to Kissinger, the NSC meeting 'could do little except to register our dilemma'.[3] He summed up the strategic problem for the President by stating:

> we and our Allies must maintain strong enough conventional forces to be able to meet Soviet aggression or the threat of it implicit in their substantial forces. Unless we and our Allies rework our NATO strategy and forces so that they can provide this capability, we will soon experience the gradual 'neutralization' of Western Europe. To avoid this situation, we must act vigorously to maintain NATO's conventional capability while developing a strategy for its use that makes sense in this fundamentally new strategic situation.[4]

In the NSC meeting, three options were discussed: (i) maintenance of a force greater than 250 000 as part of a NATO defence capable of repelling a large-scale conventional attack; (ii) reduction to a

150 000–200 000-men force capable of limited conventional defence but tailored to respond to massive attack with 'clean' battlefield nuclear weapons; and (iii) reduction to a force of 50 000 men which would signify a virtually automatic reliance on nuclear weapons to respond to anything more than a minor border incident.[5] After the NSC deliberations, the President apparently decided to eliminate the third option. By maintaining present forces over the short run he kept options (i) and (ii) open. Both options seemed consistent with NATO's strategy of flexible response.[6] But more importantly, by keeping options (i) and (ii) open, the President enhanced the flexibility of the US in future negotiations with the USSR. In a message to the NATO Ministerial Meeting of December 1970, President Nixon announced that the US would maintain current strength until at least July 1972 'unless there is reciprocal action [to reduce troops] by our adversaries'.[7]

The mix of factors that influenced the President's decision to maintain current force levels despite plans (by the Johnson Administration) to reduce some forces in Europe will never be exactly determined.[8] One factor, however, was the President's and Kissinger's conviction that the military balance in Europe and the unity of the Alliance were essential to their policy toward the USSR. Another factor was the considerable pressure applied on the Administration by the FRG (as well as other European Allies) to oppose the Senate's demands for force withdrawals. A third factor was the control function of US forces. Chancellor Brandt's *Ostpolitik* and the threat of differential detente necessitated the maintenance of current forces as support for *Ostpolitik* and as a reminder that the FRG ought not to go too far, too fast in normalizing relations with its Eastern neighbours.[9] This was one of Kissinger's main concerns. He feared that by moving too fast, Brandt would limit the Administration's ability to implement linkage thus reducing Kissinger's ability to influence the behaviour of the USSR.[10] A fourth factor was the Administration's concern with credibility. In the summer of 1970, the USSR threatened the delicate balance of power in the Middle East, and it attempted to build a nuclear submarine base at Cienfuegos in Cuba. Although these events did not directly affect the situation in Europe, the Administration may have felt that a force reduction there (with its symbolic connotations) would be interpreted as a slackening of American will in the face of new Soviet manoeuvring.[11]

Kissinger firmly opposed any reduction in US force levels in Europe, and pressed for the buildup of West European military strength. The decision to maintain over 250 000 US troops in Europe was consistent with Kissinger's conviction that maintaining NATO's capability to fight a large-scale conventional war (at least for a short period) was essential to enhance the deterrent posture of the US.[12] A strong conventional force in Western Europe would drive the USSR into a scale of military effort which would remove any doubt about its ultimate intention, therefore making the threat of massive retaliation by the US more convincing. In addition, if the NATO forces could not be overcome conventionally, the risk of initiating all-out war would shift to the USSR. This, Kissinger had argued, generates 'a very crucial psychological obstacle' to a full-scale attack on Western Europe, since it raises the risk of nuclear war to an intolerable level for the USSR.[13] Kissinger was determined that both the US and the Allies should enhance their capability to conduct ground warfare in Europe by improving equipment, supplies, and deployments. Recommendations along these lines followed from NSSM 84, and from the US-supported NATO review AD-70 (Atlantic Defence for the 1970s) initiated in 1969.[14]

Repeatedly during its first term, the Nixon Administration gave evidence of its support for NATO in ways that should have been unmistakeable to West Europeans. The most critical support derived from its stand on the Mansfield Resolution (Senate Resolution 292), which called for 'a substantial reduction of US forces permanently stationed in Europe'.[15]

Senator Mansfield and his allies marshalled a number of strategic, economic, and political arguments which revived the issues of: (a) the role of conventional forces in the defence of Western Europe; (b) burden-sharing; (c) balance-of-payments deficits; and (d) Soviet intentions. The Senator questioned the declared objective of the Nixon Doctrine to lower the American military presence abroad.[16] He also used *Ostpolitik* to justify unilateral US reductions.[17] The most important argument was that 315 000 American military personnel in Europe (along with 235 000 dependents and 14 000 civilian employees) exacerbated the 'dollar gap' in foreign exchange to the extent of $1.5 billion a year. The Administration was held directly responsible for its inability to obtain a more equitable distribution of burden-sharing within the Alliance. The offset agreements (whereby the FRG had purchased medium-term American securities to cover part of the deficit from troops stationed there) were seen as mere window dressing, since the securities would eventually be cashed by the Bundesbank for American dollars.

The intention of the resolution, according to Mansfield, was to induce the Allies to make a larger and fairer contribution to NATO, rather than to indicate that NATO's military structure was overbuilt. In the event of a contingency, American troops could be quickly flown back to Europe by air transport without sacrificing combat effectiveness. This capability was cited in the body of the resolution as one of the principal justifications for reducing standing forces. No changes were intended, the Senator claimed, beyond reducing the size of the American contribution 'without adversely affecting either our resolve or ability to meet our commitment under the North Atlantic Treaty'.[18]

The Mansfield Resolution reflected the national mood of disillusionment with the military failure in Vietnam, and the anger over Western Europe's insensitivity to America's agony. It also reflected anger over Western Europe's unwillingness to contribute more to the common defence in spite of the constant American appeals to the Allies to expand their military forces. The weakening of the dollar, due to the war-born inflation at a time when the economies of the Allies flourished and their currencies strengthened at America's expense, kept the issue alive. In addition, the Senate pressure reflected a desire to exert some influence over the executive's control of foreign policy.[19]

The Nixon Administration saw opposition to Senate troop-withdrawal pressures as an essential corollary to its policy toward the USSR. The evolution toward US–Soviet strategic parity had strengthened the need for conventional forces in NATO. The 'decoupling' (via mutual deterrence) of strategic nuclear forces from a credible military role in Europe and the continued escalation uncertainties associated with the use of tactical nuclear weapons, argued against reductions in US conventional forces in Europe. Any unilateral reductions, the Administration claimed, would jeopardize prospects for mutual force reductions in Europe. Moreover, a unilateral withdrawal would generate doubts among the Allies about the credibility of the American commitment to defend Western Europe. These arguments reflected Kissinger's view that the US required a stable East–West military balance in Europe to underpin its strategy of detente with the USSR. The Administration's stand was not therefore simply a gesture of NATO solidarity. In this issue, US Alliance policy and detente policy were mutually reinforcing.

Senator Mansfield mounted his powerful challenge on 11 May 1971, in the form of an amendment to the Draft Extension Act. The amendment required US forces in Europe to be reduced by one-half (or 150 000 men) by the end of the year.[20] Kissinger led the Administration's efforts to defeat the amendment. He considered the Mansfield Amendment a serious threat to the Administration's entire foreign policy. Introduced at a time when major negotiations were taking place on SALT, on Berlin, and on the secret trip to Peking, the amendment jeopardized every one of these policies. Kissinger was adamantly against a compromise proposed by the Administration's supporters in the Senate; this compromise avoided a specific mandatory reduction by calling upon the Administration to negotiate reductions with both the Allies and the USSR. The President was to report to Congress on 15 September 1971, and every six months thereafter, on the progress of these negotiations.[21]

Kissinger's task was facilitated by the fact that the issue of force levels in Europe had not caused intense dispute within the bureaucracy. The State Department opposed any reductions, believing that such action would undermine NATO cohesion and harm the Western bargaining position in future talks with the Warsaw Pact countries on mutual force reductions (MBFR). The Joint Chiefs, wishing to maintain the military balance in Europe, took a similar line. Only Secretary of Defense Laird recommended a 10 per cent reduction because of cost pressures. Laird's position (reportedly supported by Kissinger) reflected the fear that Congress might legislate even larger reductions if the Administration did not accept any cuts. The concern of the Treasury with the balance-of-payments aspects of the issue was overshadowed by strategic and political considerations.[22]

The popularity of the amendment required the mobilization of the bipartisan elite that had been responsible for NATO's success. On 15 May, a Presidential statement was released opposing the Mansfield Amendment. It was signed by nearly all living former Secretaries of State and Defense, their deputies, and former NATO commanders. Separate statements were obtained from Presidents Truman and Johnson.[23] The Administration lobbied actively with Senators from both parties, and a press campaign was organized.

West Europeans fully supported the Administration's stand, because (as the German Defence Minister Helmut Schmidt explained):

> nobody can deny that Western Europe, even if it were willing and able to put a European soldier in place of every GI withdrawn,

could never make up for the deterrent effect inherent in American troops and their immediate link with the strategic deterrence. In the balance of power that obtains between the two superpowers one cannot replace the soldiers of the American superpower by French, British, or German soldiers.[24]

In short, he was repeating Kissinger's argument that the defence of Western Europe must from the outset always involve American forces. The replacement of US troops by European divisions would not resolve the security dilemma of Western Europe.[25]

In Bonn, Chancellor Brandt issued a statement warning that 'a unilateral American withdrawal would leave "the irradicable impression that the United States [was] on its way out of Europe" transforming détente into appeasement'. NATO Secretary General Manlio Brosio released a letter to the President warning that a major reduction of US forces would 'withdraw all credibility from NATO's ability to keep its commitments'.[26] In addition, the Allies reiterated their commitment to the European Defence Improvement Programme (EDIP).

The Administration's efforts to defeat the Mansfield Amendment were also aided by the USSR. In a speech at Tiblisi on 14 May, Brezhnev stated for the first time that Moscow was ready to begin negotiations between NATO and the Warsaw Pact countries for mutual force reductions in Central Europe. In December 1970 the President had decided not to reduce current troop levels in Europe unless the USSR reduced its forces. Now, it seized upon Brezhnev's statement arguing that it would be foolish to withdraw troops unilaterally, thus weakening the West's bargaining hand in the negotiations (this remained the position of the Administration).[27]

The Mansfield Amendment was defeated in the Senate on 19 May 1971, by a vote of 61 to 36.[28] The next morning, President Nixon announced the breakthrough on the SALT negotiations. A subsequent effort by Senator Mansfield to revive the issue in December (with another resolution), calling for a 60 000 men reduction, was also unsuccessful. In the 1972 presidential campaign, Senator George McGovern proposed a 50 per cent reduction within a three-year period as part of a broader plan of defence cutbacks. The Administration opposed the proposal, and reiterated its commitment to maintain the current force levels in Europe.[29]

But the growing pressures in 1971 and 1972 to reduce US force levels in Europe broadened participation in the debate from a rather

narrow foreign policy elite to the general public. This set the stage
for the enactment of the Jackson–Nunn Amendment in November
1973. This Amendment directed the President to reduce US forces in
Europe by the same percentage that the Europeans failed to offset
the balance-of-payments costs of these forces for fiscal year 1974.
The Nixon Administration viewed the Jackson–Nunn Amendment
as a mixed blessing, but declined to veto it. The Administration
feared that Congress would return with legislation directly mandat-
ing force withdrawals, with or without offset. [30] In Kissinger's view
the Jackson–Nunn Amendment undermined the principle that force
structures should be based primarily on security criteria by making
burden-sharing a major American objective, and it restricted the
Executive's flexibility in the conduct of foreign affairs. But it also
strengthened the Administration's case in negotiating with the
Allies. [31]

MUTUAL AND BALANCED FORCE REDUCTIONS (MBFR)

In 1968, at its Reykjavik Ministerial meeting, NATO had signalled
its interest in exploring mutual force reductions with the Warsaw
Pact countries. MBFR was generally accepted in NATO (following
the Harmel Report) as an area for advancing East–West detente.
The Johnson Administration, however, favoured MBFR primarily as
a means to check Senator Mansfield and his supporters in the Senate,
while the Allies supported MBFR as a desirable alternative to
unilateral reductions of US forces in Europe. The Soviet invasion of
Czechoslovakia put the issue 'on ice', but NATO reactivated MBFR
in a succession of communiqués after April 1969. The communiqués
reflected the deepening US commitment to pursue MBFR which was
made by the Department of State without much review by the White
House. The President and Kissinger, absorbed with the Vietnam war
and US–Soviet detente, were not really interested in the issue. [32]
    President Nixon suggested '[t]he possibility that balanced force
reductions could become a subject of East–West discussions', in his
foreign policy report to Congress on 18 February 1970. [33] This
suggestion was seen by the Administration as an attempt to counter
the continuing Senate pressure for unilateral reductions of US force
levels in Europe. Kissinger got involved with MBFR in a low-key
manner on 13 April 1970, when he assigned NSSM 92 in an attempt to
prod the bureaucracy into sharper analysis of approaches to MBFR

negotiations.[34] He viewed NSSM 92 as a stalling action to keep the bureaucracy busy examining possible options without further committing the US at that time. The results of NSC staffwork, however, were not shared with the NATO Allies.[35]

Kissinger did not object to using MBFR as a brake on unilateral Congressional cuts, but had doubts about its complexity and inherent disadvantages. As he wrote the President:

> We have not been able to develop an approach to MBFR which would either maintain or improve NATO's military position although small mutual reductions could have a minimal adverse effect. We have not been able to identify negotiable 'collateral constraints' which would inhibit Pact mobilization and reinforcement without harming NATO at the same time. We have just scratched the surface in thinking about verification problems.[36]

In short, Kissinger was more concerned with maintaining and improving NATO's conventional forces than with pursuing MBFR. The fact that by November 1970, US forces in Europe were about 17 000 below authorized strength (two-thirds of that reduction taking place since July) strengthened his determination to prevent any further reductions.[37]

The Administration did not discourage the growing interest of West Europeans in MBFR since the Allies shared its view that it was a means to forestall unilateral American cuts. The Administration was, however, not favourably disposed toward the Allies when they sought to avoid additional expenditures to EDIP with the argument that defence improvements might be made irrelevant by new arms control agreements as a result of MBFR.[38] In addition, it opposed pressure from the Allies that were seeking to speed up the process. Chancellor Brandt wanted the Alliance to agree on certain criteria for MBFR in order to prepare for negotiations with the Eastern European States. Britain urged the immediate creation of a Standing Commission for East–West relations. But as Kissinger reports in his memoirs 'We deflected the German initiative by supporting a Canadian set of general MBFR principles of inspired vagueness. And we opposed the British proposal altogether. We wanted no institutions that would add their momentum to the already excessive pressures for relaxation of tensions based on atmospherics'.[39]

But despite the efforts of some Allies to speed up the process of MBFR, the European members of NATO were divided on its merits. France was adamantly opposed to MBFR, stressing that CSCE should be the proper focus for detente efforts. France preferred the CSCE to MBFR as a counterweight to Brandt's *Ostpolitik* (unilateral diplomacy). But in spite of its many differences with the US, France sought the maintenance of US troops in Europe (except on French territory). Paris labelled MBFR a cover for US withdrawals, and a possible constraint upon future West European defence options.[40] Britain, at best, was sceptical over the prospects for MBFR and wished to see neither greater Soviet leverage over West European defence efforts nor a reduction in NATO capabilities. London played an obstructionist role within the Alliance. A case was built to demonstrate the necessity of comprehensive NATO preparations and steep demands upon the Warsaw Pact in order to preclude the weakening of NATO's defences. The weakening of the British economy, however, was forcing London into unilateral defence cutbacks.[41] The Federal Republic originally viewed MBFR as the logical extension of *Ostpolitik*, and stressed the role of mutual force reductions in the East–West political dialogue. It was willing to accept force reductions after the parties reached consensus on principles of European arms reduction and agreed upon extensive confidence-building measures – i.e., interchange of military observers, prior warning of manoeuvres, limits on troop movements, etc. Yet the Federal Republic feared any development that would undermine NATO's cohesiveness, would create a precedent for a special zone in Central Europe not completely linked to NATO or impose excessive limitations on its own defence forces.[42] Finally, the states outside Central Europe (Italy, Greece, Denmark, Norway and Turkey) were also divided on MBFR and feared spillover effects in their areas. Moreover a split had emerged between them and the states in Central Europe over the pace of talks, intra-Alliance consultation, East–West detente, and the substance of agreements reached.

If the Administration had pressured the Allies in an attempt to arrive at a common negotiating position it would have strained the cohesion of the Alliance by bringing up chronic intra-Alliance difficulties which could never be fully settled. Kissinger's decision to stall reflected his belief that issues such as the role of conventional forces and the role of tactical and strategic weapons would not be resolved in the foreseeable future.[43] Declaratory support to pursue MBFR, and a commitment to study the possible options, were tactically useful as a demonstration of Allied consensus and as a rationale for maintaining and strengthening the conventional forces of NATO.[44] Kissinger began to focus more on MBFR after Brezhnev's speech at Tiblisi on 14 May 1971. He saw MBFR as a potentially active issue in US–Soviet relations and focused on MBFR, which at that time was also related to the fact that Senator Mansfield was putting new pressures on the Administration for unilateral troop reductions. The NSC staff began to manage the MBFR process more carefully through the Verification Panel Working Group and the Verification Panel (VP) itself which was chaired by Kissinger. The bureaucracy, however, continued to play an important role in formulating negotiating options, and in taking the lead in NATO to achieve agreement on a common position to open the preliminary talks in Vienna in October 1973.[45]

Kissinger and the President continued to be negatively disposed toward MBFR as an arms control measure. Both emphasized the necessity to strengthen the conventional capability of NATO which was the key criterion for MBFR. It was the key criterion because, as Kissinger argued in *The Necessity for Choice*:

> the inadequacies of the current NATO effort may cause the Soviets to believe that they can gain no additional security from arms control schemes or that they can achieve the objectives of arms control through unilateral Western actions. They may not take Western proposals seriously because they believe themselves already protected by their local preponderance. Thus, effective negotiations may be prevented, not by the strength of NATO but by its weakness and irresolution.[46]

In short, 'an impotent NATO provides no incentive for the Soviet leaders'. Moreover, in response to those who pushed MBFR in order to achieve political gains Kissinger reiterated his view that, 'to rest the argument for [arms] control schemes on the proposition that NATO, being unwilling to remedy its vulnerability, might as well offer to perpetuate its weakness for some political gain, is self-defeating'.[47]

In the Fall of 1971, Defense Secretary Laird, sensitive to Congressional desires for troop reductions, sent a stiff memo to the White House pressing for early decisions on the American position on MBFR and forward movement toward opening negotiations. Kissinger, however, preferring to delay the issue, did not act on this recommendation.[48] The USSR dropped the issue as suddenly as it had raised it, and thereby strengthened Kissinger's stand, as did the Soviet insistence that CSCE be convened first. Moscow sought to use

CSCE to promote detente on its own terms. The circumvention of NATO and concrete security issues in the CSCE would have restricted the leverage of the US since it would have been only one out of 35 participants, none of whom were subject to decisive American influence. The CSCE would have legitimized the status quo in Eastern Europe and raised the international standing of the GDR. In addition, Warsaw Pact states would have gained greater access to Western products, capital, and technology. Kissinger linked Western acceptance of CSCE to progress on concrete European issues (particularly Berlin), and he 'deliberately put CSCE on a slow track'.[49]

The Administration's position (accepted by all Allies except France) was that both MBFR and CSCE should proceed simultaneously. This was another example of linkage at work. By linking MBFR to CSCE, the Administration placed Moscow on the defensive and put the West on firmer ground for delaying its acceptance of Warsaw Pact proposals. The very absence of a positive reply from Moscow provided an opening for the Administration to question the depth of Soviet commitment to detente.[50] This helped Washington to rein in the Allies and preclude selective detente, thus strengthening the position of the Administration in its negotiations with Moscow.[51]

MBFR served to reemphasize the necessity of NATO in East–West negotiations. Brussels was the centre for coordinating the Western position on MBFR; by using NATO structures – i.e., the North Atlantic Council and the Ad Hoc Group in Vienna – for the coordination and announcement of Western initiatives, the Administration sought to convince Moscow that force adjustment was not only a necessary element in detente but an issue between blocs. The stated objectives of the blocs' members – i.e., lower force levels, lower costs, more confidence and more security – were to be achieved within the institutional parameters of confrontation. In short, the US and its Allies precluded in advance the possibility of any fundamental change in Alliance structures. These were essential to the maintenance of the military equilibrium, one of the two structural imperatives for the establishment of a stable international system.

The most important intervention by Kissinger in MBFR policy was probably the choice of the US position that was presented to the Allies prior to formulating a common NATO position for the opening of negotiations. The NATO opening MBFR position focused first on

US–Soviet reductions.[52] This decision was made by Kissinger or President Nixon (and probably under strong pressure from the Pentagon which controlled the 'chips'), and was opposed to indigenous Allied force reductions, a position favoured by the Department of State which cited Allied views to support its case. Other interventions by the White House were procedural. At the Moscow summit of May 1972, the President pressed for (and obtained) a Soviet commitment to negotiations in principle.[53] Kissinger clarified this Soviet commitment and strengthened the linkage to CSCE on his trip to the USSR in September 1972. During Brezhnev's visit to the US in June 1973, a date was set for the formal opening of MBFR talks. In other words – subject to overall White House coordination and guidelines, and a few important decisions – MBFR policy was made by the bureaucracy.[54]

The opening of the MBFR negotiations in Vienna on 30 October 1973 introduced the European dimension to what had been an essentially bilateral arms control process between the superpowers. When President Nixon and Brezhnev raised problems of European security in their joint statement of principles following the Moscow summit in May 1972, West Europeans expressed concern about the possible compromise of their security interests in a bilateral forum.[55] MBFR provided a multilateral framework within which Allied security concerns would figure prominently, while the bloc-to-bloc nature of the talks assured US influence. Yet none of the participants had any illusions the negotiations would result in an early and significant reduction of conventional forces in Central Europe.[56]

BURDEN-SHARING IN NATO

The Senate pressure for unilateral reductions of US troops in Europe prompted West Europeans to devise new means of burden-sharing to neutralize the criticism that they were not doing enough for the common defence, and to assist the Administration's efforts to prevent Congress from making unilateral reductions. The Allied initiative came from NATO Secretary-General Manlio Brosio. He proposed NATO conduct a defence review as a means to put a brake on Congressional demands for unilateral American withdrawals. The presumption was that Congress would do nothing irrevocable until the defence review was completed.[57] In addition, Brosio was a driving force behind the West European growing interest in MBFR.[58]

With the Administration's support, the Allies set aside preliminary work on a cost-sharing formula which involved European assumption of certain local costs of US forces in Europe, and focused on force improvement. The defence review conducted in 1970 identified military deficiencies, and the Eurogroup (consisting of Iceland and all European NATO members except France and Portugal) sought new measures to eliminate them and improve European defence. The Eurogroup's efforts were facilitated by the Administration's approach to burden-sharing, which emphasized additional European expenditures for the improvement of their conventional capabilities rather than financial gimmicks to repay the US for the stationing of troops in Europe.

The Eurogroup undertook a European Defence Improvement Programme (EDIP). In December 1970; the programme committed an additional $1 billion to modernize NATO communications, accelerate construction of shelters for NATO aircraft, and to improve national forces. These modest improvements helped the Administration to defeat the Mansfield Amendment. In December 1971, the Allies announced further increases of $1 billion to their defence budgets. These increases were allocated for tanks, anti-tank weapons, artillery, combat aircraft, helicopters and ships. In December 1972, the European Defence Ministers announced that in 1973 their additional contributions would total $1.5 billion.[59] The bulk of the additional contributions the Allies made to EDIP were already part of national procurement plans. To Kissinger, the EDIP was 'sparse and essentially irrelevant', and did not go to the heart of the problem – i.e., help to create the strong conventional capability that was essential in the age of strategic parity. But he agreed that it had achieved its immediate purpose: it had reversed the trend toward reductions.[60]

The Nixon Administration did not exert any 'real' pressure upon the Allies for further increases in order to avoid a dispute that could threaten the cohesion of the Alliance. On the contrary, the President praised EDIP in his 1971 foreign policy report to Congress. In his words: 'we were gratified. . .' because 'the program . . . represents a landmark in the history of NATO – an effort undertaken, organized, and financed entirely by our European allies'.[61] In the 1973 foreign policy report to Congress the President once again praised EDIP, and listed the improvements it had made to the common defence. He stated: 'This has been an impressive response in a period of rising costs and of growing demands of domestic programs'.[62] The President's statement, it can be safely argued, was rationalization for the unwillingness of the Allies to assume a greater share of the common defence burden, believing that real improvements of NATO's conventional defence would weaken the credibility of the nuclear deterrent. Moreover it reflected the desire of the Administration to avoid a bitter dispute with the Allies over burden-sharing at a time when the cohesion of NATO was essential to its policy towards the USSR.

The Nixon Administration reacted favourably to the establishment of the Eurogroup within NATO. When approached by Healey with the proposal for the establishment of the Eurogroup, Kissinger in a memorandum to President Nixon on 9 April 1969, recommended that the Administration 'encourage the European members of NATO to improve cooperation among themselves. But it should avoid support for a particular method'.[63] This recommendation was consistent with ideas advanced by Kissinger in 1968. In 'Central Issues of American Foreign Policy', Kissinger had argued that it would be in the American interest if the Allies 'assume much greater responsibility for developing doctrine and force levels in NATO, . . . by vitalizing such institutions as the West European Union (WEU), [or] by alternative arrangements'.[64] He had criticized 'integrationists' in the bureaucracy for strongly opposing a European identity in the defence field for fear that it would divide the Alliance while passionately supporting economic unity.

Kissinger believed the opposite was true. Kissinger was convinced that a European identity in the defence field would be less divisive than European economic unity, since in the military sphere there was no conceivable contingency in which Western Europe would be better off without American support. The American and West European vital interests were complementary while the penalty for independent West European action was overwhelming – namely that in a war with the USSR, Western Europe without the support of the US would be totally destroyed. Therefore only by arriving at independent conclusions would West Europeans see the necessity of strengthening their defence effort.[65]

Knowing Kissinger's views, Healey approached him in 1969 asking what the Administration's attitude would be toward the establishment of the Eurogroup. Kissinger responded that the Administration's reaction would be favourable 'provided that such a grouping was not used as a device to isolate France'.[66] While praising the Eurogroup's defence improvement programme, the Administration did not encourage its evolution as a European nucleus within NATO despite Kissinger's previous support for 'another force as a balance to ours' in NATO, as well as the President's speculations about a European pole in a new global balance of power. Nor did the Administration show interest in other approaches toward the same end.[67]

A number of factors explain the Administration's measured support for the Eurogroup. First, in view of the absence of France from the Eurogroup and the Administration's desire to improve relations with France, efforts to encourage the evolution of the Eurogroup as a nucleus of a future West European defence community were shunned as divisive. (Kissinger's response to Healey manifested this concern.) France wanted a united European voice, but not within NATO. Therefore, as Kissinger stated, 'it was bound to consider the British initiative as a way of getting around the issue of British membership in the Common Market.'[68] Secondly, if France joined the Eurogroup (and this was essential if the Eurogroup was to become the nucleus of a European defence community), the US would have to confront some short-term problems. Because as Kissinger noted, 'a European caucus could grow into a third force grouped around France, drawing its chief impulse to unity from anti-Americanism'.[69] However, this was not the time to deal with new problems since the President's and Kissinger's energies were devoted to US–Soviet detente and US–PRC rapprochement. Thirdly, an effective West European defence community required the development of a credible European nuclear force which in turn required the participation of the Federal Republic. As Kissinger had written, 'such a prospect is not in the interest of NATO, of European cohesion, of the Federal Republic, or of international stability'.[70] Fourthly, the Allies favoured unity in the abstract, but they feared a real European identity within NATO might give the US an excuse for reducing its military establishment in Europe. To have encouraged the development of the Eurogroup into something beyond what the Allies desired would have damaged NATO cohesion which was essential to the Administration's policy toward the USSR.

In short, the Administration's measured support for the Eurogroup was consistent with Kissinger's view that European unity in any field 'is a problem primarily for the Europeans'.[71] Moreover, given the increasingly irritable character of US–EEC relations, it seemed likely the Administration's restrained support for the Eurogroup reflected an unwillingness to encourage beyond modest limits a defence organization which could add another problematical dimension to its relations with the Allies.

West Europeans were certainly aware of this. In the foreword to the first official report on the Eurogroup, NATO Secretary General Joseph Luns stressed 'its total commitment to NATO, its informality and its pragmatic approach', and that it is 'still an informal group and likely to remain so'. The report itself emphasized that the Eurogroup 'is rooted in the existing and proven realities of the alliance... Within the framework of these fundamental convictions [i.e., the collective defence commitment and the centrality and indivisibility of the European and transatlantic security relationship], the Eurogroup concentrates on practical business without political theory or formal institutional apparatus'.[72] Indeed, Eurogroup statements abound with assurances as to the informality of the undertaking, its firm implantation within the existing NATO structure, its avoidance of matters of doctrine and 'high politics', and its intention to continue its pragmatic, low-profile course in the future. In addition, a report of the North Atlantic Assembly's Military Committee cautioned that:

> American support for the Eurogroup may wane if the efforts made by European countries to achieve co-operation in armaments production succeed to the point where US equipment sales to Europe suffer ... when the Eurogroup starts to bite, may not US reaction to it be similar to current American criticisms of the European Community for alleged discrimination and distortion of trade?[73]

Clearly, the Administration recognized there was no West European support for the formal institutionalization of the Eurogroup. The Allies made explicit the connection between the Eurogroup effort and the maintenance of American forces in Europe. In December 1971, a statement by the Federal Republic declared that it was 'appropriate to support the endeavors of the American government to maintain their forces in Europe at their present levels by calling to the attention of the American public the efforts of the Europeans themselves'.[74]

In addition to burden-sharing through force improvements, offset agreements with the FRG (which by 1969 had acquired a degree of permanence and regularity) were still concluded at two-year intervals. The 1972–3 agreement was for $2 billion, including $183 million for a programme to rehabilitate troop facilities used by American troops in the Federal Republic. This measure introduced a new concept to the agreement – i.e., budgeting budgetary relief. By undertaking expenses directly on behalf of US troops, the FRG was paying for a programme that presumably would otherwise had come from the US defense budget. This new measure, constituting both balance-of-payments and budgetary relief, at a rate of approximately $100 million annually, was very popular with both the American military and Congress.[75] The President called the offset agreements 'testimony to cooperation', but warned that not being a long-term solution they strained Alliance relations each time they came up for renewal.[76]

In 1973, Congressional pressures for troop reductions in Europe surfaced once again and, for the first time, significant efforts were made in the House as well as in the Senate.[77] To counter these pressures, the President in his 1973 foreign policy report to Congress endorsed force improvements in European forces as 'the most important aspect of sharing the defence burden'.[78] But citing the rise in the balance-of-payments deficit on military account and the German contribution through the offset agreement he added:

> Nevertheless, the Alliance as a whole should examine this problem. As a general principle, we should move toward a lasting solution under which balance of payments consequences from stationing U.S. forces in Europe will not be substantially different from those of maintaining the same forces in the United States. It is reasonable to expect the Alliance to examine this problem this year. Eliminating the periodic requirement to renegotiate a temporary arrangement with only one ally would strengthen the solidarity of the Alliance as a whole.[79]

This new approach was communicated to the Allies by Secretary of Defense James R. Schlesinger at the June 1973 meeting of the NATO Defence Planning Committee. He asked the Allies to undertake a multilateral programme to relieve the US of the balance-of-payments deficit attributable to its European forces and to assist in paying the added budgetary cost of stationing forces in Europe.[80] Given the continued emphasis on force improvements, it is highly unlikely that Kissinger was the initiator of the multilateral programme proposal. Secretary Schlesinger, who saw no intellectual reason for conceding Kissinger's preeminence (as Assistant for National Security) in defence policy, probably pushed the proposal in an attempt to check

Congressional pressures for troop reductions in Europe. Kissinger admitted that 'the White House never achieved the control over defense policy that it did over foreign policy'.[81]

The Allies responded in August 1973. The North Atlantic Council established a 'Study Group on Financial Problems Arising from the Stationing of Forces on the Territory of Other NATO Countries'. This was a technical-level body expected to address the American request. Beyond this, West European officials voiced uncertainty over whether the US was primarily interested in balance-of-payments relief, budgetary relief, or both, as well as over the degree to which force improvements were an acceptable alternative. The Allies stressed that they could not continue to improve their own forces and at the same time undertake to assist the US. They pointed out that Europe's contribution to common defence was 90 per cent of the ground forces, 80 per cent of the seapower, and 75 per cent of the airpower.[82] The Allies also argued they were continuing conscription while the US did not, and as a percentage of GNP their defence budgets were holding steady while in the US this percentage was declining. In addition they noted that the US had military balance-of-payments deficits with other developed countries (most notably Japan) from which it was not asking full relief.[83] But more importantly, it was noted that American administrations always justified US forces in Europe in terms of American security interests. If this was the case, why should Europeans pay for America's protection of its own interests?

The Administration's proposal for a multilateral programme faced its most severe difficulties from the perceptions of national interest among the Allies. Any multilateral burden-sharing programme would have had to depend primarily on the major Allies, namely the FRG, France, and Britain. The FRG was already making a contribution through offset agreements with Britain and the US. In 1972, the FRG had signed a five-year agreement with Britain encompassing both a modest payments offset and budgetary relief.[84] Therefore it was reluctant to pay additional sums through a multilateral programme, and showed a preference to continue the bilateral agreements. The negotiations of a new offset agreement with the US was proceeding at the same time as the multilateral scheme was being discussed in NATO.

Britain opposed a multilateral programme, and argued that it already devoted a larger share of its GNP to defence than any other European NATO country, that it too suffered military balance-of-payments deficits resulting from the Army of the Rhine, and that its economy and overall payments situation did not permit a greater contribution. France (having withdrawn from NATO's integrated military command) stayed out of the discussions, but pointed out it had not asked for offsets for French troops stationed in the FRG. Thus none of the three major European Allies was willing (or felt itself able) to undertake a new major commitment. The smaller NATO members (though willing to consider some adjustments in NATO financing) were constrained by their size and by European efforts to maintain a 'solid' front on Atlantic issues.[85]

In late November 1973, the Administration responded to the Jackson–Nunn Amendment by proposing an illustrative multilateral programme in NATO since the Allies had not created a proposal of their own.[86] The illustrative programme combined balance-of-payments relief through military procurement and budgetary support. But the Allied response was less than enthusiastic. The Allies pointed favourably to the report by the Study Group on Financial Problems; the report stated that force improvements should be the principal form of burden-sharing, and it would be undesirable to undercut existing national defence efforts by new measures taken to alleviate US balance-of-payments deficits. It also stated that the US would welcome an additional or supplementary European defence improvement programme as a substantive measure in burden-sharing.[87] This report made it difficult for the Administration to convince the Allies that a new multilateral programme was necessary, even with the added leverage of the Jackson–Nunn Amendment.

CONCLUSION

In 1969, the approaching strategic parity between the US and the USSR enhanced the need for the strengthening of NATO's conventional forces. This development coincided with the growing Senate pressure for the unilateral reduction of US force levels in Europe. From Kissinger's point of view, the Mansfield Resolutions were a serious threat to the Administration's entire foreign policy. A unilateral reduction of US force levels would have endangered 'strength', one of the three elements on which (according to the Nixon Doctrine) the Administration was basing the restructuring of the Atlantic relationship. It would also have endangered the equilibrium of military power, one of the two structural imperatives essential to the Administration's policy towards the USSR (and, in turn, the establishment of a stable international system). Hence it was not surprising that Kissinger led the Administration's efforts to defeat the Mansfield Resolutions.

President Nixon decided to maintain current force levels in Europe until the USSR made similar reductions. Brezhnev's statement that Moscow was ready to begin talks on MBFR helped the Administration defeat the Resolutions. From then on, the Administration argued that by unilaterally reducing force levels the US would weaken the West's bargaining position in the coming negotiations. The Administration, however, opposed pressures from the Allies who were seeking to speed up the opening of the MBFR talks in order to avoid committing additional expenditures to EDIP.

The Allies assisted the Nixon Administration in defeating the Mansfield Resolutions by stating that a reduction of US force levels would reduce the credibility of the American commitment to Europe, and by establishing the Eurogroup which undertook the EDIP. The Eurogroup's efforts were facilitated by the Administration's approach to burden-sharing, which emphasized additional European expenditures for the improvement of their conventional capabilities rather than financial gimmicks to repay the US for the stationing of troops in Europe. To Kissinger, the EDIP was essentially irrelevant since it did not help create the strong conventional capability that was essential in the age of strategic parity. But he supported it since it helped the Administration achieve its immediate purpose – that is, reversing the trend towards unilateral reductions. The Administration, however, did not exert any real pressure on the Allies for additional contributions to the EDIP, in order to avoid a dispute that could have threatened the cohesion of the Alliance as a whole.

8 US Reaction to West European Unity

INTRODUCTION

US initiatives toward Moscow and Peking, and the Congressional pressures for unilateral force reductions, were not the only causes of tension within the Alliance. Britain's effort to enter the European Economic Community (EEC), Chancellor Brandt's *Ostpolitik*, France's interest in restoring its relations with the US, and the Nixon Administration's reaction to these initiatives, also contributed to the discontent on both sides of the Atlantic.

In the 1960s, US advocates of West European unity argued that the real obstacle to Allied cooperation on a global scale was the inequality of power between the US and Western Europe. An integrated Western Europe was expected to become an equal partner with the US. Since West European and American interests were identical to some, Western Europe would share with the US the burdens and obligations of world leadership. The EEC was seen as a first step toward a politically unified Western Europe. True unification, however, could be achieved only through integration on a supranational basis – i.e., federal institutions controlled by a West European Parliament. This reflected the conviction held by American 'integrationists' that the US experience was directly applicable to Western Europe. Few of the advocates of West European unity recognized that a politically unified Europe would challenge American primacy, and would refuse to share the burdens required for the achievement of goals set by the US. Kissinger challenged the convictions of the advocates of European unity, and criticized the policies based on those convictions.[1]

This chapter examines the Nixon Administration's reaction to issues affecting West European unity. The issues were: the Soames–de Gaulle controversy, the relationship between the US and the EEC institutions, the West European initiative to expand the EEC, and President Nixon's New Economic Policy. The focus of the analysis will be on the consistency between (a) the Administration's position on these issues and Kissinger's views; and (b) the Administration's stand on West European unity and Kissinger's global strategy.

WEST EUROPEAN UNITY

The Nixon Administration inherited from the Johnson years a growing malaise in US–EEC relations. This malaise was attributed to attitude changes on both sides. The idealistic view of West European unity and Atlantic partnership that was characteristic of the Kennedy period had given way to growing American impatience and frustration by the late 1960s. De Gaulle's negative control (he vetoed Britain's entry into the EEC on 14 January 1963) over the process of West European unity precluded an active American policy. With West European unity indefinitely stalled, and with US foreign policy energies increasingly absorbed by the war in Vietnam, the American vision of partnership was replaced by Atlantic estrangement, mutual indifference, and bickering over trade issues. The Kennedy Round negotiations to adjust tariffs between the US and the EEC contributed to the new American view of the EEC as a strong trade competitor, even an adversary. The Nixon Administration shared this new view.[2]

During the Nixon Administration, the initiative for the expansion of the EEC came from the Europeans. Britain's Prime Minister Harold Wilson decided to renew his country's application to the EEC. Chancellor Brandt supported Britain's entry into the EEC,[3] while his new policy towards the East – *Ostpolitik* – raised the spectre of a more independent course by the Federal Republic, making Britain's membership in the EEC more attractive to France.[4] At the 2 December 1969 meeting of the heads of government of the members of the EEC, it was announced that the Community was prepared to negotiate with Britain and to consider political cooperation within 'the context of enlargement'.[5] The French concurred. The Administration's stand on the issue of West European unity and its desire to improve relations with France facilitated the process.

THE SOAMES–DE GAULLE CONTROVERSY

The Soames–de Gaulle controversy in early February 1969 provided the Nixon Administration with the opportunity to establish its position on West European unity. The controversy revolved around British and French views about the future of Western Europe, and clearly manifested the ongoing debate over the issue within Western Europe and the Alliance as a whole. President de Gaulle (in talks with the British Ambassador to Paris, Christopher Soames) described his concept of the future of Europe in rather novel terms, and when the British informed the other Allies about them the controversy began.

President de Gaulle's terms were three: First, to create a truly independent Western Europe that could play an effective international role, it would be necessary for West Europeans to free themselves from NATO which guaranteed the maintenance of American domination. In his view, a successful West European political organization would have to rely on a concert of the major West European powers – i.e., France, Britain, the FRG, and Italy. In this concert, the central element would have to be Anglo–French cooperation. Secondly, in this process the structure of the EEC would have to change. The EEC would be replaced by a broad, free-trade area especially for agricultural products. Thirdly, since the Anglo–French relationship would be the centre of the concert, de Gaulle indicated he was willing to hold 'private' bilateral discussions with Britain on political, economic, monetary, and financial problems. He said he would welcome a British initiative for such talks.[6]

The British considered de Gaulle's proposals very important, and were willing to discuss them further, but only with the understanding that all NATO members would be kept fully informed. The British views on NATO, relations with the US, and the desirability of a four-power concert in Western Europe differed significantly from de Gaulle's, but Britain replied that it still wished to enter the EEC and hoped that negotiations would be reopened soon.[7]

By informing the other NATO members about de Gaulle's terms, Britain unintentionally generated concern within the Alliance that the General was trying to break up NATO. French attempts to reassure NATO members that de Gaulle had no intention of breaking it up failed.

In the US, those who believed de Gaulle was a threat to the Alliance urged the Administration to seize the opportunity provided by the Soames–de Gaulle controversy to reaffirm the American commitment to a federal Europe, and to reject de Gaulle's proposal for a West European concert. President de Gaulle did not submit such a proposal to the US, therefore the Administration (which was seeking to improve relations with France) refused to continue the policies of its predecessors which President Nixon and Kissinger had criticized before assuming office.[8]

France was seen by the President and Kissinger as the pivot of

American relations – and problems – with Western Europe.[9] Priority was therefore given to the improvement of US–French relations as the key to the solution of the larger Western European issues. This approach was consistent with Kissinger's argument that American efforts to isolate de Gaulle within NATO and in Europe were 'mistaken and doomed to failure' because 'within the Europe of six, de Gaulle has never been as alone as some like to believe', and 'on the issue of East–West relations, his views without question [represented] the dominant trend in Europe'. Kissinger maintained that it was misleading to test Allied cohesion by a formal counting of votes, since within NATO the 14 to 1 line-up against France might prevail on technical issues, but would not hold together in a prolonged political contest over strategic doctrine.[10] Moreover, from Kissinger's viewpoint, Britain's views on the organization of Europe were similar to those of de Gaulle. Hence France was not the sole obstacle to European integration on the federal model.[11]

The improvement of US–French relations made the 'special relationship' between Britain and the US less of an obstacle to British membership in the EEC. In addition, France had diplomatic relations with Hanoi and Peking, and the Administration hoped to use French assistance to end the war in Vietnam and establish rapprochement with Peking.[12]

In preparation for the February 1969 trip to Europe, Kissinger briefed President Nixon about the Soames–de Gaulle controversy, and made the following recommendations: (a) the President must emphasize the US commitment to NATO, and (b) he must affirm the traditional US support for European unity, including British entry into the EEC, but (c) stress that the Administration would not inject itself into intra-European debates on the forms, methods, and timing of steps toward unity.[13] Indeed, President Nixon emphasized these points in his private discussions with West European leaders, and Kissinger repeated them often in background briefings to the press. In short, the Administration steered clear of the Soames–de Gaulle controversy by reiterating the views Kissinger had advocated in his writings.[14]

The same views were emphasized in the President's foreign policy reports to Congress. In President Nixon's words:

The structure of Western Europe itself – the organization of its unity – is fundamentally the concern of the Europeans. We cannot unify Europe and we do not believe that there is only one road to that goal. When the United States in previous Administrations turned into an ardent advocate, it harmed rather than helped progress.[15]

In short, the President was indicating that his Administration was not going to continue his predecessors' policy which he and Kissinger had criticized. They would not actively support the new British effort to enter the EEC, or advocate US commitment to a federal Europe.

The rationale for the Administration's position was evident in Kissinger's writings. Kissinger had rejected the argument that Britain's entry into EEC should be a direct objective of the US since Britain was ambivalent about its commitment to European unity.[16] He had also maintained that Britain's views on European unity were 'quite different from those of the European integrationists, who [then and now] so passionately championed her cause'. In Kissinger's view, 'Britain [was] no more prepared than de Gaulle to join an "integrated", "supranational" Europe'.[17]

The efforts to bury past differences with France and to establish a relationship of trust and confidence with de Gaulle indicated to many observers that the Administration was accepting de Gaulle's view of European political unity and of an independent role for Europe in world affairs. In a press conference, the President stated:

> He [de Gaulle] believes that Europe should have an independent position in its own right. And, frankly, I believe that too ... the world will be a much safer place and, from our standpoint, a much healthier place economically, militarily, and politically, if there were a strong European community to be a balance, basically a balance between the United States and the Soviet Union.[18]

This appeared to be a sharp break from the traditional concept of Western Europe as a component of the Atlantic pole in a bipolar (or tripolar) balance.[19] But in reality, it was not. The President was simply acknowledging the West European role in a politically multipolar international system. The emergence of strategic parity (if not Soviet superiority) led to the Administration's efforts to get the Allies to do more for their own defence – a strongly unified Europe would have contributed to this end.

It is more likely that de Gaulle's concept of a loosely unified Western Europe appealed to the President and Kissinger, since it would produce some immediate progress and provide more access points and greater opportunity for US influence than could be expected in relations with a single European political entity. In *The*

Troubled Partnership, Kissinger had written favourably of the Fouchet Plan arguing that:

> it is the one most consistent with British participation. It has the advantage that it would produce some immediate progress without foreclosing the future... It would also permit a more flexible arrangement of Atlantic relations than the 'twin pillar' concept now in vogue. A confederal Europe would enable the United States to maintain an influence at many centers of decision rather than be forced to stake everything on affecting the views of a single, supranational body.[20]

Kissinger had criticized previous administrations for equating a united Europe with supranational institutions, and disputed the relevance of the American federal experience to a Europe composed of deeply rooted nation-states.[21]

THE CALCULATED NEGLECT OF THE EEC COMMISSION

The desire of the Nixon Administration to maintain an influence at many centres of decision, its predilection for bilateral diplomacy, and the cultivation of improved relations with France, resulted in the deterioration of relations between the US and EEC institutions. J. Robert Schaetzel (US Ambassador to the EEC from 1966 to 1972) asserted that 'Washington searched for some alternative approach, for ways of by-passing the Commission and of dealing directly with the member governments'.[22] He argued that this was a reversal from traditional US policy; previous Administrations had worked with the Commission, and tried to enhance its status. But the Ambassador failed to point out that while the previous administrations favoured European unity, they had guarded rather jealously the special relationship between the US and several European states.[23]

The Nixon Administration's new policy towards the EEC institutions became evident during the President's trip to Europe in 1969. Schaetzel recalled 'it was touch-and-go whether during his Brussels stopover he would even meet with the European Commission'.[24] To emphasize the American commitment to NATO, President Nixon travelled to the NATO headquarters for extensive discussions with the Council and the Secretary General. But the Commission was invited to a meeting with the President at his suite at the Hilton, despite the fact that its headquarters was less than five minutes from

the hotel.[25] The Administration's studied neglect of the EEC
institutions, Schaetzel suggested, resulted from a desire not to offend
the French; the President and Kissinger were keenly aware of de
Gaulle's hostility to the political pretensions of the Commission. It
also resulted from Kissinger's attitudes, 'a critical factor' according
to Schaetzel. Kissinger believed 'it would be "folly" for a major
power to assist in the organization of what could become an
independent coalition of otherwise subordinate European states'.[26]
Moreover, since the EEC dealt with economic matters, Kissinger's
(and Nixon's) relative ignorance of economics contributed to the
deterioration of US–EEC relations.

The problem became compounded as the Department of State and
its European missions (which under previous Administrations had
aided the EEC in the process of institutional development) became
isolated from the policymaking machinery centred in the White
House. The President supported the informal regular consultation
which began in 1970 between the EEC Commission and the US. He
welcomed suggestions for expanding consultation, including the
possibility of a higher-level EEC representation in Washington, but
it was left to the EEC to make proposals that could be
implemented.[27]

The calculated neglect of the EEC Commission was consistent
with the views Kissinger advanced in his writings, and with his global
strategy. In *The Troubled Partnership*, Kissinger had challenged the
assumption (held by the American advocates of European unity)
that a united Western Europe and the US would inevitably conduct
parallel policies and have similar views about appropriate tactics. In
his view, this assumption ran counter to historical experience. He
had argued that 'a separate identity has usually been established by
opposition to a dominant power', and, 'the European sense of
identity [was] unlikely to be an exception to this general rule'.
Kissinger had stressed that 'this [was] all the more true because a
European sense of identity [could] no longer be nourished by fear of
the USSR'. He had maintained that even if the reality of military
threat was accepted by West Europeans (and it was not), 'it would
provide an incentive for American military protection and thus lead
to pressures for Atlantic, not European integration'.[28] Kissinger
concluded that 'a united Europe is likely to insist on a specifically
European view of world affairs which is another way of saying that it
will challenge American hegemony in Atlantic policy'.[29] This meant
that European unity would not resolve Atlantic disagreements.

Kissinger maintained that 'in many respects it may magnify rather than reduce differences. As Europe gains structure, it will be in a better position to insist on differences whose ultimate cause is structural rather than personal'.[30]

Although Kissinger was convinced that the structural problems of the Alliance could not be resolved in the foreseeable future,[31] he did not fear that they would split NATO. In the military field, he could not conceive of a contingency in which Western Europe would be better off without American support. The vital interests of the NATO members were complementary; in Kissinger's view, the penalty for independent action by West Europeans was overwhelming national destruction.[32] He recognized that although NATO had proved ineffective in containing national ambitions, American preponderance permitted the US to use NATO to exercise 'some' control over the process of detente between Eastern and Western Europe.

The EEC on the other hand had proved even more ineffective than NATO in containing national ambitions. The US was not a member of the EEC, and (more importantly from Kissinger's viewpoint) there were no penalties for noncooperation.[33] Hence the growth of a more economically and 'politically' integrated Western Europe would have further complicated the control function which Kissinger wanted to exercise through NATO. This made it highly unlikely he would have supported the strengthening of the EEC Commission since it could challenge his assumptions and his policy towards Moscow.

This was particularly true with respect to trade, the second vital element in Kissinger's linkage strategy. The US and the EEC never agreed on a common trade policy towards the East. Kissinger had written that in most economic negotiations, the position of the EEC Commission had been close to that of France despite profound differences about the political organization of Europe. The economic interests of the EEC often coincided with the political goal of France to assert a more independent role for Europe.[34] Therefore the increasing economic power of an expanded EEC was bound to complicate the US–West European relationship and threaten Kissinger's ability to use trade to influence Soviet foreign policy. The USSR was already looking to Western Europe for capital and technology to reduce the leverage of the US.

Kissinger's conclusions were precisely the opposite of those of both orthodox Atlanticism and Gaullism. Contrary to the traditional view of Atlantic partnership, Kissinger feared that West European desire for a separate identity would be magnified by a full political union. And (contrary to the Gaullist vision) he believed that de Gaulle's model of a loose, intergovernmental European grouping would: (a) preserve opportunities for US influence within the Atlantic framework; and (b) delimit and provide expression for the emergence of a true separate West European identity.[35] Therefore Kissinger's support for limited West European unity represented a necessary concession to an incipient West European consciousness in order to preserve the Atlantic cohesion which was essential for the implementation of his global strategy.

The Nixon Administration preferred to deal bilaterally with individual members of the EEC; problems that (in the whole or in part) fell within the competency of the Community were resolved on a bilateral basis. In the view of the Administration, this approach helped rather than hindered West European unity. In the 1970 annual foreign policy report to Congress, the President stated:

> We believe that we can render support to the process of European coalescence not only by our role in the North Atlantic Alliance and by our relationship with European institutions, but also by our bilateral relations with the several European countries. For many years to come, these relations will provide essential trans-Atlantic bonds; and we will therefore continue to broaden and deepen them.[36]

Subsequent annual foreign policy reports to Congress repeated this stance. Indeed, whenever the Administration had serious issues to resolve it would do so with France, Britain, and Germany, and in that order.[37]

THE WEST EUROPEAN INITIATIVE TO EXPAND THE EEC

In 1970, the EEC Commission began negotiating with Britain, Norway, Denmark, and Ireland for their full membership, and began talks with Sweden, Austria, Switzerland, and other members of the European Free Trade Association (EFTA) looking towards some lesser form of relationship. The West European initiative for expanding the EEC raised fears in the US about the negative effects an expanded EEC would have on American exports. A study prepared for the NSC noted:

In the long run we could be confronted by an 'expanded Europe' comprising a Common Market of at least ten full members, associated memberships for the EFTA neutrals, and preferential trade arrangements with at least the Mediterranean and most of Africa. This bloc will account for about half of world trade, compared with our 15%; it will hold monetary reserves approaching twice our own; and it will even be able to outvote us constantly in the international economic organizations.[38]

The business community became restless, and began to apply pressure on the Administration. The Departments of the Treasury, Commerce, and Agriculture began to seek assurances from President Nixon that American interests would be protected.

Those Departments also believed the President and Kissinger, in attempting to maintain the cohesion of the Alliance by focusing on strategic and political considerations, encouraged West Europeans to put economic pressure on the US. In the 1970 annual foreign policy report to Congress, President Nixon stated:

Our support for the strengthening and broadening of the European Community has not diminished. We recognize that our interests will necessarily be affected by Europe's evolution, and we may have to make sacrifices in the common interest. We consider that the possible economic price of a truly unified Europe is outweighed by the gain in the political vitality of the West as a whole.[39]

The President's statement intensified fears within the business community that the Administration was sacrificing the economic interests of the US in the name of Allied cohesion. The economic agencies at an interagency meeting on 13 May 1970, proposed the Administration provide an official reinterpretation of the President's statement. They also insisted that the Administration use the negotiations for British entry into the EEC to attack the Community's trade restrictions and preferential trading arrangements with other countries.[40]

For Kissinger, this was 'in effect, a declaration of war ... on the concept of the European Community'.[41] Therefore he opposed the reinterpretation of the President's statement. On this issue, he was supported by the Department of State (and especially the European Bureau, which had been the most ardent advocate of European unity in the 1960s). The Bureau feared that since France was willing to reconsider British entry into the EEC, if negotiations on British entry broke down the American opposition would provide the scapegoat.[42]

Kissinger feared that any action by the Administration would lead to a trade war, in particular that the EEC would retaliate against American agricultural exports. In a memorandum to the President on 30 June, Kissinger 'came down squarely on the side of [American] foreign policy objectives'.[43] He proposed a negotiation to place the concerns of the economic agencies before the EEC. He also put forward a mechanism to enable these agencies to air their views before the President. The NSC Under-Secretaries Committee was augmented by the economic agencies, and was instructed to consider the economic impact of an expanded EEC.[44] To Kissinger, this scheme was 'in reality a device to let the economic agencies "win" on the reinterpretation of the Presidential report, but at the same time to treat it as a foreign policy rather than economic issue through the State Department chairmanship of the committee dealing with the subject'.[45] In addition, the requirement of the economic agencies that disputed issues be referred to the President, 'guaranteed' according to Kissinger, that 'I would have an opportunity to weigh in [if not have the last word] if purely commercial considerations threatened to overwhelm foreign policy imperatives'.[46]

These developments were consistent with Kissinger's views. In *The Troubled Partnership*, Kissinger challenged the assumption of 'integrationists' that 'economic integration would inevitably lead to political unity and that institutions in the economic field could be transplanted into the political arena'.[47] By emphasizing economic unification, American policymakers were developing the dimension in which American and West European interests were most likely to diverge, and in turn, most likely to lead to competition. According to Kissinger only in the defence field (in which West European unity was discouraged by the US) were the Atlantic interests most likely to overlap.[48] Kissinger was convinced that 'a united Europe ... [would] challenge American hegemony in Atlantic policy', and suggested that 'this may well be a price worth paying for European unity'. He argued that 'American policy [had] suffered from an unwillingness to recognize that there is a price to be paid'.[49] Kissinger seemed determined during his term of office that American foreign policy would not suffer from such an unwillingness. His response to the demands of the economic agencies demonstrated Kissinger was at least willing to pay the possible economic price.[50]

The negotiations with the EEC that Kissinger proposed began on 10 October 1970. The EEC delegation was led by Ralf Dahrendorf who, in a meeting with Kissinger on 15 October emphasized his 'deep concern' about trends in American trade policy. Dahrendorf's analysis of the developments in the EEC were similar (if not the same) as Kissinger's. Dahrendorf expected British entry into the EEC, but he thought the Community was no longer thinking in terms of political unity; economic integration would be pursued for its own sake.[51] The trade negotiations with the EEC dragged on inconclusively until 15 August 1971, when President Nixon's television address outlined his New Economic Policy (NEP).[52]

While the trade negotiations were going on, the protectionist trend was gaining strength and restrictive trade legislation remained pending in Congress throughout the summer and Fall of 1970. In an attempt to reassure Congress and the economic agencies that economic interests of the US would not be sacrificed in the name of Atlantic unity, the President raised the issues of concern to them in his second annual foreign policy report to Congress on 15 February 1971. In his words:

> European unity will also pose problems for American policy, which it would be idle to ignore ... And unity happens to be coming fastest in the economic sphere – the area of policy in which competition seems to have the least immediate penalty and our common interest will take the most effort to insure. Each of us maintains restrictions on agricultural trade which limit the export opportunities of the other ... The common interest requires the prosperity of both Western Europe and the United States. This means freer and expanded trade and restraint in protecting special interests. We must negotiate a reduction in our trade restrictions ... In short, we must define our self-interest in the widest terms and fix our sights on our fundamental rather than tactical purposes.[53]

This statement was the closest President Nixon and Kissinger came to reinterpreting the previous statement as proposed by the economic agencies.

By May 1971, the last obstacles to Britain's entry into the EEC had been overcome, but the US and the Community had not been able to reach an agreement in the trade negotiations. These developments and the growing strain on the dollar intensified Congressional pressure for restrictive trade legislation, and unilateral troop reductions. As a result, US–West European relations had been strained, and were further aggravated by President Nixon's NEP and

Secretary Connally's pressure upon the West European finance
ministers for trade concessions.

NIXON'S NEW ECONOMIC POLICY

Kissinger's role in the making of the New Economic Policy was
peripheral.[54] The President made this decision after meeting with a
small group of advisors at Camp David on 13 and 14 August. Absent
from the meeting were Kissinger, Secretary Rogers or any other
representative of the State Department, as well as representatives of
the other foreign economic policy agencies such as the Commerce
Department and the Office of the Special Trade Representative.[55]
The decisionmaking process with respect to trade and other economic
issues was dominated by the Secretary of the Treasury, John
Connally, who had established a very close relationship with
President Nixon. Connally believed if Britain failed to get into the
EEC it should be a welcome development for the US. Britain was a
large importer of American agricultural products, and membership
would put it behind the EEC's protective wall. What mattered most
to Connally was not the political benefit of a united Western Europe,
but the economic damage it would cause the US by widening the area
of trade protectionism.[56]

The New Economic Policy shocked the West Europeans (the
Japanese, and the Canadians), who were not consulted in advance.[57]
The day before the President announced the policy, Paul A. Volcker
(the Under-Secretary of the Treasury for Monetary Affairs who
shared Connally's views) went to Paris to explain the thinking behind
the policy to West European finance ministers.[58] This, however, did
not reassure the Allies, who viewed the August measures as a
declaration of economic war and therefore began to harden their
position. Connally refused to put forward a specific proposal to
resolve the crisis, because he feared that any American proposal
would enable the Allies to unite against the US even though they
could not agree on a proposal of their own. In addition, he believed
that the longer the import surcharge remained, the stronger the
American bargaining position would be.

Secretary Connally's negotiating tactics injected suspicion and
tension into the Alliance. The Europeans (and especially the French)
began talking about a 'European solution', and though the Germans
were opposed to the idea (their national security depended very

heavily on the American military commitment) it appeared that there was a limit to which they could resist French pressures and risk the cohesion of the EEC.[59] Kissinger was willing to go along with Connally's hard-nosed negotiating for a time, but desired to stop short of all-out confrontation which would threaten Atlantic cohesion. When Arthur Burns (the Chairman of the Federal Reserve Board) showed Kissinger a list of retaliatory measures planned by the Allies, Kissinger concluded that the eventual outcome would have been highly disadvantageous to the US.[60]

Kissinger began to fear that unless the crisis was resolved his foreign policy would be threatened. He therefore sought to move toward articulating some specific objectives that would permit negotiations to start. Kissinger proposed the formation of a small group to establish a negotiating position. The group was composed of Kissinger, Connally, Paul W. McCracken (Chairman of the President's Council of Economic Advisers), and George P. Shultz (Director of the Budget). Arthur Burns was kept advised.[61] Kissinger's role in the group's meetings (which began in October) was limited to explaining the political implications of economic issues.[62] He encouraged a resolution of the crisis because he feared that economic tensions would spill over to weaken US security interests, thereby creating disarray in the Alliance just before the impending Peking and Moscow summits scheduled respectively for February and May 1972.

To help resolve the crisis, Kissinger also recommended that President Nixon intervene personally with West European leaders. The West European leaders were not interested in a summit (Kissinger's proposal). President Pompidou, the key to the resolution of the crisis, rejected the proposal because he knew the Europeans could not develop a common policy; the British Prime Minister (Edward Heath) was not interested because he wanted to avoid choosing sides between the US and France.[63] Chancellor Brandt was not interested because in case of a stalemate he would have been under great pressure to side with the US, thus alienating the French. The West European rejection of Kissinger's proposal for a summit led to a new American proposal for a series of bilateral meetings.[64]

The decisive meeting between President Nixon and President Pompidou was held in the Portuguese islands of the Azores on 14 December. Kissinger's role in the meeting was the key to the Nixon–Pompidou agreement that helped resolve the crisis. It was Kissinger who, over breakfast with Pompidou, settled the amount by which

France was willing to revalue the franc in exchange for the devaluation of the dollar.[65] The agreement led to a conference of the Group of Ten a week later at the Smithsonian in Washington. The Smithsonian Agreement ratified the new monetary arrangements which ended the economic crisis that began with President Nixon's unilateral decisions on 15 August 1971.

Kissinger's intervention was the key to the resolution of the economic crisis that created disarray in the Alliance, and for a short time seemed to threaten the security interests of the US.[66] This did not, however, prevent criticism of Kissinger for weakening the Alliance by his failure to dominate international economic policy. Kissinger's efforts to resolve the crisis were consistent with his view that there is a price to be paid for European unity; in pushing for the resolution of the crisis, Kissinger appeared to be paying the economic price in order to maintain Atlantic cohesion which was essential for the successful implementation of his global strategy.[67]

The treaty enlarging the EEC was signed by Britain, Ireland, Norway, and Denmark on 22 January 1972.[68] The economic crisis had, however, correctly proved Kissinger's predictions with respect to an enlarged EEC and falsified the traditional arguments in favour of European unity. Traditional idealism was replaced by a new realism that the EEC could (and would) challenge the economic primacy of the US.

CONCLUSION

The preceding analysis indicates that the Nixon Administration's reaction to the issues affecting West European unity was consistent with both Kissinger's views on European unity and his global strategy. Kissinger's proposals for dealing with the issues aimed at: (a) pacifying the domestic critics of the EEC who sought a tougher stand against the Community's trade restrictions and preferential trading arrangements that would have undermined European unity, and further damage US–EEC relations; and (b) providing support for limited West European unity, which Kissinger viewed as an essential concession to the incipient West European consciousness, to maintain the cohesion of the Alliance and thus facilitate negotiations with the USSR.

The Nixon Administration's position on West European unity was established when it responded to the Soames–de Gaulle controversy by reiterating the views Kissinger had advanced in his writings. The Administration rejected the suggestion of the European integrationists to use the controversy to reaffirm the US commitment to a federal Europe because, as Kissinger had written, de Gaulle was never as alone as his critics believed since Britain shared his views on European unity. Kissinger realized that by staying out of the controversy, the Administration was taking the first step to improving relations with France, the pivot of American relations with Western Europe. For Kissinger, the improvement of US–French relations could make the US 'special relationship' with Britain less of an obstacle to British entry to the EEC. Indeed, by not making a federal Europe (which was opposed by Britain and France) and British entry into EEC its direct objectives, the Administration facilitated the enlargement of the Community.

The Administration's position led critics to accuse it of ignoring the traditional concept of Western Europe as a component of the Atlantic pole in the global balance of power, and accepting de Gaulle's views of European unity and Europe's independent role in world affairs. The Administration was simply acknowledging the West European role in a politically multipolar international system. De Gaulle's concept of a loosely unified Western Europe was shared by Britain, and dovetailed with Kissinger's preference for bilateral relations with the major Allies since it provided more access points and thus greater opportunity for US influence. Kissinger had always warned that an economically and politically unified Western Europe would be much more difficult to deal with since it could challenge American conceptions and refuse to share the burdens necessary for the achievement of goals set by the US.

The critics charged that the Administration's preoccupation with France and bilateral diplomacy with the other Allies undermined the EEC Commission. The neglect of the Commission, however, was calculated. Kissinger was not going to enhance the power of an institution when he had written that it would challenge American primacy in the political and economic fields where temptations for independent initiatives are great and penalties for non-cooperation are small (and, in many cases, non-existent). A stronger Commission could have challenged Kissinger's Soviet policy – and, in particular, his efforts to use trade to influence the international behaviour of the USSR. The Administration did not actively oppose the strengthening of the Commission. Rather it welcomed the suggestion for high-level EEC representation in Washington to expand US–EEC consultations. As Kissinger had written, it was left to the Allies to formulate proposals that could be implemented, an unlikely prospect given French and British opposition to enhancing the power of the Commission.

The charge that Kissinger undermined West European unity is not supported by the evidence. Kissinger strongly opposed efforts of the business community and their allied economic agencies to change the declared policy that the US was willing to pay the price for European unity, and to use the negotiations for Britain's entry into the EEC for attacking the Community's trade restrictions and for seeking protection for American interests. Kissinger's actions during the crisis generated by the New Economic Policy demonstrated his willingness to pay the economic price for European unity, about which he had written. Kissinger was absent from the Camp David meeting when the decision was made, but his role in the bilateral meetings with Allied leaders (and particularly Pompidou) was the key to the resolution of the crisis. Nevertheless, his actions did not prevent critics from charging Kissinger with weakening the Alliance (and especially West European unity) by not dominating inter-national economic policy.

9 *Ostpolitik*: the Threat of 'Differential Detente'

INTRODUCTION

In 1969, the Nixon Administration confronted what Kissinger considered one of the most important issues within the Alliance, the future of Germany.[1] This issue came to the fore as a result of two developments: (a) the reemergence of the Berlin problem; and (b) Chancellor Brandt's commitment to pursue *Ostpolitik*. These developments presented the Administration with risks and opportunities. Chancellor Brandt's offers to the USSR and the GDR to renounce the use of force and accept the status quo in Central Europe raised the threat of 'differential detente'.[2] This endangered the cohesion of the Alliance and the implementation of the concept of linkage. The Berlin problem, however, could facilitate the implementation of linkage; only the US had the strength to counterbalance the isolation of Berlin. This permitted the Administration to control the process of European detente which 'really' began with Brandt's initiatives.

The prospect of selective detente began in 1966 when de Gaulle visited Moscow, opening the door for West European bilateral negotiations with the USSR. Allied leaders, encouraged by the rigid American posture toward the USSR, began to play the role of 'bridge' between East and West, assuring their people they would not permit American recklessness to start a nuclear war. Brandt's initiatives made the threat of selective detente imminent. In Kissinger's view, the offers made to the USSR and the GDR to renounce the use of force and accept the status quo in Central Europe could have: (a) aided the USSR in achieving its objectives in Europe without making any real concessions to the West; (b) increased the FRG's dependence on Soviet goodwill for the successful implementation of *Ostpolitik*; and (c) enhanced Soviet leverage over the Administration by isolating the US from its Allies.

This chapter examines Kissinger's response to Chancellor Brandt's *Ostpolitik*. The examination deals with the following: (a) the American response to the origins of *Ostpolitik* between 1955 and

1968; (b) Kissinger's critique of the American response; (c) the differences in the conceptual frameworks of Kissinger and Brandt; and (d) Kissinger's implementation of linkage to preclude 'differential detente'. The focus of the examination is on the consistency between (a) Kissinger's views on the German question and his reaction to Brandt's *Ostpolitik*; and (b) Kissinger's global strategy and the implementation of linkage.

US REACTION TO THE ORIGINS OF *OSTPOLITIK*: 1955–68

Ostpolitik is associated with Chancellor Brandt, but it actually predates his 1969 initiatives and the negotiations that led to the Moscow and Warsaw treaties of 1970, and the *Grundvertag* between the FRG and the GDR. With the integration of the FRG into the security and economic network of the Western Alliance in hand, Chancellor Konrad Adenauer had sought to improve relations with the USSR, not only to secure the release of German Second World War prisoners, but also to create more favourable conditions for the eventual prospect of reunification.

In 1955, the FRG established diplomatic relations with the USSR, and in the period between 1962 and 1964, Foreign Minister Gerhard Schroder initiated the policy of 'small steps'. The most visible manifestation of this policy was the exchange of trade missions with Poland, Romania, Hungary and Bulgaria.[3] The policy of 'small steps' was intended to provide a proper economic foundation for the development of improved political relations between the FRG and the East.

On 25 March 1966 the Erhard government sought to introduce a 'policy of movement', designed to place relations between the FRG and the countries to the East on a more normal footing. Erhard's government addressed a 'peace note' to all East European states (except the GDR) assuring them that the FRG 'was pursuing neither a policy of revenge nor of revision', and offered to sign agreements renouncing the use of force. The German question, the note said, should be resolved 'giving the whole German people the right to decide freely its political life [*Lebensform*] and fate'. The note said nothing, however, about diplomatic relations, recognition of the Oder–Neisse line, or the GDR.[4]

The action of the Erhard government was welcomed by the Johnson Administration as a contribution to detente. The Administration's reaction reflected the view that had gained ground in the US after the Cuban Missile Crisis – i.e., the only way to achieve peaceful reunification was through detente. This was a complete reversal of the prevalent view of the 1960s – that the resolution of the German problem was the *sine qua non* for the improvement of East–West relations. In 1964, when Chancellor Erhard and Foreign Minister Schroder visited the US, President Johnson told them that there would be no more initiatives by the Western powers on the German question. The President stressed it was up to the FRG to pursue the flexible 'policy of movement' (on which Schroder had already embarked) and to try to find a *modus vivendi* with the East European countries, including the GDR.[5] In October 1966, shortly before Erhard left office, President Johnson again placed detente ahead of reunification. In his words, 'we must improve the East–West environment in order to achieve the unification of Germany in the context of a larger peaceful, and prosperous Europe'.[6]

On 1 December 1966, the Erhard government was succeeded by the Grand Coalition,[7] which adopted an important new policy element by stressing that reunification no longer had to precede detente, but instead, could flow from detente. Chancellor Kurt Georg Kiesinger extended an invitation to the premier of the GDR to negotiate directly if satisfactory conditions could be established. In the Grand Coalition Foreign Minister Brandt expanded the initiatives of his predecessors toward the Eastern Bloc by restoring diplomatic relations with Romania (1967) and Yugoslavia (1968).[8] The agreements with Romania and Yugoslavia were noteworthy because they ignored the Hallstein Doctrine prohibiting relations with any country that recognized the GDR.[9] This doctrine had brought the FRG into increasing conflict with its Allies and the nonaligned countries, as more and more of them recognized the GDR, regardless of the FRG's threat to cut off relations.[10]

In March 1968, Brandt attempted to reach an accommodation with Poland by calling for respect and recognition of the existing boundaries of Europe (especially the Oder–Neisse line) until their settlement through a peace treaty. But the ensuing domestic controversy made it impossible for Brandt to pursue the matter.[11] President Johnson told Chancellor Kiesinger that the US 'would no longer fight a war of unification [for Germany]. If you want to live in peace in Europe, you have to look for an alternative'.[12] In short, the FRG's first moves in the 1960s toward the East had been taken through incitement from the US.

KISSINGER'S CRITIQUE OF US REACTION TO ORIGINS OF *OSTPOLITIK*

Kissinger criticized the Johnson Administration's argument that 'almost any measure that eases tensions also promotes German unification'.[13] This argument was based on the assumption that once detente was firmly established, the GDR might become dispensable to the USSR, and the ideological impetus for maintaining a Communist regime in the GDR could decline as the USSR pursued more national policies. In Kissinger's view, 'arguments that a detente automatically furthers the cause of German unity must be balanced against others which, on the whole, seem more likely'.[14]

Kissinger observed that the USSR, even if it became less committed ideologically, was unlikely to surrender its hold on the GDR simply as a result of detente. 'On the contrary, to the degree that a detente with the West exists, Soviet leaders may well calculate that concessions on the unification of Germany become unnecessary'.[15] For Kissinger, 'the German concern that detente may freeze the status quo in Germany is, ... not wholly unjustified'.[16] Hence, he stressed 'it is dangerous to arouse German expectations that are not likely to be fulfilled'.[17]

Kissinger criticized American policymakers for urging the FRG to take the lead in dealing with the GDR. He challenged their assumptions that increased contacts between the two Germanies would facilitate the erosion of the East German regime, and that the greater strength and unity of the FRG would give it a stronger bargaining position.[18] Kissinger argued that, at a minimum, negotiations between the FRG and the GDR might make life more bearable for the East German population while enhancing the status of the East German regime.[19]

Kissinger maintained that 'enhancing the status of East Germany [was] a dangerous course'.[20] First, it could indefinitely defer any hope for unification, since two German states would be competing for world support; secondly, it was risky because the bargaining position of the FRG was still precarious; and thirdly, in contacts between the two German states humanitarian concerns would outweigh political considerations. These contacts might not succeed in weakening the FRG's formal ties to the West, but they could produce a serious political split in the Federal Republic.[21]

Kissinger suggested that the FRG's Allies 'should not contribute to the already considerable confusion among three partly incompatible

objectives: improvement of conditions in East Germany, consolidation of the East German regime, and progress toward German
unification'.[22] He conceded that improvement of GDR conditions
was desirable for humanitarian reasons, but that this would probably
help the East German regime to consolidate itself, thereby making
unification more remote (except on its terms). As the legitimacy of
the GDR regime grew, the USSR's moral cost for maintaining the
division of Germany would diminish. This, Kissinger argued, would
reduce the Soviet desire to make concessions. In addition, as the
GDR regime gained international stature, its pressure on the FRG
would gradually increase.[23] While trying to establish its international
status the GDR would make moderate demands; but once its
legitimacy was recognized, the GDR would seek to undermine the
FRG. Kissinger believed that 'the [GDR would], in fact, be driven to
do so by its precarious position'. Within the GDR, national
aspirations clash with the existence of a Communist regime. The
FRG acts as a powerful magnet, therefore the East German regime
has every incentive to seek to undermine the FRG, by using its own
population as a hostage.[24]

In Kissinger's view, 'the superiority of West Germany's bargaining
position – which is postulated by some American policymakers –
may, therefore, be an illusion'.[25] Contrary to American policymakers' assumptions, Kissinger argued, West German political leaders
might face a growing dilemma. In return for ameliorating conditions
in the GDR, its regime could demand concrete political gains. The
West German leaders, confronted by popular pressures and moved
by humanitarian impulses, would find it very difficult to decide at
what point the seemingly marginal concessions would produce an
irreversible trend. In turn, every concession by the FRG to the GDR
would strengthen the position of those in the West favouring
recognition of the East German regime. 'The result' Kissinger
maintained, '[was] more likely to be the indefinite continuation of
two hostile, competing German states than progress toward
unification'.[26]

Kissinger also criticized the policy of 'small steps' initiated by
Schroder. Supporters claimed this policy would help isolate and
weaken the East German regime since the expanding cultural and
economic ties between the two Germanies would help spread
Western values in the GDR. Kissinger observed that the policy of
'small steps' would more probably open the way to legitimacy for the
GDR and eventually undermine the FRG. In his view, if West

German political leaders were determined to take the lead in dealing
with the East, there was nothing the US could do to prevent it, but
insisted that 'the Federal Republic should not be urged into bilateral
dealings with the East'.[27] In short, Johnson's policy of urging the
FRG to take the lead in dealing with the GDR was flawed. Kissinger
stressed that the US should make certain that the West could not be
blamed for probable consequences of policies initiated by the
political leaders of the FRG.[28] He asserted that policymakers in the
US and Britain who believed that the 'flexible' Germans would
always follow their lead could be in for some unpleasant surprises,
since the German version of flexibility could become indistinguishable from traditional nationalism.[29] As West German activity
increased toward the East, so did the fear of another Rapallo,
creating a vicious circle. The Western neighbours of the FRG would
draw closer together, and they might also seek to counter its policy by
increasing their own contacts with the USSR. This would weaken
both Atlantic and West European cohesion, and eventually lead to
the isolation of the FRG.[30] Kissinger believed that 'only a united
Atlantic Alliance facing jointly the issue of Germany's future can
minimize the danger of a sharp conflict between Germany's national
goals and its Atlantic ties'.[31]

THE CONCEPTUAL FRAMEWORK OF *OSTPOLITIK*: BRANDT VERSUS KISSINGER

Upon becoming Chancellor, Brandt indicated (more clearly than any
of his predecessors) the determination of the FRG to adopt a new
line in foreign policy. In his first policy declaration issued on 28
October 1969, Brandt recognized East Germany by its formal name,
and indicated that henceforth the GDR was to be considered a
separate state within a single German nation. In his words, 'Twenty
years after the establishment of the Federal Republic of Germany
and of the German Democratic Republic, we must prevent any
further alienation of the two parts of the German nation, that is,
arrive at a regular *modus vivendi* and from there to proceed to
cooperation'.[32] The Chancellor renounced West Germany's claim to
be the sole representative of the entire German people, and indicated
that reunification could not be achieved in the foreseeable future.[33]

What was new in the *Ostpolitik* of Chancellor Brandt was not the
interest in normalizing relations with the East, nor the public

recognition that progress in the German question was dependent on East–West detente. Rather, the new element was the decision to improve relations with the countries in the East and seek constructive change in Central Europe on the formally recognized basis of the status quo – that is, recognition of the two German states, acceptance of the existing frontiers (particularly the Oder–Neisse line and the border between the FRG and the GDR), and a willingness to bear the costs stemming from this recognition.[34]

In general, the new element in Brandt's *Ostpolitik* stemmed from the rejection of the former tendency to disregard all signs of change in the Soviet attitude toward the West as long as the USSR gave no evidence that it was willing substantially to modify its stand on the German problem. Detente between East and West began to be perceived as a more symmetrical process than had been customary in the postwar West German foreign policy. But, more importantly, Soviet foreign policy toward Europe was viewed as defensive; its main goal was to consolidate the Soviet sphere of influence in Eastern Europe.

Kissinger did not share this view. He had always maintained that Soviet foreign policy toward Europe was offensive. The USSR sought to consolidate its sphere of influence in Eastern Europe – but, more importantly, intended to extend and expand its political influence in Western Europe. Its long-term goal was to isolate the US from its Allies.

In 1969, the conceptual framework of *Ostpolitik* was attributed to Chancellor Brandt and his political confidant Egon Bahr.[35] Some of the major assumptions on which *Ostpolitik* was based can be traced to the Chancellor's perceptions of the construction of the Berlin Wall in 1961, and his experiences as Foreign Minister.[36] Brandt drew major foreign policy conclusions from the fact that the US was unable (or unwilling) to prevent the construction of the Wall. He was convinced that neither the US nor the NATO Alliance could be expected to contribute to the resolution of the German problem. As Brandt explained:

We lost certain illusions that had outlived the hopes underlying them ... Ulbricht had been allowed to take a swipe at the Western superpower, and the United States merely winced with annoyance. My political deliberations in the years that followed were substantially influenced by this day's [13 August 1961] experience, and it was against this background that my so-called *Ostpolitik* –

the beginning of détente – took shape . . . My view and inescapable realization was that traditional patterns of Western policy had proved ineffective, if not downright unrealistic.[37]

Brandt, and other political leaders in the FRG, concluded that the approaching strategic parity between the superpowers signalled the American acceptance of the status quo in Europe. Western military strength was no longer (if it ever had been) the means for altering the status quo.[38] Those conclusions had led to the policy of 'small steps'.

Kissinger had reached a similar conclusion. When the Berlin Wall was constructed Kissinger criticized the complacency with which most American policymakers accepted it. He recommended that President Kennedy order an invasion of the Eastern sector to tear the Wall down.[39] The Wall was not simply another unilateral abrogation of a treaty obligation by the USSR. Kissinger stressed that, 'In Germany . . . the partition of Berlin marked the end of the belief that German unification would more or less automatically follow the strengthening of the Atlantic Alliance'.[40] Furthermore, he saw Kennedy's reaction to the Berlin Wall as undermining the credibility of American foreign policy. Kissinger predicted that the West German leaders would eventually reach the conclusions that Brandt had reached, and take the unilateral initiatives that Brandt was now taking. He had stressed 'the challenge to Western policy [was] to prevent the Alliance from seeming an obstacle to legitimate German aspirations, while not letting German national aspirations transcend all other imperatives'.[41]

Chancellor Brandt's experience as the Grand Coalition's foreign minister shaped other major assumptions on which his *Ostpolitik* was based. A 'European peace order' became one of the primary objectives of the FRG's foreign policy under the Grand Coalition. The substance of this concept was evident in the writings and statements of Brandt and Bahr.[42]

Chancellor Brandt developed two main concepts: a 'European security system' and a 'European peace order'.[43] These concepts were elaborated in his book *A Peace Policy for Europe*, published in 1969. Additional insight into Brandt's rationale and justifications for *Ostpolitik* were provided through his acceptance speech for the Nobel Peace Prize in December 1971.

Basic to the development of Brandt's concepts was the recognition (and acceptance) of the separate identities of nations and states as fundamental elements of an all-European policy. First, according to

Brandt, the main task was to 'establish a balance between states and groups of states in which each will preserve its identity and security'.[44] Secondly, force (and the threat of force) must be renounced in relations between states; hence the existing frontiers of all states should be regarded as inviolable. The Chancellor noted that, 'the integrity of frontiers cannot mean cementing them as barriers between enemies'. Thirdly, all European states must participate in the search for specific agreements on arms limitation and control. These agreements would need to complement the renunciation of force. This process must include solid negotiations on mutual and balanced force reductions in Central Europe. Fourthly, all states must respect the principle of non-interference in the internal affairs of others. Acceptance of this principle must be accompanied by increased freedom of thought and willingness on the part of all European states to debate their divergent convictions and interests. Fifthly, the European states must endeavour to develop new forms of economic, technological, and scientific cooperation and to construct 'an all-European infrastructure'. In the Chancellor's words, 'above all, Europe evolved as a cultural community and it should again become what it was'.[45]

Chancellor Brandt acknowledged that 'the commitment of the United States is indispensable for the creation of a solid European peace order'.[46] He also maintained that 'a system of security in Europe superimposed on the blocs . . . is feasible neither without the United States nor without the Soviet Union',[47] given the military bipolarity of the international system. Brandt never defined the specific role of the superpowers in the European security system and European peace order; this omission implied that Brandt could pursue the creation of a European peace order regardless of the wishes of the US.

The Chancellor suggested that in principle the European security system could be established in two different ways. One way was by retaining NATO and the Warsaw Pact, systematically enhancing their stabilizing functions through specific arms control and arms limitation agreements and other measures. In his words, 'I am convinced that an effective European security system could, on a short-range view, be sensibly based only on agreement involving the two alliances which would go on existing'.[48] The other way was through gradual elimination of NATO and the Warsaw Pact, and establishing a new system devised to safeguard the security of all European States. In his words, 'It is also possible to dissolve the pacts and replace them by something new'.[49] The Chancellor admitted that 'differing degrees of active superpower participation would be required in either course'.[50] He explained that 'a system of European security would have to be participated in by the United States as well as the USSR. It should result from agreements related to the alliances which to begin with, would continue to exist'.[51] On practical grounds, the Chancellor felt that the first method was more likely to succeed.[52]

Chancellor Brandt believed the European peace order that would be built on the European security system required more than the elimination of the threat of war. It required active cooperation. He acknowledged that 'there is and will continue to be the delineation through ideological differences', but stressed that progress was possible 'if we speak more of interests than of ideology'.[53] In this respect Brandt's and Kissinger's conceptual approaches were similar, if not the same. An active policy of coexistence proceeds from the assumption that the prevention of nuclear war, despite differing ideologies, provides the basis on which nations with different economic and social systems can live side by side without grave conflicts. Kissinger and Brandt sought to conduct foreign policy on strictly non-ideological grounds. But unlike Kissinger – who emphasized the necessity for coordinating all Western initiatives toward the USSR – Brandt stressed that Europe had an independent role to play in the search for East–West detente. Brandt explained:

> The solution of mutual problems implies establishing links through meaningful cooperation among states beyond inter-bloc frontiers ... It means building up confidence through practical arrangements. And this confidence may then become the new basis for the solution of long standing problems. This opportunity can be Europe's opportunity in a world which as has been proven, cannot be ruled by Washington or Moscow – or by Peking – alone ... However unmistakably great the strength of the superpowers may be, it is an indisputable fact that other magnetic fields are emerging at the same time.[54]

In short, the Chancellor indicated that he would not follow the dictates of the US. This was a direct challenge to Kissinger's view that the establishment of a stable international system required the cohesion of the Alliance – and, more importantly, American primacy.

Chancellor Brandt emphatically stated: 'Small nations, too, have a part in the big game; they too can represent power in their own way; they can be a help to themselves and to others; and they can also be a danger to themselves and to others'.[55] The Chancellor believed that *Ostpolitik* could help Germany in particular and East–West detente in general. Kissinger was convinced that *Ostpolitik* would endanger both the FRG and his efforts to establish a stable international system, since it would reduce Moscow's desire to make concessions. The rationale for Kissinger's conviction was evident from his criticism of the Johnson Administration for encouraging the FRG to pursue a flexible policy in order to find a *modus vivendi* with the East European states, including the GDR.

Chancellor Brandt believed that the process of East–West detente and cooperation could not realistically proceed with the participation of the FRG alone. The process would require a specific German contribution. He declared:

> know that peace policy must be something more than merely applauding others ... a country like the Federal Republic of Germany could not remain tied to a vaguely general [role], but had to define a specific contribution. We could not leave to others answers which we could give ourselves. Nobody can relieve us of a task when, owing to the realities of the situation, it is one that only we ourselves can fulfill ... These [realities] we cannot recognize if we are prone to self-deception or if we confuse politics with legal arguments. The Kremlin is no local court ... and I would extend this metaphor to include Washington.[56]

The Chancellor was stressing that detente and cooperation required more from the FRG than simply applauding the efforts of the superpowers.

An accommodation between the FRG and the USSR, according to Brandt, was central to the process of East–West detente and the establishment of a European peace order. Brandt stated, 'The special importance of the Soviet Union – it is obvious – is rooted in its position as a world power and for us, to be sure, also in its position as one of the four powers that are still responsible for the problem of Germany'.[57] He pointed out that in the Grand Coalition 'we have not let ourselves be deflected, either by crossfire from abroad or by a lack of understanding in our own country, from seeking an objective dialogue with the Soviet Union ... I will not be made to deviate from this goal, nor shall I let myself be deflected from energetically continuing a conversation, initiated with so much difficulty, as

purposefully and as intensively as possible'.[58] Brandt's determination
to conduct a dialogue with the USSR and Kissinger's determination
to prevent this from moving too far, too fast, made tensions between
the two Administrations inevitable.

The establishment of a European peace order would precede the
fulfilment of the national aspirations of the German people. For
Brandt:

> The question of the future of Germany and of the position of
> Germans in Europe is the question of an enduring European peace
> order. Only in a peacefully ordered Europe which has succeeded in
> building a bridge between East and West and in which nations as
> equals among equals will vie with each other for peace, justice, and
> prosperity, will the past be overcome in a positive way.[59]

In short, a European peace order would open up possibilities for – or
at least would not hinder a settlement of – the German question,
implying the ending of the division of the German nation.

The elaboration of the concepts of a European security system and
a European peace order revealed that the Chancellor's initial
conception of detente was different from Kissinger's. Brandt viewed
detente as a continuing, self-perpetuating peace process in Europe,
based on the recognition of the status quo, on reciprocal political
concessions, economic interdependence, and – ultimately – on
military disengagement by both sides. But Kissinger (and Brezhnev)
conceived detente as a policy for managing the fundamentally
irresolvable East–West conflict under new international conditions
and with slightly altered methods.[60] For the US and the USSR the
East–West relationship was essentially conflictual and would remain
so, indefinitely. Brandt recognized the conflictual nature of East–
West relations, and continuously affirmed the FRG's commitment to
NATO, insisting that his *Ostpolitik* was based on a firmly rooted
Westpolitik.[61] The Chancellor constantly stated, 'If the Federal
Republic is following a line of greater independence in its foreign
policy today, no estrangement from America can be deduced from
this.[62] 'The Atlantic alliance is indispensable to us.'[63]

The elaboration of Brandt's concepts also revealed that (for him)
detente meant regional rapprochement, centred on the FRG's
relations with the East European states, in particular the USSR and
the GDR. Kissinger's detente policy, on the other hand, had a
bipolar orientation, and was worldwide in scope; hence, it lacked a
specifically European focus. Brandt's conceptualization postulated

the East's fear of Germany as 'the problem' (or one of the problems), wide-scale cooperation as the solution, and the reunification of Germany as the end result. The USSR and its East European Allies were to be drawn into a gradually expanding web of political, economic, cultural and military agreements aimed at deepening trust and amity among the people and governments of Europe to the point where – with the traditional suspicions of German militarism overcome – the unification of Germany would no longer be seen as a threat. As outlined by Chancellor Brandt, Bonn's 'peace policy for Europe', comprising a European security system and a European peace order, did constitute the long-range goals of *Ostpolitik*.

In the long term, Chancellor Brandt expected *Ostpolitik* to achieve what previous governments and policies had failed to accomplish – that is, to gain Soviet acquiescence for a permanent solution to the German problem which would be acceptable to the German people. *Ostpolitik* would accomplish this: (a) by providing the opportunity for all Germans within the German 'nation' to normalize their communication and to regain a form of cultural, economic, and social unity, despite (or because of) the low prospects for political unity in the foreseeable future; and (b) by a gradual opening of Eastern Europe, a loosening of Soviet control, and the development of a European peace order which would allow (or result from) the disappearance of the military and ideological confrontation between East and West in Europe. The achievement of these two goals would provide the German 'nation' with an opportunity freely to decide if it desired political reunification.[64]

In the short term, *Ostpolitik* could achieve the following goals. First, it would establish *modus vivendi* with the GDR which would allow greater communication between Germans living in the two German states; for Chancellor Brandt, it was essential to reverse the increasing trend toward a greater separation between the two. Secondly, the Chancellor hoped that *Ostpolitik* would lead to greater West German political influence and trade in Eastern Europe. The FRG's acceptance of the status quo in Central Europe would reduce the Soviet desire (and ability) to block the development of productive relations between the FRG and the East European states. As a result, it would capitalize on East European needs for goods, credits and technology. The Chancellor hoped that an expansion of influence would induce East European states to pressure the GDR to be more cooperative in its relations with the FRG. Thirdly, the Chancellor was seeking assurances that the USSR and the GDR would accept the status quo in Berlin for the indefinite future, and would not interfere with West German access to the city. And fourthly, Chancellor Brandt hoped that an active dialogue with the USSR and the other East European states would confer upon the FRG the prestige and independence in the foreign policy field which (until then) had been the prerogatives of its major Allies.[65]

In summary, Brandt and Kissinger shared the conviction that foreign policy should be conducted on a non-ideological basis. But they had different perceptions about the nature and objectives of Soviet foreign policy and different conceptions of detente. Those differences, and their determination to implement their conceptions, suggested the inevitability of friction between the two.

IMPLEMENTING 'LINKAGE': BERLIN AND BRANDT'S *OSTPOLITIK*

Before the 1969 American Presidential inauguration, the Berlin problem reemerged as a result of the FRG constitutional cycle which made 1969 their presidential year. In December 1968, the USSR formally protested at the assembly of the Federal Convention in Berlin, charging it was 'illegal' and a 'deliberate provocation', although the convention had been held without incident in the old Reichstag Building in West Berlin since 1954.[66] The Johnson Administration left the response to the Soviet protest to its successor.

The State Department sent President Nixon a draft rejecting the Soviet protest, but the prepared reply was delayed by Kissinger's recommendation; he (although agreeing with the reply) sought to avoid an acrimonious exchange with Moscow. Through a memorandum, Kissinger proposed that the President use his first meeting on 17 February 1969 with Ambassador Dobrynin to convince the Soviets that their interference with access to Berlin was a matter of direct concern to the US. Dobrynin reassured the President that Moscow sought no confrontation. But on 22 February, the day before President Nixon left for Western Europe, Dobrynin by a note to Kissinger urged the Administration to intervene with Chancellor Kurt Kiesinger to call off the Berlin election and avoid tensions. Kissinger rejected the Soviet proposition and 'warned Dobrynin sternly against unilateral acts'. At the same time, the President (on Kissinger's recommendation and despite strong opposition from the

State Department) ordered increased US military traffic over the access routes to Berlin, reaffirming the American commitment to the city.[67] These actions were consistent with views advanced in Kissinger's writings.

President Nixon agreed with Kissinger that since 'Berlin [had] become the touchstone of the West's European policy ... a defeat for the West [would] demoralize the Federal Republic ... [and] become a warning to all other states in Europe of the folly of resisting Communist pressure ... [and] illustrate the irresistible nature of the Communist advance to the rest of the world'.[68] Both men were convinced that their demonstration of resolution in Berlin was essential to enhance US credibility, which was a prerequisite for a successful foreign policy.[69]

During his Berlin visit on 27 February 1969, at the Siemens Factory, President Nixon's speech reiterated the US commitment to defend the city and expressed the hope that Berlin could become the object of 'negotiation ... and reconciliation'.[70] This was the first indication that the Administration was willing to move toward discussions with the Soviets on improving conditions in and around Berlin, and resulted from the lobbying efforts of Chancellor Kiesinger and Foreign Minister Brandt.[71] The President was not at all convinced his initiative would succeed; discussing Soviet policy with the Chancellor in Bonn, he said that Moscow's desire for agreement on the projected SALT talks would enable him to extract concessions in the Middle East and Vietnam. But whether the Soviets would make concessions on Berlin was another matter. Nevertheless Chancellor Kiesinger urged President Nixon to include Berlin on his agenda for negotiations with the USSR and informed him that Bonn would undertake its own initiatives to improve relations with Eastern Europe.[72]

The election of the FRG president, Gustav Heinemann, took place on 5 March in the Reichstag Building without a crisis, and harassment stopped. A number of reasons could explain Soviet restraint. Evidently Moscow did not want to jeopardize the SALT talks, which were just beginning to take shape.[73] Worsening relations between Moscow and Peking also played a crucial role. In March 1969, armed clashes took place between Soviet and Chinese troops along the disputed Ussuri River boundary; the Soviet leadership, acutely aware of its vulnerability in the East, sought to secure its Western front.[74] There was little doubt that Moscow's need for Western technology was another consideration.

Following the American initiative on Berlin and the Soviet border clashes with the PRC, Moscow embarked on an 'agonized appraisal of its European policy. On 17 March 1969 in Budapest, at a meeting of the Political Consultative Committee of the Warsaw Treaty Organization, the Soviets formally proposed an early conference on European security. The Budapest Appeal called for recognition of the GDR and FRG; renunciation by Bonn of possession of nuclear weapons in any form and of its claim to represent the entire German people; strengthening of political, economic, and cultural contacts; and recognition of West Berlin's separation from the FRG. The Budapest Appeal was the Soviet programme for Europe put forward in the name of enhancing European security. Of particular importance was the omission of the anti-German polemics that had characterized earlier pronouncements on this subject. But the appeal did not mention US participation in the negotiations, thus seriously alienating the Administration.[75]

The Administration's initial reaction (shared by some of the Allies) was very cool. It viewed the Budapest Appeal as a Soviet ploy to achieve the formal ratification of the status quo in Europe without making any concessions. The Administration changed its position, however, after the April 1969 NATO Ministerial meeting in Washington. In a communiqué released at the end of the meeting, the Allies offered to explore 'concrete issues' with the Warsaw Pact, and insisted on US and Canadian participation. The Administration's initial reaction changed due to the lobbying efforts of Foreign Minister Brandt, and Kissinger's fear that a total rejection of the Soviet overture would isolate the US within NATO.

During the NATO meeting, Brandt had urged the Allies critically to examine the idea of a European security conference, arguing that 'it would be a mistake for the West to pursue detente on a selective basis'. The Administration, he felt, should not expect West Europeans to reject Moscow's conciliatory gestures while it negotiated with the USSR.[76] Italian Foreign Minister Pietro Nenni supported Brandt's recommendation by proposing that the West take the lead in calling for a security conference.[77] The French supported Brandt in order to involve the FRG in a multilateral framework and preclude independent German initiatives towards the East, while the British advocated a European security conference as a means to transcend the cold War.[78] The three Allies (France, Britain and the US) responsible for Berlin were urged by Brandt to approach the USSR.

Kissinger, seeing that the conciliatory tone of the Soviet offer had evoked Alliance eagerness for a European security conference, proposed that the Administration make its agreement in principle dependent on progress on other European issues, especially Berlin. In a memorandum dated 8 April 1969, he noted:

> Without such progress, a conference would probably find the East European countries closely aligned with a rigid Soviet position, while the western participants would be competing with each other to find ways to 'break the deadlock'. The new result ... woud tend to set back prospects for an eventual resolution of European issues. Consequently, our emphasis should be on the need for talks on concrete issues and for consultations within NATO designed to develop coherent western positions on such issues.[79]

This became the American position. Brandt reported that during the NATO ministerial meeting, President Nixon informed the Allies about the prelude to the SALT talks, and declared that in moving toward an 'age of negotiation ... the West must not ... be drawn into a selective detente which would leave the Soviet Union more or less free to determine where it considered detente appropriate or a continuation of the Cold War expedient'. According to Brandt, 'Kissinger's handwriting was clearly discernible [in the President's statement]'.[80]

The linkage between Soviet concessions on Berlin and the European security conference had been established by Kissinger despite the objections of the State Department. The State Department viewed the conference as a forum that could produce results on MBFR, or on principles of coexistence. Thus on Kissinger's recommendation the European security conference was deliberately put on a slow track, and no action was taken until the next NATO ministerial meeting on December 1969.[81] President Nixon, to test Soviet flexibility and satisfy Brandt's need for movement on Berlin, repeated his offer to discuss Berlin in a letter on 26 March to Soviet Premier Alexei Kosygin.[82] Kosygin, encouraged by American domestic criticism of the Administration's linkage approach, replied on 27 May 1969, by forcefully challenging linkage. He argued that 'taking into account the complexity of each of these problems by itself, it is hardly worthwhile to attempt somehow to link one with another'.[83] He indicated that Moscow had no 'objections' to a discussion of Berlin, arguing that Bonn was to blame for any tensions that might take place there. Kissinger – concerned with Allied reaction (and especially Brandt's) – recommended against pursuing the issue of Berlin in a bilateral US–Soviet channel. In view of the forthcoming parliamentary election in the FRG (September 1969), Kissinger proposed that the Administration discuss the issue with the new government, and then decide whether (and how) to pursue the subject with Moscow.[84]

Thwarted by Washington, Moscow turned to the public arena to put pressure on the Administration. On 10 July 1969, in a speech to the Supreme Soviet, Gromyko suggested 'an exchange of opinions' with the three Western powers on 'how to prevent complications on West Berlin now and in the future', but stressed that in such talks Moscow would not 'allow anything to impinge' on its interests or 'the legitimate interests' of the GDR, or to 'violate the special status of West Berlin'.[85] Western public opinion warmly welcomed Moscow's willingness to discuss Berlin, but Washington, Paris, and London were very sceptical. Only Bonn urged rapid acceptance of Gromyko's offer; Bonn's response was in part related to Chancellor Kiesinger's and Foreign Minister Brandt's awareness of the benefit that easing of tensions could have in their September 1969 election. The Allies responded on 6 and 7 August to Gromyko's offer, shortly after President Nixon's visit to Romania. Although highly suspicious of Moscow's intentions, in almost identical notes they suggested a more detailed exchange of opinions on Berlin to test Soviet flexibility.[86]

The disappointing Soviet reply came on 12 September 1969, repeating Gromyko's 10 July offer for Four-Power talks, and containing the familiar Soviet preconditions for relaxing tensions in Central Europe – i.e., the talks were to focus on curbing the FRG's activities in Berlin, inviolability of existing boundaries, etc. It opposed any discussion for improving access to Berlin. Nevertheless its tone was encouraging; for the first time since 1955, the Soviets seemed willing to discuss Berlin in a peaceful atmosphere.[87]

Soviet efforts to isolate the US from its Allies resumed on 20 October, when Ambassador Dobrynin met President Nixon and proposed a formal exchange of views through the bilateral channel. Kissinger – sensitive to Brandt's charges that the Administration was pursuing selective detente, and given the Soviet unwillingness to discuss improvements in access to Berlin – cautioned the President against it, stating:

I think we should not encourage the notion of bilateral US – Soviet talks on Berlin at this stage. The Soviets would use them to stir up suspicions among the Allies and to play us off against each other. I believe we would do best to keep this issue in the quadripartite forum for the moment and not to press too much ourselves.[88]

Kissinger was primarily concerned with precluding any independent European initiatives toward Moscow. Only then would linkage work.

Brandt's election as Chancellor by the Bundestag on 21 October caught the Nixon Administration by surprise.[89] The new coalition of Social Democrats and Free Democrats came into office pledging new initiatives toward the East, so Moscow shifted its focus to Bonn. These developments alarmed Washington. This was evident in Kissinger's memorandum to President Nixon. Kissinger stated:

> It should be stressed that men like Brandt, Wehner, and Defence Minister [Helmut] Schmidt undoubtedly see themselves as conducting a responsible policy of reconciliation and normalization with the East and intend not to have this policy come into conflict with Germany's Western association. There can be no doubt about their basic Western orientation. But their problem is to control a process which, if it results in failure, could jeopardize their political lives and, if it succeeds, could create a momentum that may shake Germany's domestic stability and unhinge its international position.[90]

This was a reiteration of the same warning advanced in Kissinger's writings.[91] Kissinger feared that Brandt's *Ostpolitik*, which many viewed as a progressive policy for establishing detente, could turn into an new form of classic German nationalism. In Kissinger's view, the essence of Germany's nationalist foreign policy would be to manoeuvre freely between East and West. But, as Kissinger had warned in *The Necessity for Choice*, 'An attempt by Germany to play off the West against the East would prove disastrous for the peace of the world'.[92]

Aware of Washington's alarm, and before being formally installed, Brandt asked the White House to receive Egon Bahr, his political confidant, to iron out their differences.[93] During their first meeting on 13 October 1969, Bahr informed Kissinger of the course Brandt intended to follow and stressed that the Chancellor wanted to pursue it in cooperation with Washington. Bahr, however, made it clear that *Ostpolitik* itself was not subject to discussion,[94] and rejected Kissinger's view that *Ostpolitik* was more likely to lead to a permanent division of Germany than toward unification.[95] In this meeting, a backchannel was established so that Kissinger and Bahr could resolve important issues outside formal procedures. Chancellor Brandt shared the President's distrust of the foreign policy bureaucracy, and kept his foreign office in the dark.[96]

Bonn's announcement on 11 November 1969 that it would initiate talks with Moscow concerning an agreement on the mutual renunciation of force was followed by a formal proposal to the USSR on 16 November. At the same time Bonn (perhaps in deference to Washington) declared its hope that negotiations with Moscow would coincide with the holding of Four-Power talks on Berlin. On 17 November Washington announced the start of the long-delayed SALT talks in Helsinki.[97]

The Administration, despite its reservations and concern about the possible negative consequences of Brandt's initiative, did not seek to derail it because, as Kissinger admitted, 'we had no alternative to offer'.[98] In his view, 'the sole option available to [the Administration] was to give the inevitable a constructive direction.[99]

The SPD–FDP coalition had been elected on the programme the Chancellor sought to implement. Therefore, the US could derail *Ostpolitik* only by intervening heavily in the internal politics of the FRG. Opposing the initiative would have alienated the other Allies. President Pompidou and Prime Minister Wilson endorsed it publicly, and privately pressed the Administration to do the same because they feared a German 'liberation policy'. President Pompidou also feared that only the refashioning of NATO into a US–FRG Alliance for the liberation of Eastern Europe might stop Brandt.[100] Domestically, the Administration would have been charged with destroying hopeful prospects for improving the harsh conditions of the division of Germany; as Kissinger put it, public opinion would not understand a policy of insisting on German reunification against the wishes of the German government: 'We could not be more German than the Germans'.[101]

Those who participated in the NSC staff meetings (when the Brandt initiatives were discussed) reported that Kissinger was strongly opposed to *Ostpolitik*.[102] But the rationale of Kissinger's opposition was evident in his writings where he criticized the Johnson Administration for urging Bonn to take independent initiatives towards the East.[103] Kissinger repeated the warnings advanced in his writings through a memorandum to President Nixon on 16 February 1970. He wrote:

The most worrisome aspects of *Ostpolitik*, however, are somewhat more long-range. As long as he is negotiating with the Eastern countries over the issues that are currently on the table – recognition of the GDR, the Oder–Neisse, various possible arrangements for Berlin – Brandt should not have any serious difficulty in maintaining his basic pro-Western policy...

But assuming Brandt achieves a degree of normalization he or his successor may discover before long that the hoped-for benefits fail to develop ... Having already invested heavily in their Eastern policy, the Germans may at this point see themselves as facing agonizing choices. It should be remembered that in the 1950s, many Germans not only in the SPD under Schumacher but in conservative quarters traditionally fascinated with the East or enthralled by the vision of Germany as a 'bridge' between East and West, argued against Bonn's incorporation in Western institutions on the ground that it would forever seal Germany's division and preclude the restoration of an active German role in the East. This kind of debate about Germany's basic position could well recur in more divisive form, not only inflaming German domestic affairs but generating suspicions among Germany's Western associates as to its reliability as a partner.[104]

From this, one realizes Kissinger was not inconsistent, as critics have charged.

Recognizing that Brandt's initiatives could not be derailed, Kissinger endeavoured to control the pace of European detente.[105] Kissinger knew that despite Brandt's determination, he could not conduct *Ostpolitik* on a purely national basis. As Kissinger stated, 'we were not without recourse'[106] since the security of the Allies depended on the American strategic umbrella. The rationale of Kissinger's convictions was evident in *The Troubled Partnership*, where he concluded that 'as long as NATO strategy was nuclear and the United States had no obvious alternative to nuclear retaliation, our Allies were ready to acquiesce in the hegemonial position of the United States'.[107] The concept of sufficiency advanced by Kissinger permitted the US continual deployment of strategic weapons in order to sustain the credibility of its NATO commitments while negotiating strategic arms limitations with the USSR.

In 1968, in 'Central Issues of American Foreign Policy', Kissinger found it 'hard to visualize a "deal" between the Soviet Union and Europe which would jeopardize [American] interests without jeopar-

dizing European interests first'.[108] Brandt's *Ostpolitik* compromised
this conclusion. Now Kissinger feared that *Ostpolitik*, if not related to
other issues involving the Alliance as a whole, would produce a
'deal', – i.e., the formal recognition of the status quo in Europe –
which would endanger the implementation of his global strategy.
Kissinger sought to gain Soviet concessions before giving that
recognition.

Through overtures to Bonn, Moscow sought to manoeuvre
Washington into appearing as the obstacle to the relaxation of East–
West tensions, thus isolating the US within the Alliance. From
Kissinger's viewpoint (given the West European interest in mutual
force reductions and the Soviet proposal for a European security
conference), 'the prospect was real that a "differential detente"
would develop'. The USSR could exploit the West European
attitudes while remaining intransigent on global issues of concern to
the Administration – i.e., Vietnam and the Middle East.[109]

Kissinger 'opposed the [Berlin] talks from the very beginning',[110] a
stand consistent with views advanced in his writings. Kissinger
considered Berlin the touchstone of Western policy, and had
criticized the Western powers for negotiating on Berlin only to make
concessions that further undermined the freedom of the city. More
importantly, such concessions undermined the credibility of American foreign policy. He had written that because of Berlin's
vulnerability 'the range of possible concessions is unfortunately
limited'. Therefore in 1969 he probably felt that negotiations would
lead only to more Western concessions.[111]

But in view of Brandt's initiatives, Kissinger decided that 'Berlin
became the key to the whole puzzle'.[112] The treaties negotiated by
Brandt had to be ratified by the Bundestag where his coalition had a
slim twelve-vote majority. Therefore, he could ill afford to provide
more ammunition for the Christian Democratic opposition which was
already charging him with a complete sellout of German interests in
the East. In Kissinger's view 'an agreement improving the security of
Berlin was the most tangible and convicing *quid pro quo* for Brandt's
controversial treaties ... It became clear that only with a Berlin
agreement would Brandt's Eastern treaties be ratified'.[113] A Berlin
agreement required the concurrence of the four wartime powers, and
this gave the Administration a major voice in the negotiating process,
regardless of how it started.

The linkages the Administration sought were formally established
at the NATO foreign minister's meeting in Brussels in December

1969. At the Administration's urging, the Allies (for the first time) made the holding of a European security conference conditional on Soviet diplomatic movement on Berlin, on progress in the FRG–Soviet negotiations, and on talks about mutual and balanced force reductions.[114] This decision was in line with Kissinger's concept of linkage in international relations – i.e., cooperation with the USSR in one area of detente cannot be divorced from progress in others.[115]

The Four-Power talks on Berlin began at the Ambassadorial level on 26 March 1970. The Allies believed that the talks represented a 'test case' regarding the seriousness of Soviet interest, both in detente and in long-term cooperation in Europe.

Being a political–diplomatic negotiation, the Quadripartite Talks gave the State Department the strongest hand in inter-agency discussions. State Department men staffed the Bonn Group and the Berlin Task Force, and its Assistant Secretary for European Affairs (Martin J. Hillenbrand) chaired the European Inter-Departmental Group which met as a sub-committee of the NSC. The Bonn Group met at the level of heads of the political sections of the American, French and British embassies in Bonn, and worked closely with the head of the German section of the Foreign Ministry of the FRG. Its objective was to form a consensus within the Alliance and draft position papers. Occasionally the Group met at the Ambassadorial level to discuss particularly difficult problems. The Berlin Task Force, under the direction of Hillenbrand, formulated states' recommendations for the negotiations. The position papers it drafted were forwarded to the European Inter-Departmental Group (which included representatives for the Pentagon, the CIA and the NSC staff), seeking to establish the basic American position for the Berlin negotiations.[116]

Kissinger controlled the process through the Senior Review Group which evaluated the agreed positions of the European Inter-Departmental Group. To establish the US objectives and develop options for the Berlin negotiations, Kissinger assigned the preparation of two National Security Study Memoranda (NSSM). NSSM 111, issued on 29 December 1970, represented the American draft of an Allied proposal for a Berlin agreement. It was presented (with modifications) to the Soviets on 8 February 1971. NSSM 136, dated 30 July 1971, consisted of specific concessions which could be granted to the USSR to obtain its agreement on such critical issues as access, visits across the Wall by Berliners, and recognition of Bonn's ties to West Berlin. During the course of the Berlin talks, these were the only major position papers to clear the complex bureaucratic machinery for Presidential approval.[117]

As Hillenbrand, who chaired the European Inter-Departmental Group, wrote, 'once initial Presidential approval had been obtained for US participation in the negotiations and the broad outlines of the US position to be followed, there was for a year practically no White House involvement in the actual formulations of positions'.[118] Kissinger's role became somewhat more pronounced in the later stages of the negotiations.

Once the basic US position (or change in it) had been formulated and approved, it was sent to the US Ambassador Kenneth Rush in Bonn. Ambassador Rush's direct access to President Nixon and Kissinger facilitated progress when the negotiations threatened to become deadlocked. Their instructions to the Ambassador frequently caught the State Department off guard. At the same time, the Ambassador kept Kissinger informed for his backchannel negotiations with Dobrynin and Bahr. Kissinger was particularly concerned with Bonn's propensity to move too fast and claim credit with the Soviets for all concessions made.[119] If Bonn succeeded in speeding up the Berlin negotiations' pace, it would have undermined Kissinger's efforts to implement linkage to influence the international behaviour of the USSR.

Brandt, having started the negotiations with Moscow and Warsaw in December 1969, decided to break the stalemate arising from Moscow's insistence that the FRG recognize the GDR by appointing Bahr to lead the second round of talks. Through Bahr and a letter to the President on 25 February 1970, he urged the Administration to speed up the Berlin talks so that they would not fall behind his negotiations with Moscow. The Administration, however, was reluctant to do so. Kissinger believed that Brandt wanted to speed up the Berlin talks so that he could use them for leverage in Moscow – and, more importantly, feared that if necessary Brandt would use the talks to 'shift the onus for any failure of his *Ostpolitik* to the [Administration].[120] This was not a new concern. In *The Troubled Partnership*, Kissinger had stated, 'to be sure, if German political leaders are determined to pursue [negotiations with the East], there is nothing we can do to prevent it. But we should make certain that the West cannot be blamed'.[121] Kissinger refused to make concessions in the Four-Power rights in Berlin for progress in the inter-German negotiations,[122] and recommended a slower pace.

Kissinger's position on the Berlin talks was influenced by considerations of linkage. This was demonstrated a number of times during the negotiations. On 10 February 1970, the USSR (which had stalled the Berlin talks) formally invited the Western Three to begin negotiations on 18 February. Bonn had just escalated the level of talks with Moscow, so Kissinger viewed the short deadline as a Soviet ploy to divide the FRG from its Allies by using two simultaneous sets of talks. He recommended to President Nixon that the Soviet proposal be accepted, but that the negotiations be phased to deprive Moscow of the opportunity. The Administration's position led (in Kissinger's words) 'to a careful minuet in which neither we nor our German ally could make our positions explicit'.[123] Indeed, as Chancellor Brandt reported, 'I never encountered what I have called "doubts" about our *Ostpolitik* in conversation with Nixon and Kissinger'. But in discussions with Kissinger during his visit to Washington in April, Brandt 'gained the impression ... that [Kissinger] would rather have taken personal charge of the delicate complex of East–West problems in its entirety'.[124]

For Kissinger, the fast pace of Brandt's negotiations with Moscow and Warsaw increased the leverage of the Administration. He believed once these negotiations were completed the Western position over Berlin 'would be vastly improved because the Soviets would be eager to see the Eastern treaties ratified'.[125] They therefore would probably be more willing to make concessions on Berlin. In addition, the bitter attacks on Brandt's initiatives by the Christian Democrats made it highly unlikely the Eastern treaties would be ratified unless the Berlin agreement was satisfactory.[126] In short, Brandt's slim parliamentary majority made it impossible for him to make concessions that did not have Washington's approval. This approval was given at the semi-annual meeting of the NATO Foreign Ministers in Rome on 26–27 May 1970. Brandt received the solid support of the Allies.

The Bonn–Moscow negotiations which had resumed on 12 May produced an agreement on 22 May on 'principles'. With the support of the Allies and a victory in a local election in June, Brandt decided to complete the negotiations with Moscow. Foreign Minister Scheel was sent to Moscow on 27 July to renegotiate the terms of the draft Treaty. On 12 August 1970, the Bonn–Moscow Treaty was signed by Brandt in Moscow. The provisions of the Treaty pledged both governments to a mutual renunciation of force as a means of settling disputes and to respect the territorial integrity of all states in Europe within their existing frontiers. The latter point was a matter of great controversy with the FRG, because it amounted to *de facto* recognition by Bonn of the division of Germany and to the loss of German territory east of the Oder–Neisse line.[127]

Recognizing this, and seeking to facilitate the ratification of the Treaty, the Soviets accepted two auxiliaries to it. The first, in a form of a letter from Brandt, provided a written safeguard of the German right to unity through peaceful means. The other consisted of an exchange of notes between the FRG and the three Western powers, reaffirming that the Treaty was not a Peace Treaty (ending the Second World War), and thus did not infringe on Allied rights in Berlin.[128]

In Moscow, the Chancellor informed the Soviet leaders the Treaty would not be submitted to the Bundestag for ratification until a satisfactory settlement of the Berlin problem had been reached. The linkage made by Brandt drew a negative reaction from the Allies, even though they had themselves sought it.[129] Kissinger, insisting on this linkage, viewed Brandt's move with concern because (as he told President Nixon) 'we were being set up [by Brandt] as the fall guy should the intricate set of negotiations collapse'. But he conceded that 'matters had gone too far for that. We had become the deciding element, though neither Moscow nor the Federal Republic was to understand this fully for five more months'.[130] At the urging of the Administration, the Allies responded by reiterating the European security conference that Moscow was seeking was conditional on the successful conclusion of the Berlin negotiations.

Kissinger's concern stemmed from tactical considerations and not the substantive provisions of the Bonn–Moscow Treaty. This was evident in his writings. In *The Troubled Partnership* he wrote, 'it is essential to recognize that acceptance by Germany of its eastern frontiers will have to be part of any responsible program for unification'. He explained, 'the perpetuation of German claims to the territories east of the Oder–Neisse line complicates progress on the issue of unification. It provides the Soviets with a convenient excuse for maintaining their hold on Eastern Germany; it cements Soviet relations with Eastern Europe'. But Kissinger also stressed, 'it is an important tactical question at what point the Federal Republic should renounce its claims'.[131] In August 1970, he felt that Brandt had renounced the German claims too soon, thus depriving the West of the opportunity to get any substantive Soviet concessions for recognizing the status quo in Europe. 'Bonn forswore its national claims in return for an improvement of the atmosphere and easing of inter-German contacts, which should never have been interrupted to begin with'.[132]

The Administration's preoccupation with linkage reappeared after the signing of the Bonn–Warsaw Treaty on 7 December 1970. On the eve of the signing ceremony, the chief spokesman for Brandt's government, Conrad Ahlers, told a press conference there was 'no juridicial connection' between ratification and a Berlin settlement. In view of the deadlock in the Berlin Talks, Washington was disturbed by Bonn's refusal directly to link the solution of the Berlin problem with the ratification of the Treaty. The disturbing fact was that Bonn's position appeared to be at variance with the position taken by Foreign Minister Scheel in private talks with the Western powers at the NATO ministerial meeting held the week before in Brussels. Scheel had assured them Brandt would not submit the Treaty to the Bundestag until there was a satisfactory agreement on Berlin. Bonn's position regarding the Bonn–Warsaw Treaty was no different than that pertaining to the Treaty with Moscow.[133]

The Chancellor fuelled the Administration's concern by pressing Washington, Paris, and London to turn the Berlin Talks into a continuous conference.[134] Brandt's suggestion to 'institutionalize' the Berlin Talks stemmed from his conviction (after his discussions with Brezhnev and Kosygin) that the Soviet leadership wanted a Berlin settlement before its party congress in March 1971. The Chancellor's idea was pushed in Washington by State Secretary Horst Ehmke. He informed Kissinger that Bonn no longer considered itself bound to wait for a formal directive from the Four Powers before beginning discussions with the GDR on issues such as access to Berlin. This was particularly upsetting to the Administration because, until then, Bonn and the Allies had agreed on a coordinated step-by-step approach. This approach called first for quadripartite agreement on the principles of a Berlin settlement and then for direct talks between the GDR and the FRG to work out the specific details of implementation. Kissinger was concerned about Brandt's independent approach, fearing it would jeopardize the Allied claim that only the Four Powers had jurisdiction over Berlin, and suspected that Brandt's need for a Berlin agreement might lead him to settle for less than what the Western Three deemed acceptable.[135]

The Administration's uneasiness with the growing tendency of Bonn to deal bilaterally with the USSR and other East European states was evident in President Nixon's Foreign Policy Report to

Congress. On 25 February 1971, he stated:

> the Western countries do not have identical national concerns and cannot be expected to agree automatically on priorities or solutions. Each ally is the best judge of its own national interest. But our principal objective should be to harmonize our policies and insure that our efforts for detente are complementary. A differentiated detente, limited to the USSR and certain Western allies but not others, would be illusory. It would cause strains among allies. It would turn the desire for detente into an instrument of political warfare. Far from contributing to reconciliation in Europe, it would postpone it indefinitely'.[136]

Nixon criticized Brandt for proceeding too rapidly and without adequate consultation with his Allies. Also indicated was the belief that Brandt had given much more than he had received in the treaties with Moscow and Warsaw.

The linkage between the Berlin Talks and US–Soviet detente had never been made explicit by the Administration. This linkage did become evident in May 1971, when the Soviets tried to exploit Kissinger's double backchannel system. The Soviet SALT negotiator, Vladimir Semenov, approached the US SALT negotiator, Gerard C. Smith, with an ABM agreement which Kissinger had rejected six weeks before in talks with Dobrynin. Unaware of Kissinger's move, Smith (believing the SALT talks were on the verge of a breakthrough) urged the Administration to accept it. Kissinger viewed this circumvention of the backchannel as a Soviet ploy to put public and Congressional pressure on the Administration to accept an old Soviet position. Kissinger exploited the Soviet need for an early agreement on Berlin; he delayed the agreement by instructing Ambassador Rush to postpone the 19 May 1971 meeting with the Soviet Ambassador. The SALT breakthrough came the next day, and Kissinger permitted the Berlin negotiations to proceed.[137]

The prospect for speedy agreement on Berlin looked good on 7 July when Soviet Ambassador Falin informed Ambassador Rush (and Bahr) that Moscow approved the concessions he had made in June. But Kissinger, after talks with Dobrynin in June, realized that Moscow was seeking additional concessions on Berlin and a European security conference by making the final agreement to a Moscow summit (tentatively scheduled for September 1971) conditional on the speedy conclusion of the Berlin talks. In early July, with no summit in sight, Kissinger again instructed Ambassador Rush to delay the talks. The objective in delaying the Berlin talks until after the announcement of his visit to Peking was to gain leverage that would prevent Moscow from using the opening to PRC as a pretext to launch a new round of crises. The Allies, seeing Moscow's willingness to make concessions, pressed the Administration to conclude the talks.

President Nixon announced Kissinger's visit to Peking on 15 July 1971, and Kissinger then permitted the Berlin talks to resume. An agreement was reached on 18 August, and the draft text was initialled on 23 August. The agreement on Berlin was facilitated by the opening to PRC. On the one hand Moscow accepted the Western conditions on Berlin in order to preclude its isolation in the West; the Administration, on the other, made concessions to prevent the disruption of US–Soviet detente by assuring Moscow that rapprochement with Peking was not an attempt to isolate the USSR. The Brandt cabinet unanimously approved the draft agreement on 25 August, and the Quadripartite Agreement was officially signed on 3 September 1971.[138]

Kissinger believed that the Quadripartite Agreement on Berlin demonstrated 'that calculations of national interest were better solvents of East–West deadlocks than appeals to a change of heart. Linkage was working even if rejected by theorists; we had kept SALT and Berlin in tandem and substantially achieved our goals'.[139] The USSR had for the first time guaranteed unimpeded access from FRG to West Berlin, and accepted the right of West Berliners to visit the GDR and East Berlin. Also accepted was the right of West Berliners to travel on FRG passports, and Bonn's right to represent West Berlin in international agreement bodies.

The Allies agreed to permit a Soviet consulate in West Berlin.[140] Kissinger viewed the concession (which he had made through the backchannel with the personal approval of President Nixon) as a face-saving device because 'it was of no help to the Soviet theory of separating West Berlin from the Federal Republic, since Soviet consulates exist[ed] in West German cities'.[141] In addition, the Allies and Bonn agreed to a reduction of the FRG's presence in West Berlin – i.e., the Federal President would no longer be elected in West Berlin (this activity had never been recognized by the Allies). In sum, the Quadripartite Agreement provided substantial improvement in the lives and safety of Berlin's population. Kissinger's critics even acknowledged that their fears were unfounded.[142]

CONCLUSION

The preceding discussion has demonstrated that Kissinger's response to Brandt's *Ostpolitik* was derived from views advanced in his writings, and was consistent with his global strategy. Kissinger's criticism of the Johnson Administration's urging of the Federal Republic to take the lead in dealing with East European countries indicated that he would not pursue a similar policy. His initial reaction to Brandt's initiatives was negative, confirming this was indeed the case. Kissinger did not seek to derail Brandt's policy because, as he admitted, the Administration had no alternative to offer for resolving the German problem. This implied if another viable option existed, the Administration might have opposed Brandt's *Ostpolitik*.

The view that German flexibility was indistinguishable from traditional nationalism could partly account for Kissinger's opposition to Brandt's *Ostpolitik*. Kissinger feared that in pursuing its traditional role as a bridge between East and West, the FRG could weaken the basis of its incorporation into Western institutions. This was evident in his memoranda to President Nixon recommending what actions the Administration should take in response to Brandt's policy. As a criticism of Johnson's response to *Ostpolitik*, Kissinger predicted that as the FRG's activity toward the East increased other West European countries would draw closer together while increasing their own contact with the USSR, resulting in a weakened Atlantic cohesion. Kissinger's prediction was substantiated by the immediate British and French endorsement of Brandt's initiatives, and West European impatience toward pursuing the Soviet proposal for a European Security conference.

For Kissinger, Berlin was the touchstone of Western policy. He maintained that the acceptance of the Berlin Wall would demoralize the Federal Republic and undermine American foreign policy by demonstrating to the world the irresistible nature of the Communist advance. Brandt's determination to pursue *Ostpolitik* demonstrated the extent of the FRG's demoralization. Kissinger's actions during the Berlin 'mini'-crisis in early 1969 revealed that he was prepared to demonstrate America's resolution to use its strength, thus enhancing US credibility which he viewed as an essential requisite for a successful foreign policy.

In 1968, Kissinger found it 'hard to visualize a "deal" between the Soviet Union and Europe which would jeopardize [American] interests without jeopardizing European interest first'.[143] Brandt's *Ostpolitik* compromised this conclusion. If Kissinger had failed to link ratification of the Moscow and Warsaw Treaties and a European security conference with Soviet concessions on Berlin, *Ostpolitik* would have produced such a deal. The formal recognition of the status quo in Europe through *Ostpolitik* would have precluded the Soviet concessions to guarantee unimpeded access from FRG to West Berlin and accept the FRG's right to represent West Berlin in international agreements and bodies. The Soviet guarantee deprived the USSR of an issue (access to Berlin) which could have further undermined American credibility by repeatedly demonstrating the 'unrealistic' nature of the US commitment to defend Berlin.

In his writings, Kissinger observed that if the FRG's political leaders were determined to take the lead in dealing with the East, there was nothing the US could do to prevent it. But, he warned, the US should make certain that the West would not be blamed for the probable consequences of the FRG's policies. This warning is reiterated in Kissinger's memorandum to President Nixon when Brandt publicly linked ratification of the Moscow Treaty to a satisfactory settlement on Berlin. Kissinger, who had insisted on this linkage, feared that the failure of *Ostpolitik* could be blamed on the US, thereby exacerbating the tensions between the Allies. Kissinger had no objections to the FRG's recognition of its eastern frontiers as long as the West extracted Soviet concessions for this recognition.

Allied acceptance of the Administration's proposal to put the Four-Power talks and a European security conference on a slow track demonstrated that Kissinger was correct in stating '[a]s long as NATO strategy was nuclear and the United States had no obvious alternative to nuclear retaliation, [the] Allies were ready to acquiesce in the hegemonial position of the United States'.[144] The established linkages proved that Kissinger was prepared to use American military dominance to control the Allied initiatives toward the East to protect American interests as he defined them. On the other hand, Brandt's *Ostpolitik* corroborated Kissinger's view that 'because an isolated strategy is indeed impossible, allies have unprecedented scope for the pursuit of their own objectives. And the more detente – real or imaginary – proceeds, the more momentum these tendencies will gather'.[145]

Kissinger's diplomatic moves during the Four-Power talks and the timing of Soviet concessions verified the linkage between Berlin and US–Soviet detente despite the Administration's reluctance to make this explicit. On the one hand, the timing of Soviet concessions corroborated Kissinger's view that US–PRC rapprochement would make the USSR more responsive to American demands. On the other, the timing of Kissinger's concessions indicated that he sought to prevent the disruption of US–Soviet detente by assuring Moscow that US–PRC rapprochement was not an attempt to isolate the USSR.

10 Conclusions

The aim of this study was to examine the consistency between Kissinger's West European policy and the conceptions advanced in his academic writings. Consistency was examined in the context of the linkage between Kissinger's Soviet policy and Alliance policy. The policies Kissinger formulated and implemented derived from his models of stable and revolutionary international systems and the notion of limits. Kissinger's world view was dominated by his conception of peace which he defined as *stability* based on an equilibrium of forces within a legitimate international order. Intellectually, the notion of limits was the touchstone of Kissinger's conservatism, and emanated from the cool calculation of power upon which US–Soviet detente and US–West European relations rested. The consistency between those conceptions and Kissinger's policies has been demonstrated throughout this study.

Kissinger's models of stable and revolutionary international systems – upon which his perception of the contemporary international system was based – provided the intellectual underpinnings of his global strategy. Kissinger viewed the contemporary international system as revolutionary because it contained two revolutionary powers, the USSR and the PRC. These powers reject the notion that harmony between different social systems can exist and are committed to a transformation of the existing international order. For Kissinger, the revolutionary character of the international system is further complicated by: (a) the large increase in the number of new nations that inject the revolutionary fervour that gained them independence into their foreign policy; and (b) the advent of nuclear weapons which, while making international relations truly global for the first time, imposed limits on statesmens' ability to relate power to national objectives.

The conception of peace defined as stability dominated Kissinger's world view, leading him to concentrate on superpower relations. Only the US and the USSR possess the preponderant military power that could transform the existing international system or destroy the world if each unilaterally attempted to do so. Kissinger felt no other country or group of countries could challenge the military preeminence of the superpowers. Rather, the gap in military strength between the superpowers and the rest of the world would increase. He recognized military bipolarity as a source of rigidity in foreign policy because the existing balance of power between the superpowers is both precarious and inflexible making a gain for one side appear as an absolute loss for the other. According to Kissinger, US–Soviet relations were complicated due to the need of each superpower to strengthen its security *vis-à-vis* the other, maintain its preeminence among its Allies, and increase its influence among the uncommitted. He maintained that some of these objectives were incompatible therefore choices had to be made.

Kissinger recognized that military bipolarity encouraged political multipolarity. Allies, convinced their defence is in the interest of their senior partner, see no need to purchase its support by acquiescence in its policies therefore making it extremely difficult, if not impossible, for the superpowers to maintain preeminence in their respective Alliances. The new nations, feeling protected by the rivalry of the superpowers, made bolder assertions of national will. Kissinger saw the new nations only as pawns in a deadly game played by the superpowers, but agreed that their integration into the international structure was essential to establish an equilibrium of forces. In establishing an equilibrium of forces, the cohesion of the Alliances was essential as well. Coinciding with the nuclear stalemate which precluded the use of force in the case of the superpowers, political multipolarity reduced foreign policy rigidity without guaranteeing stability.

Stability would result from the establishment of a legitimate (or stable) international system that could contain the clash of national interests, power rivalries, and ideological antagonisms from engulfing the world in a nuclear holocaust. Such a system had two structural imperatives: (a) an equilibrium of military power; and (b) acceptance by the superpowers of certain fundamental principles of legitimate and illegitimate state action in the international system. Neither imperative was sufficient by itself; for Kissinger, unless a stable international order can be achieved the quest for peace will be self-defeating.

Stability based on an equilibrium of forces was conceivable only when the international system accepted that certain principles could not be compromised even for the sake of peace. A stable international order does not eliminate conflicts, rather it limits their scope. Kissinger rejected the conception of peace as the avoidance of war because it left the international system at the mercy of revolutionary powers. Limited wars are 'necessary' to maintain the existing international structure. In short, Kissinger believed that the primary objective of nations is not to preserve peace (avoid war), but to achieve stability, and this required both military strength and the will to use it.

A stable international system does not eliminate conflict, but it could prevent a nuclear holocaust since the superpowers who have the capability to wage full-scale nuclear war would reach an agreement on the nature of workable arrangements and the permissible aims and methods of foreign policy. This agreement between a status quo power and a revolutionary power was facilitated by nuclear weapons (a conservative force) which, by imposing limits on statesmen, necessitated self-restraint. According to Kissinger the Soviet leadership, regardless of its commitment to transform the international system, shared the view that strategic parity served as a deterrent against irresponsible behaviour in world affairs. This recognition of mutual vulnerability led to US–Soviet detente.

For Kissinger, US–Soviet detente was the first step in achieving his ultimate goal of the establishment of a stable international system. In establishing this system, Kissinger subordinated the long-standing relationship with the Allies to America's strategic interest in maintaining its global position. Kissinger believed that the highest obligation was neither the Alliance nor the preservation of Western values, but American security interests and ultimately national survival because, unless the US survived, no principles would be realized. The cohesion of the Alliance was an essential requisite to Kissinger's Soviet policy, but he felt that damage to the US–West European relationship (resulting from its subordination to US–Soviet detente) could be controlled since the Allies have more to gain from NATO than the US.

Kissinger's Soviet policy was based on (a) the strategic nuclear balance which served as a deterrent against irresponsible behaviour by the superpowers; and (b) the Sino–Soviet split which broke the ideological unity of Communism, thereby prompting the revolutionary powers toward greater participation in the international system to gain leverage over each other. The willingness of the revolutionary powers to seek greater participation in the international system dovetailed with Kissinger's desire to conduct a non-ideological foreign policy. He did not believe the USSR and the PRC would abandon Communism, but given the nuclear stalemate and the Sino–Soviet split, he was convinced they were ready to contribute toward establishing a stable international system. Kissinger was not interested in the ideological dispute between the USSR and the PRC. But he shared the PRC's need to check Soviet geopolitical ambitions. The US–PRC rapprochement was a means of gaining leverage over the USSR to make it more willing to make concessions to American interest. By preceding US–Soviet detente, it increased momentum and provided concrete substance to Kissinger's concept of an emerging multipolar world, and his opposition to an ideologically oriented foreign policy. This triangular relationship emerged as Kissinger's global strategy.

The concept of linkage was a basic postulate of Kissinger's global strategy. Kissinger linked the USSR's need for technology and concern with US–PRC rapprochement to issues of concern to the US, specifically Vietnam and the Middle East. He also linked the Soviet desire for ratification of the Moscow and Warsaw Treaties and a European security conference to Soviet concessions on Berlin and MBFR. This study demonstrates that in some instances linkage worked. The SALT agreements and the Quadripartite Agreement on Berlin were in large part a result of Soviet willingness to make concessions to preclude its isolation due to US–PRC rapprochement.

The central element in Kissinger's global strategy was the US–Soviet relationship which rested on the strategic arms limitations talks (SALT), and economic cooperation. SALT was facilitated by the mutual US–Soviet perceptions of strategic parity, the mutual vulnerability it produced, and technological advances that made verification by national technical means possible. Economic cooperation rested exclusively on the weakness of the Soviet economy. The SALT agreements (the ABM Treaty and the Interim Agreement) were consistent with Kissinger's goal of establishing a stable international system since they produced one of the two structural imperatives of the system, the equilibrium of military power.

The ABM Treaty and the Interim Agreement made possible the agreement on Basic Principles of US–Soviet relations, and the Agreement on Prevention of Nuclear War which placed the US–Soviet relationship on a broader foundation. The Basic Principles and the Agreement on the Prevention of Nuclear War were seen by Kissinger as a first step in achieving the second structural imperative of a stable international order – i.e., superpower agreement on what constituted legitimate state action in the international arena.

Kissinger's models for stable and revolutionary international systems and the notion of limits, that led him to concentrate on superpower relations, were also the foundations of his West

European policy. Kissinger subordinated the US–West European relationship to US–Soviet detente in order to establish a stable international system that could prevent a nuclear war and assure national survival. He was not prepared to subordinate the requirements of the overall strategic balance to Alliance policy because, unless survival was assured, no Western principles could be realized. He recognized that the cohesion of the Alliance was essential to maintain an equilibrium of forces, but felt that US–Soviet detente would not split the Alliance since the Allies had more to gain than the US. According to Kissinger independent initiatives by the Allies (Brandt's *Ostpolitik* being the primary example) were a greater threat to Allied unity; the USSR could have driven a wedge between the US and its Allies by playing to West European attitudes for reduced tensions while remaining intransigent on global issues of concern to the US. By achieving selective detente, the USSR would have precluded the first steps in establishing a stable international system.

The West European policies Kissinger formulated and executed were derived from conclusions drawn from analysing the Alliance's dilemmas – i.e., strategic doctrine, nuclear weapons control, and West European unity. Kissinger concluded that those dilemmas were caused by the linkage of sovereignty with nuclear weapons which, by transforming the nature of alliances, imposed limits on statesmen's ability to resolve them as long as NATO remained composed of sovereign states. In his view, the risk of nuclear war could not be reliably combined with the key attribute of sovereignty, the unilateral right of a sovereign state to alter its strategic and political views. This view led Kissinger to criticize the Kennedy and Johnson Administrations, not for failing to resolve the dilemmas, but for their propensity to propose solutions (multilateral force and the doctrine of flexible response) that confused the issues and exacerbated discord in the Alliance. Kissinger-the-policymaker did not raise the issues of nuclear weapons control or strategic doctrine, and in this sense he was consistent.

The consistency between the Nixon Administration's policies and Kissinger's conceptions have been demonstrated throughout this study. The doctrine of strategic sufficiency advanced by Kissinger, although a unilateral change of US strategy, was not an attempt by the Administration to replace the NATO strategy of flexible response. By incorporating the concepts of superiority and parity, the ambiguity of the doctrine permitted the US to continue the deployment of nuclear weapons to sustain the credibility of its NATO commitments while negotiating strategic arms limitation with the USSR. West European doubts about the credibility of the American commitment to defend West Europe were overcome by:

(a) the Administration's opposition to sharp cutbacks in strategic programmes
(b) its willingness to 'consult' the Allies regarding SALT (and the Agreement on the Prevention of Nuclear War) while rejecting Soviet demands to discuss forward based systems (FBS) and the British and French nuclear forces
(c) its willingness to consider the views of the Allies on issues directly affecting their security – i.e., FBS and MBFR
(d) its opposition to the Mansfield Resolutions calling for unilateral troop reduction in Europe
(e) its acceptance of the nuclear forces of France and Britain, and
(f) its acquiescence in the Nuclear Planning Group's decision for the demonstrative use of tactical nuclear weapons.

NATO's strategic dilemmas were not at the top of Kissinger's agenda, nor for that matter, at the top of the agenda of the West European leaders who shared his view the dilemmas could not be resolved given the limits imposed by the linkage of sovereignty with nuclear weapons. SALT did not resolve the strategic dilemmas of NATO, but the Administration's actions reassured the Allies who viewed SALT as consonant with their efforts to secure a more general relaxation of East–West tensions. The NPG decision regarding the 'demonstrative use' of tactical nuclear weapons did not resolve the issue, but by acquiescing to the decision the Administration fulfilled the West European need for reassurance. For Kissinger, the NPG decision demonstrated the West's lack of political will to the USSR. To rectify this dangerous perception, Kissinger ordered the nuclear alert during the Yom Kippur War to demonstrate Western resolution to use of its military strength to maintain an equilibrium of forces which was essential to stability.

Limitations imposed by the linkage of sovereignty with nuclear weapons also affected the role of conventional forces in the defence of Western Europe. This issue was not resolved by the defeat of the Mansfield Resolutions. Recognizing the controversial nature of the issue, Kissinger did not really pressure the Allies to strengthen their conventional forces. He simply accepted the European Defence

Improvement Programme (EDIP) undertaken by the Eurogroup in order to assist the Administration in defeating unilateral troop reductions. The EDIP was facilitated by the Administration's approach to burden-sharing which emphasized additional European expenditures for improving Allied conventional forces rather than financial gimmicks to pay for the stationing of US troops in Europe.

Kissinger's position on unilateral troop reductions was not simply a gesture of NATO solidarity. US–Soviet strategic parity necessitated a strong conventional NATO capability. The 'decoupling', by means of mutual deterrence of strategic nuclear forces from a credible military role in Europe and the continued escalation uncertainties associated with the use of tactical nuclear weapons, argued against reductions in US troop levels in Europe. Kissinger sought to reassure the Allies – but, more importantly, to maintain the equilibrium of military power in Europe to underpin US–Soviet detente. In this issue, his West European policy and Soviet policy were mutually reinforcing; in addition, unilateral troop reductions would have further complicated the control function Kissinger sought to exercise through NATO.

The charge Kissinger undermined West European unity is not supported by the evidence. By not making a federal Europe (which was opposed by Britain and France) and the British entry into the EEC its direct objectives, the Administration facilitated the enlargement of the Community. The neglect of the EEC Commission was a calculated action by Kissinger, reflecting the linkage between US–Soviet detente and his West European policy. He was not prepared to increase the power of an institution which would challenge American primacy in the economic and political fields where temptations for independent initiative are great, and penalties for non-cooperation are almost non-existent. A stronger EEC Commission would have further complicated the control function Kissinger sought to exercise through NATO by challenging his Soviet policy – and, in particular, his efforts to use trade to influence the USSR's international behaviour.

The Administration did not actively oppose the strengthening of the Commission. It left West Europeans to formulate proposals that could be implemented (an unlikely prospect given French and British opposition to enhancing the power of the Commission). Kissinger's actions during the crisis generated by President Nixon's New Economic Policy demonstrated his willingness to 'pay the [economic] price' for European unity. His actions, however, did not avert the charge that he weakened the Alliance by failing to dominate international economic policy.

This study corroborates Kissinger's view that as long as NATO strategy is nuclear and the US has no other alternative to nuclear retaliation, the Allies are ready to acquiesce in the US's hegemonial position. The Allies, although reluctantly, accepted Kissinger's recommendation purposely to put the Berlin talks and a European security conference on a slow track. It also demonstrates that Kissinger was correct in maintaining that the impossibility of an isolated strategy gives the Allies unprecedented scope to pursue their own objectives, a tendency that increases as detente – real or imaginary – proceeds. Chancellor Brandt informed the Administration of the initiatives he would take, but left no doubt he would take them regardless of the Administration's views.

Today the Alliance is confronted with the same dilemmas – i.e., strategic doctrine, nuclear weapons control, the role of tactical nuclear weapons, the role of conventional forces, and West European unity. In the US, demands continue for unilateral troop reductions, a new nuclear strategy, increased defence spending by the Allies, and the removal of EEC restrictions on American products. In Western Europe, doubts about the credibility of the American commitment increase, as does the fear that American recklessness could start a nuclear war; the Allies demand US reassurance while pursuing their independent initiatives. In short, Kissinger's argument – that the dilemmas could not be resolved as long as the Alliance remained composed of sovereign states – is still valid.

Notes

1 Introduction

1. John G. Stoessinger, *Henry Kissinger: The Anguish of Power* (1976) p. 137.
2. Henry Kissinger, *The Troubled Partnership* (1965) p. 40; Stephen R. Graubard, *Kissinger: Portrait of a Mind* (1973) p. 205.
3. Stoessinger, *Henry Kissinger*, pp. 137–8; George W. Ball *Diplomacy for a Crowded World* (1976) pp. 155–6; Peter W. Dickson, *Kissinger and the Meaning of History* (1978) pp. 113–14; Jeffry R. Bendel 'Scholar Versus Statesman: The Record of Henry Kissinger; The United States and Western Europe', Ph.D. dissertation, University of Massachusetts (1982); Richard A. Falk, *What's Wrong with Henry Kissinger's Foreign Policy* (1974) pp. 5–6; David Landau, *Kissinger: The Uses of Power* (1972) pp. 114–15; Zbigniew Brzezinski, 'US Foreign Policy: The Search for Focus', *Foreign Affairs*, 51 (1973) 708–27; Also by Brzezinski, 'Recognizing the Crisis', *Foreign Policy* 17 (Winter 1974–75) 63–74; 'The Deceptive Structure of Peace', *Foreign Policy* 14 (Spring 1974): 35–55. 'The Balance of Power Delusion'. *Foreign Policy* 7 (Summer 1972)', 54–59. 'Half Past Nixon', Foreign Policy 3 (Summer 1971) 3–21. Stanley Hoffmann, 'Choices', *Foreign* 12, (1973) 3–42; J. Robert Schaetzel, 'Some European Questions for Dr Kissinger', *Foreign Policy*, 12 (1973) 66–74.
4. Kissinger, *The Troubled Partnership*, p. 5; Graubard, *Kissinger*, p. 203.
5. Warren G. Nutter, *Kissinger's Grand Design* (1975) p. 10.
6. Bob Woodward and Carl Bernstein, *The Final Days* (1976): the authors show the similarities between President Nixon and Kissinger.
7. Oriana Fallaci, 'Kissinger: An Interview', *The New Republic*, 167 (16 December 1972) pp. 20–1; Danielle Hunebelle, *Dear Henry* (New York: 1972) p. 43. According to Hunebelle, Kissinger actually regarded Richard Nixon as a personal confidante during his early years at the White House. Kissinger is quoted as saying 'when you're under pressure and in control of yourself, you really feel like opening up sometimes. So, at night, I often go up and chat with the President'.
8. Dickson, *Kissinger and the Meaning of History*, p. 146.
9. Marvin Kalb and Bernard Kalb, *Kissinger* (1974) p. 15.
10. Kalb and Kalb, *Kissinger*, pp. 15–16; Landau, *Kissinger*, p. 88.
11. Henry Kissinger, *A World Restored: Europe after Napoleon* (1973) pp. 326–7.
12. Kissinger, *White House Years* (1979) p. 12.
13. Kalb and Kalb, *Kissinger*, p. 89; the Kalb brothers state that President Nixon 'wanted to be his own Secretary of State; therefore he appointed the best front man he could find to run the State

Department . . . and then appointed the finest mind in foreign policy that he could find anywhere to work exclusively for him'. See also Kissinger, *White House Years*, p. 11.

14. Richard M. Nixon, *The Memoirs of Richard Nixon*, vol. 1 (1978) p. 422. Landau, *Kissinger* (1972) pp. 92–3. Landau states that the divergence between the two men on concrete policy issues was not that great. Many of Nixon's private views on foreign policy were not measurably different from Kissinger's. Falk, *What's Wrong with Henry Kissinger's Foreign Policy*, p. 7. Falk states: 'I believe that Nixon and Kissinger shared an interpretation of the dynamics of the state system and of the main targets of diplomatic opportunity that existed in 1969. I do not mean that Kissinger was always in agreement with the tactical judgments of Nixon . . . While Nixon's view of the state system seems indistinguishable from that of Kissinger, Kissinger's diplomatic flair has probably added a measure, perhaps a decisive measure, of effectiveness to what Nixon might have achieved with "ordinary" as distinct from "exemplary" execution of his policies'. Roger Morris, *Uncertain Greatness: Henry Kissinger and American Foreign Policy* (1977) p. 3. Morris reports that from the beginning aides to both men were anxious to cite differences between them, but no one was able to document major distinctions in their approach to policy. 'I'll never know where one ended and the other began', admitted an official closest to their decisions according to Morris.

15. Nixon, *The Memoirs of Richard Nixon*, p. 423.

16. Kalb and Kalb, *Kissinger*, p. 91; Landau, *Kissinger*, p. 142.

17. Morris, *Uncertain Greatness*, pp. 91–2. Morris reports that as Kissinger's power and fame widened, the system became less and less used. The most important decisions were taken without the benefit of NSSM options.

18. Stoessinger, *Henry Kissinger*, p. 210.

19. Kissinger, *White House Years*, pp. 28–9; Kissinger states that the President 'excluded his Secretary of State from his first meeting with Soviet Ambassador Anatoly Dobrynin on February 17, 1969, [and that this] practice, established before [his] own position was settled, continued: Throughout his term, when a State visitor was received in the Oval Office by Nixon for a lengthy discussion, I was the only other American present'. Kissinger also states that President Nixon asked him to inform Ambassador Dobrynin when the Secretary of State went beyond the President's thinking. But Kissinger acknowledges that this practice created problems when policies were implemented. U. Alexis Johnson and Jef Olivarius McAllister, *The Right Hand of Power* (1984) pp. 552–3. Ambassador Johnson makes the same points as Kissinger.

20. Bruce Mazlish, *Kissinger: The European Mind in American Policy* (1976) p. 215.

21. Kissinger, *White House Years*, p. 48; Morris, *Uncertain Greatness*, p. 145. Morris reports that by the early spring of 1969 (and even after) Kissinger had acquired, through mutual interest a near monopoly on the time, attention, and respect of the President on all matters of

foreign policy. His was literally the first and final word on policy
decisions.

22. Graubard, *Kissinger*, pp. 272–3.
23. Stoessinger, *Henry Kissinger*, p. 37. Stoessinger claimed: 'What *can*
be proved, however, is that the intellectual convictions that Kissinger
developed a quarter of a century ago survived almost unchanged and
were applied by him in a conscious and deliberate effort to pursue his
vision of a stable world order'; Mazlish, *Kissinger*, pp. 233–4; 287.
Mazlish concludes: 'there is no question that [Kissinger] has a
coherent, consistent concept behind his various policies', but maintains that: 'there is a definite gap between what Kissinger the
academic wrote and what Kissinger the adviser to the President did'.
He acknowledges, however, that 'most of Kissinger's writings were on
Europe, and most of his foreign policy actions in non-European
areas'. This recognition in my view weakens Mazlish's conclusion
about the gap between concepts and policy with respect to policies
toward Western Europe.
24. Dickson, *Kissinger and the Meaning of History*, pp. 118–19.
25. Graubard, *Kissinger*, pp. xi–xvi; also see Dickson, *Kissinger and the
Meaning of History*, pp. 83–116; Mazlish, *Kissinger*, pp. 177–86.
26. Dickson, *Kissinger and the Meaning of History*, pp. 83–116. Dickson
recognized the importance of the doctrine of limits in Kissinger's
political philosophy, and devoted a chapter to it. Mazlish, *Kissinger*,
pp. 177–86; Mazlish provides a brief examination of the notion of
limits.
27. Mazlish, *Kissinger*, pp. 177; 180–2.
28. Dickson, *Kissinger and the Meaning of History*, p. 100.
29. Mazlish, *Kissinger*, pp. 12–13. Mazlish maintains that Kissinger 'had a
strong hand in our policies and actions ... Whatever the specific case
or country, Kissinger has subsumed his position toward it under his
larger concern for international stablity and order. All of his policies,
just as is his own personality, are linked in covert or dramatic fashion
to this overriding concern. Above even this concern, or, rather,
haunting it, is the concern with the nuclear threat. For Kissinger, if
international stability and order fail to hold, if the center gives, there
is the real and constant possibility of holocaust'.
30. Mazlish, *Kissinger*, p. 234. Mazlish states that: 'the overriding theme
... is Kissinger's constant concern with the Soviet Union. For him,
only the Soviets are a realistic threat to international stability, and a
potential source of holocaust'. Landau, *Kissinger*, p. 104. Stoessinger,
Henry Kissinger, p. 214. Stoessinger stated: 'I believe that Henry
Kissinger was right when he declared that the overriding reason for
detente with Russia was the avoidance of a nuclear catastrophe. I
believe that if such a world cataclysm has become less likely, this is in
no small measure to be credited to Kissinger.'
31. Kissinger, *American Foreign Policy* (1969) p. 75; Dickson, *Kissinger
and the Meaning of History*, p. 119.
32. Mazlish *Kissinger*, pp. 271–3. Mazlish claims that Kissinger's desired
purpose for the power he secured was to help establish a world of

stability and order. Graubard, *Kissinger*, p. 274. Graubard states that
Kissinger's object was to secure a stable international order. That
purpose transcended all others; in his mind, it was the necessary
precondition of peace. Landau, *Kissinger*, pp. 12–13. Landau argues
that the central issue in Kissinger's political life has been the
establishment of a stable international order. Stoessinger, *Henry
Kissinger*, pp. 37; 45. Stoessinger argued that '[Kissinger's] objective
above all, was to secure a stable international order. All specific
policies were subordinated by him to this fundamental quest'.

33. Henry A. Kissinger, *Nuclear Weapons and Foreign Policy* (1969) pp.
     220–3; Dickson, *Kissinger and the Meaning of History*, pp. 20–1.
34. Graubard, *Kissinger*, pp. ix; 273.
35. Dickson, *Kissinger and the Meaning of History*, p. 81.
36. Dickson, *Kissinger and the Meaning of History*, p. 82.
37. Dickson, *Kissinger and the Meaning of History*, pp. 90; 95; 100; 103.
38. Dickson, *Kissinger and the Meaning of History*, pp. 115–18; 120; 125;
     143.
39. Mazlish, *Kissinger*, p. 11.
40. Mazlish, *Kissinger*, pp. 177; 180–2.
41. Mazlish, *Kissinger*, pp. 233–4; 271–3; 282; 287.
42. Nutter, *Kissinger's Grand Design*, pp. 7–8.
43. Nutter, *Kissinger's Grand Design*, pp. 15–16; 25.
44. Nutter, *Kissinger's Grand Design*, p. 16.
45. Falk, *What's Wrong with Henry Kissinger's Foreign Policy*, p. 3.
46. Falk, *What's Wrong with Henry Kissinger's Foreign Policy*, p. 6.
47. Falk, *What's Wrong with Henry Kissinger's Foreign Policy*, p. 7.
48. Falk, *What's Wrong with Henry Kissinger's Foreign Policy*, p. 14.
49. Falk, *What's Wrong with Henry Kissinger's Foreign Policy*, p. 17.
     Given the discussion in the preceding paragraph, Falk here seems to
     contradict himself. However, no contradiction exists if one keeps in
     mind that Falk considers the 'extreme patterns of injustice in the
     Third World' where 'exploitation and mass misery are the norms of
     existence' as revolutionary threats.
50. Morris, *Uncertain Greatness*, p. 70.
51. Morris, *Uncertain Greatness*, p. 285.
52. Morris, *Uncertain Greatness*, p. 298.
53. Morris, *Uncertain Greatness*, p. 300.
54. Landau, *Kissinger*, p. 12.
55. Landau, *Kissinger*, p. 103.
56. Landau, *Kissinger*, p. 104.
57. Landau, *Kissinger*, p. 104.
58. Landau, *Kissinger*, p. 125.
59. Landau, *Kissinger*, pp. 125–6.
60. Stoessinger, *Henry Kissinger*, p. 37.
61. Stoessinger, *Henry Kissinger*, p. 111.
62. Stoessinger, *Henry Kissinger*, p. 214.
63. Stoessinger, *Henry Kissinger*, p. 214.
64. Stoessinger, *Henry Kissinger*, p. 134.
65. Stoessinger, *Henry Kissinger*, p. 144.

66. Mazlish, *Kissinger*, pp. 233–4.
67. Jeffry R. Bendel, 'Scholar Versus Statesman: The Record of Henry Kissinger; The United States and Western Europe', p. 143.

2 The Intellectual Underpinnings of Kissinger's Global Strategy

1. Cited by James E. Dougherty and Robert L Pfaltzfraff Jr (eds), *Contending Theories of International Relations* (1981) p. 111.
2. Kissinger, *A World Restored*, p. 1.
3. Kissinger, *A World Restored*, p. 1.
4. Kissinger, *A World Restored*, p. 1.
5. Kissinger, *A World Restored*, p. 1.
6. Kissinger, *A World Restored*, p. 1.
7. Kissinger, *A World Restored*, p. 2.
8. Kissinger, *A World Restored*, p. 2. Landau, *Kissinger*, p. 28.
9. Kissinger, *A World Restored*, p. 3.
10. Kissinger, *A World Restored*, p. 172.
11. Kissinger, *A World Restored*, p. 2.
12. Kissinger, *A World Restored*, p. 145.
13. Kissinger, *A World Restored*, p. 145.
14. Kissinger, *A World Restored*, p. 2.
15. Kissinger, *A World Restored*, pp. 2–3.
16. Kissinger, *A World Restored*, p. 3.
17. Kissinger, *A World Restored*, p. 3.
18. Kissinger, *A World Restored*, p. 5.
19. Kissinger, *A World Restored*, p. 114.
20. Kissinger, *A World Restored*, p. 79.
21. Kissinger, *A World Restored*, p. 2.
22. Kissinger, *A World Restored*, p. 169.
23. Kissinger, *A World Restored*, p. 16.
24. Kissinger, *A World Restored*, p. 120.
25. Kissinger, *A World Restored*, p. 138.
26. Mazlish, *Kissinger*, p. 234.
27. Kissinger, *Nuclear Weapons and Foreign Policy* p. 3; Mazlish, *Kissinger*, pp. 173; 175. Mazlish states: 'Most importantly, Kissinger views our time as a revolutionary one in which the revolutionary forces of Hitlerism and communism have supplanted the nineteenth-century French revolutionaries and Napoleon . . . in 1955 the revolutionaries were perceived by Kissinger as the Sino–Soviet bloc, which is determined to prevent the establishment of an equilibrium'.
28. Kissinger, *Nuclear Weapons and Foreign Policy*, p. 3.
29. Kissinger, *American Foreign Policy* p. 53; *The Necessity for Choice* (1961) p. 2; Falk, *What's Wrong With Henry Kissinger's Foreign Policy*, p. 14. Falk states that in *The Necessity for Choice, Kissinger's analysis showed a shift* in emphasis from the revolutionary actor to the revolutionary situation.
30. Kissinger, *American Foreign Policy*, p. 80.
31. Kissinger, *American Foreign Policy*, p. 80.

214 *Notes*

32. Kissinger, *American Foreign Policy*, p. 81. Stoessinger, *Henry Kissinger*, p. 220.
33. Kissinger, *Nuclear Weapons and Foreign Policy*, p. 4
34. Kissinger, *American Foreign Policy*, p. 85.
35. Kissinger, *American Foreign Policy*, p. 61.
36. Kissinger, *American Foreign Policy*, p. 61.
37. Kissinger, *American Foreign Policy*, p. 60.
38. Kissinger, *American Foreign Policy*, p. 60. Kissinger states that: 'China [PRC] gained more in real military power through the acquisition of nuclear weapons than if it had conquered all of Southeast Asia. If the Soviet Union had occupied Western Europe but had remained without nuclear weapons, it would be less powerful than it is now with its existing nuclear arsenal within its present borders'.
39. Kissinger, *American Foreign Policy*, p. 55.
40. Kissinger, *American Foreign Policy*, p. 55.
41. Kissinger, *Nuclear Weapons and Foreign Policy*, pp. 2–3.
42. Kissinger, *American Foreign Policy*, pp. 55–6.
43. Kissinger, *American Foreign Policy*, p. 56.
44. Kissinger, *American Foreign Policy*, p. 56.
45. Kissinger, *American Foreign Policy*, p. 56.
46. Kissinger, *American Foreign Policy*, p. 56.
47. Kissinger, *American Foreign Policy*, pp. 56–7.
48. Kissinger, *American Foreign Policy*, pp. 56–7.
49. Kissinger, *American Foreign Policy*, p. 57.
50. Kissinger, *American Foreign Policy*, p. 58.
51. Kissinger, *American Foreign Policy*, p. 58.
52. Kissinger, *American Foreign Policy*, p. 75; *The Troubled Partnership*, p. 169. Dickson, *Kissinger and the Meaning of History*, p. 119.
53. Kissinger, *American Foreign Policy*, p. 75; *The Troubled Partnership*, p. 169.
54. Kissinger, *The Troubled Partnership*, p. 106.
55. Kissinger, *American Foreign Policy*, p. 72.
56. Kissinger, *American Foreign Policy*, p. 72.
57. Kissinger, *American Foreign Policy*, p. 79.
58. Kissinger, *American Foreign Policy*, p. 79.

3 Kissinger's Global Strategy: a Triangular Relationship?

1. *The New York Times*, 13 October 1974.
2. Seyom Brown, *The Crises of Power: An Interpretation of United States Foreign Policy During the Kissinger Years* (1979) pp. 16–17.
3. Brown, *The Crises of Power*, pp. 16–17. David Landau, *Kissinger* pp. 103–4. Landau states that: 'Kissinger has supervised a policy that is remarkably rhythmic in pattern. There is an exquisite internal harmony, a self-contained consistency in it that bears the unmistakable stamp of its creator. In order to grasp the Kissinger policy, one would do well to envision the working of a finely tuned watch. The face of the

watch is obliged to change from one minute to the next; but these changes are merely gestures, no more than outward manifestations of the underlying grand design. Beneath the surface, the mechanism remains fixed, emitting identical signals through every hour of every day, churning constantly forward with the same relentless virtuosity. The eternal fluctuations of competing political and military forces are ever subject to its endless pulse. This conceptual vision has made a clear impact on the conduct of American policy. And it derives from the assumptions which Kissinger has nurtured throughout his intellectual life'.

4. Nixon, *The Memoirs of Richard Nixon*, vol. 1, p. 422.
5. Richard M. Nixon, *US Foreign Policy for the 1970s: A New Strategy for Peace* (1970) p. 2.
6. Graubard, *Kissinger*, p. 271. Graubard states that all the annual foreign policy reports to Congress were prepared by Kissinger.
7. Nixon, *US Foreign Policy for the 1970s: A New Strategy for Peace*, pp. 2–3.
8. Nixon, *US Foreign Policy for the 1970s: A New Strategy for Peace*, pp. 3–5.
9. Nixon, *US Foreign Policy for the 1970s: A New Strategy for Peace*, pp. 4–12.
10. *Time*, 3 January 1972, pp. 14–15; Ball, *Diplomacy for a Crowded World*, p. 157. Ball states that while we may dismiss the President's statement with a shrug, that was not the reaction of many Europeans, who perceived Nixon's vision as an American wish to break with the policy grounded on the Western Alliance. Landau, *Kissinger*, pp. 34; 46–9. Landau argues that: 'for Kissinger, the Metternich system was no mere analogy drawn from the depths of a bygone history, but a period and a world system to which he would very much have liked to return'. He adds that Kissinger was led to believe in limited nuclear war through his faith in the universal applicability of Metternich-style diplomacy. Stoessinger, *Henry Kissinger*, pp. 27–8. Stoessinger maintained that: 'The fatal weakness of Kissinger's doctrine [graduated deterrence] lay in his belief that nineteenth century diplomacy, with its common ground rules of limited objectives, could be applied to nuclear diplomacy'. However, unlike Landau, Stoessinger explained that in *The Necessity for Choice*, Kissinger retracted his belief in tactical nuclear war. Theodore Draper, 'Detente', *Commentary*, 57 (June 1974) p. 29.
11. Kissinger, *American Foreign Policy*, p. 75; *The Troubled Partnership*, p. 169; Dickson, *Kissinger and the Meaning of History*, p. 119; Falk, *What's Wrong with Henry Kissinger's Foreign Policy*, p. 10. Falk states: 'what Kissinger admired was Metternich's understanding of the revolutionary character of the Napoleonic challenge and his leadership in bringing about a new era of international stability after Napoleon's military defeat. But Kissinger never intended such admiration to be understood as tantamount to proposing Metternichian solutions for comparable contemporary problems'. Stoessinger, *Henry Kissinger*, p. 213.

12. Kissinger, *American Foreign Policy*, p. 57; Falk, *What's Wrong with Henry Kissinger's Foreign Policy*, p. 15.
13. Nixon, *US Foreign Policy for the 1970s: Shaping A Durable Peace* (1973) p. 232; Dickson, *Kissinger and the Meaning of History*, pp. 126–7.
14. Brown, *The Crises of Power*, pp. 32; 41. Brown states that Kissinger placed the triangular relationship at the centre of his geopolitical strategy; Robert E. Osgood *et al.*, *Retreat From Empire?: The First Nixon Administration* (1973) pp. 5–7. Osgood argues that the Nixon Administration in fact, while capitalizing on an incipient tripolar diplomatic relationship, was almost as opposed as preceding Administrations to a full-scale pentagonal world.
15. Stoessinger, *Henry Kissinger*, pp. 43–4; Graubard, *Kissinger*, p. 252. Graubard states that Rockefeller promised: 'I would begin a dialogue with Communist China. In a subtle triangle of relations with Washington, Peking, and Moscow, we improve the possibilities of accommodations with each as we increase our options toward both . . . in such a framework we can talk with Soviet leaders with new purposefulness and hope about a basic settlement'. Both Stoessinger and Graubard point out that all of Rockefeller's statements on foreign policy were written by Kissinger. See Kalb and Kalb, *Kissinger*, pp. 216–21. The Kalb brothers point out that: 'for the first six months of 1969, Kissinger was a mere passenger on the Administration's China train. The President was clearly its sole engineer'. To support their argument, the Kalbs point to President Nixon's 1967 article in *Foreign Affairs*. See Brown, *The Crises of Power*, pp. 157–8, which argues that: 'accounts designed to make Nixon look like the original mind behind the breakthrough to China present highly selected excerpts from this article. Unfortunately, the Kalbs' book . . . is no exception. A rereading of the article itself shows Nixon reiterating the standard rationale for continuing the established containment policy. If anything, the 1967 article was a rebuttal to the minority in the policy community who in 1966 had begun to talk of a policy of "containment without isolation" toward China'. In my view, Brown's argument is more accurate.
16. Stoessinger, *Henry Kissinger*, pp. 80–91. Stoessinger discusses developments in the US–Soviet relationship after the Cuban missile crisis, and states that: 'Henry Kissinger's perception of the Soviet Union was deeply altered by these events. Before the Cuban missile crisis, he had viewed the Soviet Union as the world's leading "revolutionary" power, insatiably bent on global conquest. By the time he joined the government in 1969, Kissinger had changed his mind'. Mazlish, *Kissinger*, pp. 234–5. Mazlish reports that Kissinger has evolved in his view of the USSR. At first he saw it as a purely revolutionary force, necessarily transgressing the limits and irreconcilably threatening international stability. More lately he has seen it as becoming, like the US, a status quo power. Falk, *What's Wrong with Henry Kissinger's Foreign Policy*, 13–14. Graubard, *Kissinger*, p. 273.
17. Landau, *Kissinger*, p. 105.

18. Nixon, *US Foreign Policy for the 1970s: Building for Peace* (1971) p.
     105.
19. Nixon, *US Foreign Policy for the 1970s: Building for Peace*, p. 157.
20. Falk, *What's Wrong with Henry Kissinger's Foreign Policy*, pp. 13–14;
     17–18; 30; Landau, *Kissinger*, pp. 7; 10; 105.
21. Nixon, *US Foreign Policy for the 1970s: A New Strategy for Peace*, p.
     142.
22. Nixon, *US Foreign Policy for the 1970s: A New Strategy for Peace*, p.
     136.
23. Kissinger, *White House Years*, p. 129. Landau, *Kissinger*, pp. 125–6;
     143. Landau maintained that 'linkage [was] a policy of risk'. It was:
     'little more than unreconstructed Cold Warriorism'. He argued that
     the linkage approach did not lead to serious conflict because the
     'Soviets show[ed] occasional good sense', by not adopting it as well,
     'despite the fact that they [were] provoked outright [by Washington]
     into doing so'. In addition, Landau argued that the linkage approach
     further consolidated Kissinger's role. Kissinger, by retaining control of
     the two pivotal issues – Vietnam and SALT – was able to control the
     policy in its entirety because he insured that a Soviet action on any
     front would be answered in one of the central arenas.
24. Mazlish, *Kissinger*, pp. 235–7. Mazlish states that the key issue
     Kissinger sought to link with SALT was Vietnam. In this he was
     following his President. But on the issue of SALT it seems to have
     been ... Kissinger who moved Nixon around to favouring it. Yet it
     was also Kissinger who counselled holding off from negotiations on
     SALT, which the Russians desired, until they were prepared to 'give'
     elsewhere – e.g., in Vietnam. Thus Kissinger approached SALT as a
     part of an overall linkage, and strongly influenced Nixon in taking this
     same stand.
25. Mazlish, *Kissinger*, pp. 12–13. Mazlish argues that: 'whatever the
     specific case or country, Kissinger has subsumed his position toward it
     under his larger concern for international stability and order. All of
     his policies ... are linked in covert or dramatic fashion to this
     overriding concern'. Graubard, *Kissinger*, p. 274. Graubard states
     that Kissinger's object was to secure a stable international order. That
     purpose transcended all others. Landau, *Kissinger*, pp. 12–13.
     According to Landau, the central issue in Kissinger's political life has
     been the establishment of a stable international order. Stoessinger,
     Henry Kissinger, p. 45.
26. Landau, *Kissinger*, pp. 7; 10. Falk, *What's Wrong with Henry
     Kissinger's Foreign Policy*, p. 17.
27. Kissinger, *White House Years*, p. 183.
28. Kissinger, *White House Years*, p. 764.
29. Mazlish, *Kissinger*, pp. 244–6. Mazlish reports that although it was
     Nixon who devised the strategy regarding US–PRC rapprochement, it
     was Kissinger who devised the tactics that led to the President's trip to
     Peking. By the time Nixon made his famous trip Kissinger seemed to
     be the key figure in the rapprochement, and Nixon had to keep
     assuring Chou that 'it was really me' (i.e., Nixon) who was to be

credited. Kalb and Kalb, *Kissinger*, p. 124; Falk, *What's Wrong with Henry Kissinger's Foreign Policy*, p. 7; Morris, *Uncertain Greatness*, 202–8. Morris argues that 'just as the China opening could not have begun or continued without Nixon's vision, it would never have been so skilfully executed without Kissinger'.

30. Mazlish, *Kissinger*, p. 245. Mazlish argues Kissinger began his relations with the PRC uninterested in the Chinese Communists as such and concerned only with putting the screws on the Russians. The overture to China was part of the linkage.

31. Landau, *Kissinger*, pp. 104–5. Landau states that the Nixon–Kissinger policy has been geared primarily to the behaviour of the America's only rival for worldwide power and influence, the USSR. Every foreign policy decision since 1969 has had the purpose of making a certain impression upon the Soviets, if not of responding directly to them. Mazlish, *Kissinger*, p. 234. Stoessinger, *Henry Kissinger*, p. 214.

32. Nixon, *US Foreign Policy for the 1970s: Building for Peace*, p. 157.

33. Nutter, *Kissinger's Grand Design*, p. 15. Nutter reports that Kissinger has never altered his position that the transformation of Soviet society, insofar as it takes place, will be a slow evolutionary process essentially beyond the influence of outside pressure.

34. Stoessinger, *Henry Kissinger*, p. 81.

35. Morris, *Uncertain Greatness*, p. 210. Morris claims that: 'Kissinger's general diplomatic vision of detente was as clear and premeditated as Nixon's political instincts on the subject. The shape and negotiating techniques of a post-cold war settlement between America and Russia were central themes in his later writings on U.S. policy and already implicit in 1957 in *A World Restored*. Détente, with all its operational contradictions and fundamental logic after 1972, reflected his concept of a great two-power condominium, joined together by a framework of personal contacts and formal agreements, which might mitigate rivalries and lead even to collaboration on common problems. But that vision would have remained an academic theory without his matching appreciation of the real bureaucratic obstacles and opportunities'.

36. Morris, *Uncertain Greatness*, p. 97.

37. Kissinger, *White House Years*, pp. 152–3.

38. Kissinger, *White House Years*, pp. 153–4. He made this recommendation to President Nixon in a briefing paper on 21 May, 1969, before a NSC meeting on East–West trade.

39. Dickson, *Kissinger and the Meaning of History*, pp. 18–19. Dickson argues that although Kissinger's personality and his inordinately complex pattern of behaviour seem to defy analysis, Kissinger has left one clue that unlocks the door to his deepest throughts about himself and his objectives. This clue resides in his tendency to juxtapose the words 'history' and 'morality' in his academic writings and his speeches as a Secretary of State. This is most evident in Kissinger's discussions of detente.

40. Kissinger, *White House Years*, p. 132.

41. Kissinger, *The Necessity for Choice*, pp. 165–7.

42. Landau, *Kissinger*, pp. 114; 118.

43. Graubard, *Kissinger*, p. 260.

44. Kissinger, *White House Years*, pp. 530–1; Dickson, *Kissinger and the Meaning of History*, pp. 130–1. Dickson argues that 'most political commentators are mistaken when they attribute the SALT I accords and the Quadripartite Agreement on Berlin to Kissinger's theory of linkage'. The opening to the PRC according to Dickson was the 'principal factor encouraging the Soviets to be more flexible at the negotiating table'. In his view, the policy of linkage was a 'complete failure'.

45. Stoessinger, *Henry Kissinger*, p. 82; Mazlish, *Kissinger*, p. 235. According to Mazlish on the issue of SALT it seems to have been Kissinger who moved Nixon around to favouring it.

46. Graubard, *Kissinger*, p. 274. Graubard states that: 'Kissinger's object was to secure a stable international order. That purpose transcended all others; in his mind, it was the necessary precondition of peace'. Stoessinger, *Henry Kissinger*, pp. 36–7; 45.

47. Kissinger, *The Troubled Partnership*, p. 109.

48. Mazlish, *Kissinger*, p. 236. According to Mazlish although Nixon as a candidate in 1968 had advocated superiority, he was brought over to Kissinger's view of sufficiency.

49. Richard M. Nixon, *US Foreign Policy for the 1970s: Building for Peace*, p. 170.

50. Nixon, *US Foreign Policy for the 1970s: Building for Peace*, p. 170.

51. Kissinger, *Nuclear Weapons and Foreign Policy*, p. 36.

52. Kissinger, *Nuclear Weapons and Foreign Policy*, pp. 42; 117.

53. Richard M. Nixon, *US Foreign Policy for the 1970s: The Emerging Structure of Peace*, p. 158.

54. Nixon, *US Foreign Policy for the 1970s: The Emerging Structure of Peace*, p. 158.

55. Nixon, *US Foreign Policy for the 1970s: Building for Peace*, pp. 170–1.

56. On 29 May 1972, President Nixon and General Secretary Brezhnev signed the agreement on Basic Principles of US–Soviet Relations.

57. Morris, *Uncertain Greatness*, p. 212. Morris argues that: 'almost certainly the most important external factor was the triangular Realpolitik with China. Only a day after the critical negotiating round on ABM had begun in July 1971, Kissinger first landed in Peking; and the progress in SALT over the ensuing months gathered speed as the Sino–American detente became a decisive new international reality.'

58. Nixon, *US Foreign Policy for the 1970s: The Emerging Structure of Peace*, p. 175. These agreements had been worked out in parallel with the main arms negotiations.

59. Dickson, *Kissinger and the Meaning of History*, pp. 130–2. Dickson argues that most political commentators are mistaken when they attribute SALT and the Quadripartite Agreement on Berlin to Kissinger's theory of 'linkage'. The policy, to the extent that it existed, was a complete failure. Regarding these breakthroughs

according to Dickson, it would not be far off the mark to suggest that the Administration's decision to establish diplomatic relations with the PRC was the principal factor encouraging the Soviets to be more flexible at the negotiating table. Dickson concludes that American policy toward the PRC as a version of power politics, not the so-called 'linkage' policy, was the prime factor accounting for Kissinger's success with the Soviets at the negotiating table.

60.   Nixon, *US Foreign Policy for the 1970s: Shaping a Durable Peace*, p. 37.
61.   Nixon, *US Foreign Policy for the 1970s: Shaping a Durable Peace*, p. 37.
62.   Nixon, *US Foreign Policy for the 1970s: Shaping a Durable Peace*, p. 37.
63.   Nixon, *US Foreign Policy for the 1970s: Shaping a Durable Peace*, p. 37.
64.   Henry A. Kissinger, *Years of Upheaval* (1982) p. 285.
65.   Kissinger, *Years of Upheaval*, p. 286.
66.   United States Department of State, *United States Foreign Policy, 1972: A Report of the Secretary of State* (1973) pp. 27–8; 509–14.
67.   Morris, *Uncertain Greatness*, pp. 283–4. According to Morris, detente was not the cause of the disarray of the American domestic food market and skyrocketing grocery prices. The Department of Agriculture's advocacy for high prices and bureaucratic incompetence and inertia, as well as the actions of the huge American grain companies, had the same disastrous consequences as the imagined Communist conspiracy.
68.   Stoessinger, *Henry Kissinger*, p. 99.
69.   Stoessinger, *Henry Kissinger*, p. 110.

4 The US and Western Europe: a Troubled Partnership

1.   Kissinger, *The Necessity for Choice*, pp. 165–8; *The Troubled Partnership*, pp. 245–9.
2.   Kissinger, *American Foreign Policy* p. 65. See Kissinger, *The Necessity for Choice*, p. 99.
3.   Kissinger, *The Troubled Partnership*, p. 5.
4.   Kissinger, *The Troubled Partnership*, p. 40.
5.   Graubard, *Kissinger*, p. 203.
6.   Kissinger, *The Troubled Partnership*, p. 5.
7.   Mazlish, *Kissinger*, pp. 177–83: Dickson, *Kissinger and the Meaning of History*, pp. 83–116.
8.   Nutter, *Kissinger's Grand Design*, p. 16.
9.   Kissinger, *The Troubled Partnership*, p. 7.
10.   Kissinger, *The Troubled Partnership*, p. 7.
11.   Kissinger, *The Troubled Partnership*, p. 23.
12.   Kissinger, *The Troubled Partnership*, pp. 7–8.
13.   Kissinger, *The Troubled Partnership*, p. 27.

14. Kissinger, *The Troubled Partnership*, pp. 26–7.

15. Kissinger, *The Troubled Partnership*, p. 8.

16. Kissinger, *The Troubled Partnership*, p. 9.

17. Kissinger, *American Foreign Policy*, p. 71.

18. Kissinger, *American Foreign Policy*, p. 9.

19. Kissinger, *American Foreign Policy*, p. 72.

20. Kissinger, *American Foreign Policy*, p. 72.

21. Walter LaFeber, *America, Russia and the Cold War 1945–1975* (1976) p. 230.

22. Kissinger, *The Troubled Partnership*, p. 247.

23. Kissinger, *The Troubled Partnership*, p. 10.

24. Kissinger, *American Foreign Policy*, p. 74; *The Troubled Partnership*, p. 243; Graubard, *Kissinger,* p. 222.

25. Kissinger, *American Foreign Policy*, p. 74; *The Troubled Partnership*, pp. 242–3.

26. Kissinger, *The Troubled Partnership*, p. 169.

27. Kissinger, *American Foreign Policy*, p. 75; *The Troubled Partnership*, p. 169.

28. Kissinger, *American Foreign Policy*, p. 75; *The Troubled Partnership*, p. 106.

29. Graubard, *Kissinger*, p. 203.

30. Kissinger, *Nuclear Weapons and Foreign Policy*, pp. 117–18. Also Kissinger, *The Troubled Partnership*, p. 11.

31. Kissinger, *The Troubled Partnership*, pp. 11–12.

32. The North Atlantic Treaty, *Department of State Bulletin* (20 March 1949) pp. 340ff.

33. Kissinger, *The Troubled Partnership*, p. 12.

34. Kissinger, *The Troubled Partnership*, p. 101. Also Secretary McNamara's speech at Ann Arbor, Michigan (16 June 1962), *Department of State Bulletin* (9 July 1962) pp. 64–9.

35. Kissinger, *The Troubled Partnership*, pp. 100–1; 119.

36. Kissinger, *The Troubled Partnership*, p. 166.

37. Kissinger, 'The Unsolved Problems of European Defence', *Foreign Affairs*, 40, 4 (July 1962) 537–40.

38. Graubard, *Kissinger,* p. 204.

39. Kissinger, *The Troubled Partnership*, p. 139.

40. Kissinger, *The Troubled Partnership*, p. 139.

41. Kissinger, *The Troubled Partnership*, p. 15.

42. Kissinger, *Nuclear Weapons and Foreign Policy*, pp. 11–12.

43. Kissinger, *The Troubled Partnership*, p. 169.

44. Kissinger, *The Troubled Partnership*, p. 15.

45. Kissinger, *The Troubled Partnership*, pp. 114–15.

46. Kissinger, *The Troubled Partnership*, pp. 116–17; Nutter, *Kissinger's Grand Design*, p. 13.

47. Kissinger, *The Troubled Partnership*, p. 183.

48. Kissinger, *The Troubled Partnership*, pp. 181–2.

49. Kissinger, *The Troubled Partnership*, p. 117.

50. Kissinger, *The Necessity for Choice*, p. 121.

51. Kissinger, *The Troubled Partnership*, p. 125.

52. Kissinger, *The Necessity for Choice*, pp. 125–6.
53. Kissinger, *The Troubled Partnership*, pp. 16–17.
54. Kissinger, *The Troubled Partnership*, p. 17.
55. Kissinger, *The Troubled Partnership*, p. 17.
56. Kissinger, *The Troubled Partnership*, pp. 117–18.
57. Kissinger, *The Necessity for Choice*, p. 101.
58. Kissinger, *The Necessity for Choice*, pp. 105–6.
59. Kissinger, *The Troubled Partnership*, p. 181.
60. Kissinger, *The Necessity for Choice*, p. 107.
61. Kissinger, *The Necessity for Choice*, p. 106.
62. Kissinger, *The Necessity for Choice*, p. 109.
63. Kissinger, *The Necessity for Choice*, p. 109.
64. Kissinger, *The Necessity for Choice*, pp. 109–10.
65. Kissinger, *The Necessity for Choice*, p. 254.
66. Kissinger, *The Necessity for Choice*, p. 157.
67. Kissinger, *The Necessity for Choice*, p. 149.
68. Kissinger, *The Necessity for Choice*, p. 158.
69. Kissinger, *The Troubled Partnership*, p. 223. Also Kissinger, *The Necessity for Choice*, p. 130.
70. Kissinger, *The Necessity for Choice*, p. 129.
71. Kissinger, *The Troubled Partnership*, p. 189.
72. Kissinger, *The Troubled Partnership*, p. 209.
73. Kissinger, *The Troubled Partnership*, p. 216.
74. Kissinger, *The Troubled Partnership*, p. 211.
75. Kissinger, *The Troubled Partnership*, p. 220.
76. Kissinger, *The Troubled Partnership*, p. 220.
77. Kissinger, *The Necessity for Choice*, p. 130. Also Kissinger, *The Troubled Partnership*, p. 69.
78. Kissinger, *The Troubled Partnership*, p. 223.
79. Kissinger, *The Necessity for Choice*, p. 139. Also Nutter, *Kissinger's Grand Design*, p. 5.

5 The Nixon Doctrine and Western Europe: a 'Genuine Partnership'?

1. Henry Kissinger, *The Troubled Partnership*, pp. 159; 186; and Stoessinger, *Henry Kissinger*, p. 137.
2. Kissinger, *White House Years*, pp. 68; 104–14. President Nixon shared Kissinger's admiration for President de Gaulle. Nixon, *The Memoirs of Richard Nixon*, vol. 1, pp. 460–2; and George W. Ball, *Diplomacy for a Crowded World*, pp. 159; 338.
3. See preceding chapters, and Stoessinger, *Henry Kissinger*, p. 138.
4. Walter F. Hahn, 'The Nixon Doctrine: Design and Dilemmas', *ORBIS*, 2 (Summer 1972) 361.
5. Lawrence S. Kaplan, 'NATO and The Nixon Doctrine Ten Years Later', *ORBIS*, 1 (Spring 1980) 149.
6. Kaplan, 'NATO and the Nixon Doctrine'. Kaplan argues that: 'both the Truman Doctrine and the Nixon Doctrine have had vital roles in

the evolution of American policy towards the Atlantic Alliance'.

7. Hahn, 'The Nixon Doctrine: Design and Dilemmas', p. 361. Hahn argues that: 'This tendency has been more pronounced with respect to domestic philosophy – witness Roosevelt's "New Deal", Truman's "Fair Deal", Kennedy's "New Frontier", and Johnson's "Great Society". But the imperative operates in foreign policy as well'.

8. Informal remarks with newsmen, 25 July 1969, in *Public Papers of the Presidents*, (Washington, DC: GPO, 1971) p. 544; Marshall Green, 'The Nixon Doctrine: A Progress Report', *US Department of State Bulletin*, (8 February 1971) p. 161. Not until 3 November did the President recognize that he had said something significant at Guam about 'what has been described as the Nixon Doctrine' notes Green.

9. Nixon, *US Foreign Policy for the 1970s: A New Strategy for Peace*, p. 6.

10. Nixon, *US Foreign Policy for the 1970s: A New Strategy for Peace*, p. 7.

11. Nixon, *US Foreign Policy for the 1970s: A New Strategy for Peace*, p. 6.

12. Nixon, *US Foreign Policy for the 1970s: A New Strategy for Peace*, pp. 6–7.

13. Nixon, *US Foreign Policy for the 1970s: Building for Peace*, pp. 12–13.

14. Nixon, *The Memoirs of Richard Nixon*, vol. 1, p. 422.

15. Henry Brandon, *The Retreat of American Power* (1973) p. 40; and Hahn, 'The Nixon Doctrine: Design and Dilemmas', p. 362.

16. Kissinger, *American Foreign Policy*, p. 97.

17. Kissinger, *American Foreign Policy*, p. 58.

18. Kissinger, *American Foreign Policy*, p. 134; and Nixon, *US Foreign Policy for the 1970s: A New Strategy for Peace*, pp. 68–72. Kaplan makes the same point in 'NATO and the Nixon Doctrine', p. 150.

19. Nixon, *US Foreign Policy for the 1970s: A New Strategy for Peace*, p. 27; *US Foreign Policy for the 1970s: Building for Peace*, p. 24.

20. Nixon, *US Foreign Policy for the 1970s: A New Strategy for Peace*, p. 29; Nixon, *The Memoirs of Richard Nixon*, vol. 1, p. 463. Nixon stated: 'I felt that the European trip had accomplished all the goals we set for it. It showed the NATO leaders that a new and interested administration which respected their views had come to power in Washington. It served warning on the Soviets that they could no longer take for granted – nor take advantage of – Western disunity'.

21. Radio address, 13 October 1968, 'The Time to Save NATO', in *Atlantic Community Quarterly* (Winter 1968–69) 481–2. According to Nixon: 'Actions have been taken by the United States which vitally affected the security of our European partners, without even the courtesy of prior consultation... It's time we began paying Europe more attention. And if our ideals of Atlantic interdependence are to mean anything in practice, it's time we began lecturing our European partners less and listening to them more'.

22. Nixon, *US Foreign Policy for the 1970s: A New Strategy for Peace*, p. 8; *US Foreign Policy for the 1970s: Building for Peace*, p. 24. Also see Hahn, 'The Nixon Doctrine: Design and Dilemmas', 369–70; and

Werner Kaltefleiter, 'Europe and the Nixon Doctrine: A German Point of View', *ORBIS*, 1 (Spring 1973) 75–7.

23. Nixon, *US Foreign Policy for the 1970s: A New Strategy for Peace*, pp. 28–31; *US Foreign Policy for the 1970s: Building for Peace*, pp. 24–8.
24. Kissinger, *The Troubled Partnership*, pp. 21–2.
25. Nixon, *US Foreign Policy for the 1970s: Building for Peace*, pp. 30–1.
26. Nixon, *US Foreign Policy for the 1970s: Building for Peace*, p. 11.
27. Kissinger, *American Foreign Policy*, p. 71.
28. Nixon, *US Foreign Policy for the 1970s: Building for Peace*, p. 11.
29. Nixon, *US Foreign Policy for the 1970s: Building for Peace*, p. 36.
30. Kissinger, *The Troubled Partnership*, pp. 6–7; and in *American Foreign Policy*, p. 68. See also *US Foreign Policy for the 1970s: Building for Peace*, pp. 12; 26.
31. Nixon, *US Foreign Policy for the 1970s: A New Strategy for Peace*, p. 30.
32. Nixon, *US Foreign Policy for the 1970s: Building for Peace*, p. 12.
33. Kissinger, *A World Restored*, p. 1.
34. Nixon, *US Foreign Policy for the 1970s: Building for Peace*, p. 39.
35. Nixon, *US Foreign Policy for the 1970s: The Emerging Structure of Peace*, p. 40.
36. Nixon, *US Foreign Policy for the 1970s: A New Strategy for Peace*, p. 32. *US Foreign Policy for the 1970s: Building for Peace*, pp. 28–31.
37. Nixon, *US Foreign Policy for the 1970s: Building for Peace*, p. 25.
38. Nixon, *US Foreign Policy for the 1970s: Building for Peace*, pp. 13–14.
39. Nixon, *US Foreign Policy for the 1970s: Building for Peace*, p. 14.
40. US Department of Defence, *Defense Report: Fiscal Year 1972–1976 Defense Program and the 1972 Defense Budget*, p. 15.
41. Nixon, *US Foreign Policy for the 1970s: A New Strategy for Peace*, pp. 122–4; *US Foreign Policy for the 1970s: Building for Peace*, p. 174.
42. Kissinger, *American Foreign Policy*, pp. 61–4; and Nixon, *US Foreign Policy for the 1970s: A New Strategy for Peace*, p. 111; see also *US Foreign Policy for the 1970s: Building for Peace*, pp. 33–4.
43. Nixon, *US Foreign Policy for the 1970s: A New Strategy for Peace*, pp. 128–9. The '2½ War' principle is that 'US forces would be maintained for a three month conventional forward defense of NATO, a defense of Korea or Southeast Asia against a full-scale Chinese attack, and a minor contingency all simultaneously'.
44. Nixon, *US Foreign Policy for the 1970s: A New Strategy for Peace*, p. 129; and *US Foreign Policy for the 1970s: Building for Peace*, p. 178.
45. Nixon, *US Foreign Policy for the 1970s: Building for Peace*, p. 179.
46. Hahn, 'The Nixon Doctrine: Design and Dilemmas', 369.
47. Nixon, *US Foreign Policy for the 1970s: A New Strategy for Peace*, p. 4.
48. Kissinger, *American Foreign Policy*, pp. 72–4.
49. Kissinger, *The Troubled Partnership*, p. 227.
50. Nixon, *US Foreign Policy for the 1970s: Building for Peace*, p. 20.
51. Kissinger, *The Troubled Partnership*, p. 223.
52. Kissinger, *American Foreign Policy*, p. 75.

53. Landau, *Kissinger*, p. 114.
54. George Liska, *Beyond Kissinger: Ways of Conservative Statecraft* (1975), p. 65; and Stanley Hoffmann, *Primacy or World Order* (1978) p. 47.
55. Liska, *Beyond Kissinger*, p. 64.
56. Liska, *Beyond Kissinger*, p. 64.
57. Hoffmann, *Primacy or World Order*, pp. 46–8.
58. Hoffmann, *Primacy or World Order*, pp. 46–8.
59. Nixon, *US Foreign Policy for the 1970s: A New Strategy for Peace*, p. 7. See also Hahn, 'The Nixon Doctrine: Design and Dilemmas', 370.
60. Hahn, 'The Nixon Doctrine: Design and Dilemmas', 370. Hahn makes the same point, but in terms of a vision of a pentagonal international system.
61. Nixon, *US Foreign Policy for the 1970s: The Emerging Structure of Peace*, pp. 8–9.
62. Hahn, 'The Nixon Doctrine: Design and Dilemmas', 374.
63. Nixon, *US Foreign Policy for the 1970s: Building for Peace*, p. 30.
64. Congressional support for troop withdrawals can be interpreted as a manifestation of the public view on the issue. Senator Mansfield would not have pushed for such a policy if he believed that both the Administration and the public were opposed to it.
65. Kissinger, *The Troubled Partnership*, pp. 116–17.
66. Kissinger, *The Troubled Partnership*, p. 241.
67. Kissinger, *The Troubled Partnership*, p. 40.
68. Kissinger, *The Troubled Partnership*, pp. 26–7.
69. Nixon, *US Foreign Policy for the 1970s: Building for Peace*, p. 14.
70. Osgood *et al.*, *Retreat From Empire?*, p. 7.
71. Kissinger, *The Troubled Partnership*, p. 149.
72. Kissinger, *The Troubled Partnership*, pp. 149–50.
73. Osgood *et al.*, *Retreat From Empire?*, p. 8.
74. Osgood *et al.*, *Retreat From Empire?*, p. 8.
75. Hoffmann, *Primacy or World Order*, pp. 49–50.
76. Kissinger, *American Foreign Policy*, p. 75; Dickson, *Kissinger and the Meaning of History*, p. 119.
77. Hoffmann, *Primacy or World Order*, p. 48.
78. Hoffmann, *Primacy or World Order*, p. 49.
79. Kissinger, *The Troubled Partnership*, pp. 169–72.
80. Osgood *et al.*, *Retreat From Empire?*, p. 18.

6 The Dilemmas of Common Defence: US Initiatives, Allied Reactions

1. Kissinger, *White House Years*, p. 382.
2. Kissinger, *White House Years*, p. 382.
3. Kissinger, *The Troubled Partnership*, pp. 25–7.
4. Osgood *et al.*, *Retreat From Empire?*, pp. 173–5.
5. Landau, *Kissinger*, pp. 104–5.
6. The Nixon Doctrine is examined in Chapter 5.

7. Kissinger, *The Troubled Partnership*, p. 118.
8. Kissinger, *White House Years*, p. 220.
9. Kissinger, *White House Years*, pp. 215–16.
10. Kissinger, *White House Years*, pp. 215–16.
11. Kissinger, *White House Years*, p. 217. Also Nixon, *US Foreign Policy for the 1970s: A New Strategy for Peace*, pp. 121–4.
12. Kissinger, *White House Years*, p. 217.
13. Osgood *et al.*, *Retreat From Empire?*, p. 182.
14. Nixon, *US Foreign Policy for the 1970s: Building for Peace*, p. 170.
15. Nixon, *US Foreign Policy for the 1970s: Building for Peace*, pp. 170–5.
16. Brown, *The Crises of Power*, p. 25.
17. Kissinger, *The Troubled Partnership*, p. 106.
18. Jerome Kahan, *Security in the Nuclear Age: Developing US Strategic Arms Policy* (1975) pp. 142–96.
19. Willy Brandt, *People and Politics: The Years 1960–1975* (1976) p. 285.
20. Kissinger, *The Troubled Partnership*, pp. 177–86.
21. Nixon, *US Foreign Policy for the 1970s: A New Strategy For Peace*, pp. 33–4; *US Foreign Policy for the 1970s: Building For Peace*, p. 32; *US Foreign Policy for the 1970s: The Emerging Structure of Peace*, pp. 42–4; *US Foreign Policy for the 1970s: Shaping a Durable Peace*, p. 85.
22. Lawrence W. Martin, 'Military Issues: Strategic Parity and its Implications', in Osgood *et al.*, *Retreat From Empire?*, p. 167. Kissinger, *White House Years*, p. 219. The NPG was composed of four permanent members and three members rotated at eighteen-month intervals. The permanent members were the US, Britain, the FRG, and Italy (France, to maintain its independence in nuclear matters refused to participate).
23. Chapter 3 examines the structural problems of NATO that preclude the resolution of the strategic issues.
24. Paul Buteux, *The Politics of Nuclear Consultation in NATO 1965–1980* (1983), pp. 110–45. Also Kissinger, *White House Years*, pp. 218–20.
25. Kissinger, *White House Years*, pp. 223–7. The US, Buteux states, was far more sceptical as to the value of a demonstration option than were the authors of the Anglo–German working paper from which the political guidelines on initial use of tactical nuclear weapons were developed; they, it was reported, favoured an earlier and more limited use of nuclear weapons than did the Americans. Also, *The Times* (London) 31 May 1969.
26. Kissinger, *White House Years*, p. 219.
27. Kissinger, *White House Years*, pp. 587–9. The US nuclear forces are normally in various states of alert called DEFCONS (for Defence Condition), in descending order from Defcon I to Defcon V. Defcon I is war. Defcon II is a condition in which attack is imminent. Defcon III increases readiness without the determination that war is likely; it is in practice the highest stage of readiness for essentially peacetime conditions. Most of the US forces were on Defcon IV and V, except those in the Pacific which because of the Vietnam War were in 1973 permanently on Defcon III. Kissinger during the Yom Kippur War ordered Defcon III. In addition, the 82nd Airborne Division was put

on alert, and the aircraft carriers *Franklin Delano Roosevelt* (at the time off Italy) and *John F. Kennedy* (in the Atlantic) were ordered to go to the Eastern Mediterranean south of Crete. Morris, *Uncertain Greatness*, pp. 247–9.

28. Nixon, *US Foreign Policy for the 1970s: The Emerging Structure of Peace*, pp. 43–4.
29. William C. Cromwell, 'Europe and the "Structure of Peace" ', *ORBIS*, 1 (Spring 1978) 23–4.
30. Kissinger, *Years of Upheaval*, pp. 712–13.
31. Kissinger, *Years of Upheaval*, p. 712.
32. Kissinger, *White House Years*, p. 220.
33. Kissinger, *White House Years*, p. 84.
34. Nixon, *US Foreign Policy for the 1970s: A New Strategy for Peace*, p. 34; *US Foreign Policy for the 1970s: The Emerging Structure of Peace*, p. 43.
35. Kissinger, *The Troubled Partnership*, p. 166.
36. Kissinger, *White House Years*, p. 389.
37. Osgood *et al.*, *Retreat From Empire?*, p. 182.
38. Ian Smart, 'Perspectives from Europe', in Mason Willrich and John B. Rhinelander (eds), *SALT: The Moscow Agreements and Beyond* (1974) p. 187; also William R. Kinter and Robert L. Pfaltzgraff Jr, 'The Strategic Arms Limitation Agreements of 1972: Implications for International Security', in William R. Kinter and Robert L. Pfaltzgraff Jr, *SALT: Implications for Arms Control in the 1970s* (1973) p. 397. According to Kinter and Pfaltzgraff West European fears of American strategic decoupling were much more a function of perceived intentions than of specific quantitative calculation of size of forces or nuclear megatonnage.
39. Smart, 'Perspectives from Europe', p. 187.
40. Smart, 'Perspectives from Europe', p. 187.
41. Smart, 'Perspectives from Europe', pp. 187–8.
42. Kissinger, *White House Years*, pp. 403–4.
43. Smart, 'Perspectives from Europe', p. 189.
44. Kissinger, *White House Years*, p. 404. Kissinger reported in his memoirs that Josef Luns (then Dutch Foreign Minister) said to President Nixon that the notion of parity was one of the most shocking propositions that he had ever heard. Chancellor Kissinger commented that it had come to something of a 'thought-provoking' surprise to realize how close the two sides were to equality. The British representative at the NATO Council questioned whether this was the moment for talks.
45. Smart, 'Perspectives from Europe', p. 188.
46. Smart, 'Perspectives from Europe', p. 185.
47. Kissinger, *White House Years*, pp. 404–5.
48. Roger Morgan, *The United States and West Germany 1945–1973: A Study in Alliance Politics* (1974) pp. 209–10.
49. J. Robert Schaetzel, *The Unhinged Alliance: America and the European Community* (1975) pp. 52–3.
50. Kissinger, *A World Restored*, pp. 324–7.

51. Kissinger, *American Foreign Policy*, pp. 72–4.
52. Kissinger, *White House Years*, p. 387.
53. Kissinger, 'American Policy and Preventive War', *Yale Review*, 44, 3 (March 1955) 336.
54. Smart, 'Perspectives from Europe', 187; 190.
55. Gerard Smith, *Doubletalk: The Story of the First Strategic Arms Limitation Talks* (1980) pp. 145–6; 323. Smith states that the Soviets argued that since a SALT freeze would not affect British and French forces the US might evade its terms by helping the European members of NATO to build up their strategic forces. Hence the Soviets sought to limit the international transfer of strategic systems (and their technology) by a SALT agreement.
56. Smith, *Doubletalk: The Story of the First Strategic Arms Limitation Talks*, p. 361. Smith states that the Soviets often cited Secretary of Defence Laird as to the Allies' contribution to America's overall strategic defence posture.
57. The Soviet Union had 700 IRBMs/MRBMs in the western part of the country, 100 SS-5s and 600 SS-4s, with respective ranges of 2300 and 1200 miles.
58. Smart, 'Perspectives from Europe', p. 192.
59. Smith, *Doubletalk*, pp. 182–8; and Smart, Perspectives from Europe', 192–3.
60. The conventional role of the FBS was (and is) a concern of the US that may not have been (or is) equally shared by the Allies who emphasize the nuclear role of the FBS.
61. Morgan, *The United States and West Germany 1945–1973*, p. 210.
62. Kissinger, *White House Years*, p. 1273. Kissinger admitted that 'criticisms did not come from heads of government, all of whom wrote congratulatory letters (which may or may not have accorded with their private views). But there was an influential stratum of middle-level officials and publicists who gave vent to a lingering uneasiness, which reflected in part Europe's inability to articulate its own objectives'.
63. Geoffrey Kemp and Ian Smart, 'SALT and European Nuclear Forces', in Kintner and Pfaltzgraff (eds), *SALT: Implications For Arms Control*, pp. 209–10.
64. Roger P. Labrie (ed.), *SALT Hand Book* (1979) p. 18. Smart, 'Perspectives from Europe', p. 194. Kintner and Pfaltzgraff (eds), *SALT: Implications for Arms Control*, pp. 396; 420. According to the unilateral US interpretation: 'In regard to this Article [IX] . . . The US side wishes to make clear that the provisions of this Article do not set a precedent for whatever provision may be considered for a treaty on Limiting Strategic Offensive Arms. The question of transfer of strategic offensive arms is a far more complex issue, which may require a different solution'. *The New York Times*, 14 June 1972, p. 18.
65. Smart, 'Perspectives from Europe', p. 194. Martin, 'Military Issues: Strategic Parity and Its Implications', p. 148.
66. Smart, Perspectives from Europe', p. 194.
67. Kissinger, *Years of Upheaval*, pp. 276; 1235.

68. Kissinger, *Years of Upheaval*, p. 275.
69. Kissinger, *Years of Upheaval*, p. 277.
70. Kissinger, *Years of Upheaval*, p. 275.
71. Kissinger, *Years of Upheaval*, p. 278. Kissinger reported that in the summer of 1972 the Administration briefed the major European Allies and the leadership of the PRC on the outlines of the Soviet proposal.
72. Kissinger, *Years of Upheaval*, p. 286. Kissinger reported that for reasons of their own the leaders of Britain and the Federal Republic had not kept their bureaucracies informed. Also, Cromwell, 'Europe and the "Structure of Peace" ', p. 21.
73. Kissinger, *Years of Upheaval*, pp. 278–86. Kissinger discussed the role played by the British in the drafting of the agreement and especially the Foreign Office's Soviet expert Sir Thomas Brimelow.
74. *The New York Times*, 11 December 1973; see the report by Robert Kleiman.
75. Kissinger, *The Troubled Partnership*, p. 26.
76. Kissinger, *American Foreign Policy*, p. 75.
77. Kissinger, *American Foreign Policy*, pp. 72–4.
78. Chapter 2 deals with Kissinger's definition of peace (especially pp. 31–2).
79. Kissinger, *Years of Upheaval*, p. 285.
80. Kissinger, *Years of Upheaval*, p. 286.
81. Kissinger, *Years of Upheaval*, p. 286. Mazlish, *Kissinger*, pp. 256–7. Mazlish states that the Yom Kippur War disclosed that Kissinger had effectively superseded Nixon in the formulation of American foreign policy. Late on 24 October, Kissinger, consulting Nixon only in the most *pro forma* way, if that, replied to Soviet moves in Egypt by ordering a military alert. The threat of force, a basic element in Kissinger's diplomacy, worked. In Mazlish's view, the military alert showed that Kissinger had become the president for foreign affairs. Morris, *Uncertain Greatness*, p. 249.
82. Kissinger, *Years of Upheaval*, p. 286. Kissinger stated that according to the US interpretation of the agreement the USSR could not bring pressure on Peking without violating its provisions. But the leadership in Peking did not share the Administration's interpretation.

7 US Troops in Europe

1. Kissinger, *White House Years*, p. 386.
2. Wilfrid L. Kohl, 'The Nixon–Kissinger Foreign Policy System and the US–European Relations: Patterns of Policy Making', *World Politics*, XXVIII, 1 (October 1975) 27–8. John P. Leacacos, 'Kissinger's Apparat', *Foreign Policy*, 5 (Winter 1971–2) 25–7.
3. Kissinger, *White House Years*, p. 402.
4. Kissinger, *White House Years*, p. 402.
5. John Yochelson, 'The American Military Presence in Europe: Current Debate in the United States', *ORBIS*, 15 (Fall 1971) 793.

6. Yochelson, 'The American Military Presence', p. 793.
7. *The New York Times*, 4 December 1970, p. 1.
8. United States Senate, Committee on Foreign Relations, *United States Security Agreements and Commitments Abroad: United States Forces in Europe* (1970) p. 20; *White House Years*, pp. 394; 399. The Johnson Administration in an effort to get a greater contribution from the Allies had begun 'a process of thinly disguised withdrawal'. In 1967–8 part of one Army division and some Air Force units, almost 60 000 troops had been withdrawn. Kissinger reported that by November 1970, forces in Europe were about 17 000 below authorized strength; almost two-thirds of that reduction had taken place since July. Yochelson, 'The American Military Presence', p. 790.
9. Yochelson, 'The American Military Presence', p. 794.
10. Kissinger, *White House Years*, pp. 529–34.
11. Yochelson, 'The American Military Presence', p. 794; Kohl, 'The Nixon–Kissinger Foreign Policy System and US–European Relations', p. 29.
12. Nutter, *Kissinger's Grand Design*, p. 13. Nutter states that despite all the other changes in his thinking, Kissinger has not wavered in his insistence on strong conventional forces to defend Europe. He has steadfastly opposed any reduction in US forces and pressed for a build-up in European military strength.
13. Kissinger, *The Necessity for Choice*, p. 107.
14. Kohl, 'The Nixon–Kissinger Foreign Policy System and US–European Relations', p. 28.
15. United States Congress, *Congressional Record*, 115, 91st Congress, 1st Session, 1 December 1969, pp. 36147; 36167; Kaplan, 'NATO and the Nixon Doctrine', p. 152.
16. Yochelson, 'The American Military Presence', p. 799–802.
17. John Newhouse *et al., US Troops in Europe: Issues, Costs and Choices*, (1971) p. 5; *Congressional Record*, 18 May 1971, p. S7217; Kissinger, White House Years, p. 399.
18. *Congressional Record*, 115, 91st Congress, 1st Session, 1 December 1969, pp. 36147–9.
19. Yochelson, 'The American Military Presence', p. 796–7.
20. *Congressional Record*, 117, 92nd Congress, 1st Session, 11 May 1971.
21. Kissinger, *White House Years*, p. 241.
22. Yochelson, 'The American Military Presence' 794–5; *The New York Times*, 25 December 1970, p. 6; Kohl, 'The Nixon–Kissinger Foreign Policy System and US–European Relations', p. 28–9.
23. Kissinger, *White House Years*, pp. 942–6; Kohl, 'The Nixon–Kissinger Foreign Policy System and US–European Relations', p. 29; Kaplan, 'NATO and the Nixon Doctrine', p. 153; For President Johnson's statement, see *The New York Times*, 13 and 16 May 1971.
24. Wolfram F. Hanrieder (ed.), *Helmut Schmidt: Perspectives on Politics* (1982) p. 16.
25. Kissinger, *The Necessity for Choice*, p. 109.
26. Kissinger, *White House Years*, p. 945.
27. Kohl, 'The Nixon–Kissinger Foreign Policy System and US–European

Relations' 29–30; Yochelson, 'The American Military Presence', p. 785.

28. *Congressional Record*, 117, 92nd Congress, 1st Session, 19 May 1971, p. 15960.
29. C. Gordon Bare, 'Burden-sharing in NATO: The Economics of Alliance', *ORBIS*, 2 (Summer 1976) 426.
30. Bare, 'Burden-sharing in NATO', p. 431.
31. Kissinger, *The Years of Upheaval*, pp. 706–7; Bare, 'Burden-sharing in NATO', pp. 430–1.
32. Kohl, 'The Nixon–Kissinger Foreign Policy System and US–European Relations', p. 31.
33. Nixon, *United States Foreign Policy for the 1970s: A New Strategy for Peace*, p. 35.
34. Leacacos, 'Kissinger's Apparat' 16; 26; Kohl, 'The Nixon–Kissinger Foreign Policy System and US–European Relations', p. 31.
35. Kohl, 'The Nixon–Kissinger Foreign Policy System and US–European Relations', p. 31.
36. Kissinger, *White House Years*, pp. 401–2.
37. Kissinger, *White House Years*, pp. 401–20.
38. Kissinger, *White House Years*, p. 401.
39. Kissinger, *White House Years*, p. 534.
40. Brandt, *People and Politics*, p. 259; Michel Debré, 'The Defence of Europe and Security in Europe', *The Atlantic Community Quarterly*, 11, 1 (Spring 1973) 93–118.
41. 'Fear of Symmetry', *The Economist*, 25 November 1972, pp. 14–16.
42. Press and Information Office of the Federal Republic of Germany, *White Paper 1971/1972: The Security of the Federal Republic of Germany and the Development of Federal Armed Forces*, (1971) pp. 9–11.
43. John N. Yochelson, 'MFR: West European and American Perspectives', in Wolfram F. Hanrieder (ed.), *The United States and Western Europe*, (1974) pp. 258–9.
44. Kissinger, *White House Years*, p. 947.
45. Kohl, 'The Nixon–Kissinger Foreign Policy System and US–European Relations', pp. 31–3.
46. Kissinger, *The Necessity for Choice*, p. 157.
47. Kissinger, *The Necessity for Choice*, p. 154.
48. Kohl, 'The Nixon–Kissinger Foreign Policy System and US–European Relations', p. 32.
49. Kissinger, *White House Years*, p. 415.
50. In June 1971 Moscow refused to receive NATO's emissary Brosio for exploratory talks on MBFR, arguing that it did not wish to participate in bloc-to-bloc negotiations.
51. Kissinger, *White House Years*, pp. 416; 534.
52. The initial Western proposal tabled in November 1973 called for the reduction of ground force manpower on both sides to the common collective ceiling of 700 000 men in two phases. In the first phase the US would withdraw 29 000 men, leaving their equipment behind. The USSR would withdraw a tank army, consisting of 68 000 men and 1700 tanks.
53. In the Moscow communiqué of 29 May the two sides agreed that 'the

goal of ensuring stability and security in Europe would be served by a reciprocal reduction of armed forces and armaments, first of all in Central Europe ... [and that] Appropriate agreement should be reached as soon as practicable between states concerned on the procedures for negotiations on this subject in a special forum'. United States Department of State, *United States Foreign Policy 1972: A Report of the Secretary of State* (1973) p. 87.

54.   Kohl, 'The Nixon–Kissinger Foreign Policy System and US–European Relations', pp. 32–3.
55.   Robert E. Hunter, 'Beyond Military Security in Europe', in Wolfram F. Hanrieder (ed.), *The United States and Western Europe*, pp. 234–5.
56.   The Mutual and Balanced Force Reductions (MBFR) negotiations began in Vienna, Austria, on 30 October 1973. On the Western Side, the 'direct' participants (those with armed forces in the agreed area of reductions) were Belgium, Canada, the Federal Republic of Germany (FRG), Luxembourg, the Netherlands, the UK, and the US. 'Indirect' participants (those without armed forces in the agreed area of reductions) were Denmark, Greece, Italy, Norway, and Turkey. For the East, the direct participants were Czechoslovakia, the German Democratic Republic (GDR), Poland and the USSR. Indirect participants were Bulgaria, Hungary, and Romania. The agreed area of reductions (the NATO Guidelines Area, or NGA) included the FRG, the Netherlands, Belgium, Luxembourg, the GDR, Czechoslovakia, and Poland. For an excellent summary of the history of MBFR which includes an analysis of proposals submitted by Eastern and Western participants over the years, see John G. Keliher, *The Negotiations on Mutual and Balanced Force Reductions: The Search for Arms Control in Europe* (1980); Also see Linda P. Brady, 'Negotiating European Security: Mutual and Balanced Force Reductions', *International Security Review*, VI, II (Summer 1981) 207.
57.   Kissinger, *White House Years*, p. 400.
58.   Kissinger reported that Brosio frankly admitted to President Nixon when they met privately in Naples in September 1970 that the defence review and the growing NATO interest in MBFR were designed as devices to put a brake on unilateral American decisions.
59.   Nixon, *US Foreign Policy for the 1970s: The Emerging Structure of Peace*, p. 45; *US Foreign Policy for the 1970s: Shaping a Durable Peace*, p. 83; United States House of Representatives, Committee on Armed Services, *US Military Commitments to Europe*, 93rd Congress, 2nd Session (1974) pp. 7; 12; Bare, 'Burden-sharing in NATO', p. 422.
60.   Kissinger, *White House Years*, pp. 401–2.
61.   Nixon, *US Foreign Policy for the 1970s: Building for Peace*, p. 36.
62.   Nixon, *US Foreign Policy for the 1970s: Shaping a Durable Peace*, p. 83.
63.   Kissinger, *White House Years*, p. 386.
64.   Kissinger, *American Foreign Policy*, pp. 75–6.
65.   Kissinger, *American Foreign Policy*, p. 75; Kissinger, *White House Years*, p. 385.
66.   Kissinger, *White House Years*, p. 385.

67. Cromwell, 'Europe and the "Structure of Peace"', p. 16.
68. Kissinger, *White House Years*, p. 386.
69. Kissinger, *White House Years*, p. 385.
70. Kissinger, *The Troubled Partnership*, p. 149.
71. Kissinger, *American Foreign Policy*, p. 74.
72. *The Eurogroup* (1972) pp. 4; 7–8.
73. Cromwell, 'Europe and the "Structure of Peace"', p. 17.
74. Press and Information Office of the Government of The Federal Republic of Germany, *The European Group in the North Atlantic Alliance*, a Report by the Planning Office of the Federal Ministry of Defence (1972) p. 11. Also William C. Cromwell, *The Eurogroup and NATO* (1974) p. 3.
75. Bare, 'Burden-sharing in NATO' 420.
76. Nixon, *US Foreign Policy for the 1970s: The Emerging Structure of Peace*, p. 45.
77. The House of Representatives voted 242 to 163 against a troop-reduction amendment in July 1973.
78. Nixon, *US Foreign Policy for the 1970s: Shaping a Durable Peace*, p. 83.
79. Nixon, *US Foreign Policy for the 1970s: Shaping a Durable Peace*, p. 84.
80. See *The New York Times*, 8 June 1973, p. 10, and 28 July 1973, p. 4; Bare, 'Burden-sharing in NATO' 427.
81. Kissinger, *White House Years*, p. 396.
82. Brandt, *People and Politics*, p. 290.
83. Bare, 'Burden-sharing in NATO' 428.
84. United States Congress, *Report on the Fifth Meeting of Members of Congress and of the European Parliament*, 93rd Congress, 2nd Session, (1974) p. 27.
85. Bare, 'Burden-sharing in NATO'. pp. 428–9.
86. Bare, 'Burden-sharing in NATO', pp. 431.
87. United States Senate, Committee on Foreign Relations, *US Security Issues in Europe* (1973) p. 3; Bare, 'Burden-sharing in NATO', pp. 431–2.

8 US Reaction to West European Unity

1. For Kissinger's views on the issue see Chapter 3 and Chapter 4. Also Kissinger, *White House Years*, p. 86.
2. Brandt, *People and Politics*, pp. 282–3.
3. Chancellor Brandt stated: 'In reality *Ostpolitik* was one of our reasons for wanting progress in the West'. In short, Britain's entry into the EEC would balance his independent initiatives to the Communist bloc: in *People and Politics*, p. 254.
4. Brandt, *People and Politics*, p. 245. The French proposed the EEC summit conference according to Brandt.
5. Brandt, *People and Politics*, pp. 245–6; Kissinger, *White House Years*, p. 389.
6. Edward A. Kolodziej, *French International Policy Under de Gaulle*

and Pompidou (1974) pp. 401–3; Kissinger, *White House Years*, pp. 86–91.

7.   Kissinger, *White House Years*, pp. 86–91.
8.   Nixon, *The Memoirs of Richard Nixon*, vol. 1, pp. 457–8.
9.   Kissinger, *The Troubled Partnership*, p. 32. Kissinger had been arguing that France has the power to prevent the US from realizing its objectives in Europe.
10.   United States Senate, Committee on Foreign Relations, *United States Policy Toward Europe and Related Matters* (1966) p. 137.
11.   Kissinger, *The Troubled Partnership*, pp. 76; 239–40.
12.   Nixon, *The Memoirs of Richard Nixon*, vol. 1, p. 457.
13.   Kissinger, *White House Years*, p. 89.
14.   Chapter 4 deals with Kissinger's views on the issue of West European unity.
15.   Nixon, *US Foreign Policy for the 1970s: A New Strategy for Peace*, p. 32.
16.   Kissinger, *American Foreign Policy*, p. 74; *The Troubled Partnership*, pp. 76; 242–3.
17.   Kissinger, *The Troubled Partnership*, pp. 76; 239–40.
18.   President Nixon's press conference, 4 March 1969; in *Department of State Bulletin*, 24 March 1969.
19.   Cromwell, 'Europe and the "Structure of Peace" ', p. 12.
20.   Kissinger, *The Troubled Partnership*, p. 244; Also see Kissinger's statement in United States Senate, *United States Policy Toward Europe*, p. 175.
21.   Kissinger, *The Troubled Partnership*, pp. 37–8.
22.   Schaetzel, *The Unhinged Alliance*, p. 49.
23.   Graubard, *Kissinger*, p. 206.
24.   Graubard, *Kissinger*, p. 51.
25.   Graubard, *Kissinger*, p. 51.
26.   Graubard, *Kissinger*, p. 51; Cromwell, 'Europe and the "Structure for Peace" ', p. 18.
27.   Nixon, *US Foreign Policy for the 1970s: Building for Peace*, p. 30.
28.   Kissinger, *The Troubled Partnership*, pp. 39–40.
29.   Kissinger, *The Troubled Partnership*, p. 40.
30.   Kissinger, *The Troubled Partnership*, p. 232.
31.   Chapter 3 deals with Kissinger's analysis of the structural problems of NATO.
32.   Kissinger, *White House Years*, p. 385; *The Troubled Partnership*, pp. 166; 169; *American Foreign Policy*, p. 75.
33.   Kissinger, *The Troubled Partnership*, p. 169.
34.   Kissinger, *The Troubled Partnership*, p. 8.
35.   Cromwell, 'Europe and the "Structure of Peace" ', p. 15.
36.   Nixon, *US Foreign Policy for the 1970s: A New Strategy for Peace*, p. 32.
37.   Schaetzel, *The Unhinged Alliance*, p. 49; Martin J. Hillenbrand, 'The Future of the European Community as a Problem of American–European Relations', in Karl Kaiser and Hans-Peter Schwarz (eds), *America and Western Europe* (1977) pp. 317–18.

38. Kissinger, *White House Years*, p. 426.
39. Nixon, *US Foreign Policy for the 1970s: A New Strategy for Peace*, p. 32.
40. Kissinger, *White House Years*, p. 426.
41. Kissinger, *White House Years*, p. 426.
42. Kissinger, *White House Years*, pp. 426–7.
43. Kissinger, *White House Years*, pp. 427–8.
44. The Under-Secretaries Committee was chaired by the Under-Secretary of State, and included the Deputy Secretary of Defense, the Chairman of the JCS, the Director of the CIA, and Kissinger. Its task was to implement decisions. Kalb and Kalb, *Kissinger*, p. 86.
45. Kissinger, *White House Years*, p. 428.
46. Kissinger, *White House Years*, p. 428.
47. Kissinger, *The Troubled Partnership*, p. 39.
48. Kissinger, *American Foreign Policy*, p. 75.
49. Kissinger, *The Troubled Partnership*, p. 40.
50. Cromwell, 'Europe and the "Structure of Peace"', p. 14. Cromwell argues that in the Nixon Administration Kissinger was even less prepared to pay such a price than were his predecessors.
51. Kissinger, *White House Years*, pp. 428–9.
52. The US, the President stated, would levy a 10 per cent surcharge on all imports, end the convertability of the dollar into gold, and establish wage and price controls.
53. Nixon, *US Foreign Policy for the 1970s: Building for Peace*, pp. 29–30.
54. Kohl, 'The Nixon–Kissinger Foreign Policy System and US–European Relations', p. 19. Also Kissinger, *White House Years*, p. 950.
55. Kohl, 'The Nixon–Kissinger Foreign Policy System and US–European Relations', p. 19.
56. Brandon, *The Retreat of American Power*, p. 229.
57. Brandon, *The Retreat of American Power*, p. 227. the US deficit with Japan and with Canada was about $2 billion each; with Europe the US had a surplus of about $1.5 billion.
58. Brandon, *The Retreat of American Power*, p. 224.
59. Brandon, *The Retreat of American Power*, p. 235.
60. Kissinger, *White House Years*, p. 957.
61. Burns supported Kissinger in his efforts to resolve the crisis. Brandon, *The Retreat of American Power*, pp. 233; 235–6. Also Kohl, 'The Nixon–Kissinger Foreign Policy System and US–European Relations', p. 38.
62. Kissinger, *White House Years*, pp. 957–8.
63. Heath became Prime Minister in June 1970.
64. Meetings were scheduled with Pompidou in the Azores for 13 December, with Prime Minister Heath in Bermuda for 20–21 December and with Brandt in Key Biscayne for 28–29 December.
65. Brandon, *The Retreat of American Power*, pp. 240–1; Kohl, 'The Nixon–Kissinger Foreign Policy System and US–European Relations', p. 38; Kissinger, *White House Years*, pp. 959–62.
66. Brandon, *The Retreat of American Power*, p. 234. Brandon reports

that Richard Cooper of Johns Hopkins University and Francis Bator of Harvard wrote a memo, on Kissinger's request, warning that the crisis could impinge on vital American political and security interests and encourage neo-Gaullism in Europe. They argued for early removal of the surcharge and for approaching the Allies informally with proposals for a solution.

67. Brandon, *The Retreat of American Power*, p. 241. Brandon states that at the Azores meeting Pompidou began by offering to revalue the Franc by 6 per cent. Connally countered with a demand for 9½ per cent. Pompidou moved up to 7 and finally 8.57 per cent. Connally tried to hold out for 9 per cent but the President accepted Pompidou's last offer as Kissinger had suggested. The President agreed to increase the price of gold to $38 dollars (an increase of only $3 dollars), and thereby devalue the dollar. Brandon states that Pompidou had made such a substantial concession, not because he thought it was particularly financially advantageous, but because he wanted to make a contribution to US–French understanding, Kissinger, *White House Years*, pp. 960–2.

68. The British House of Commons voted for entry into the EEC by a clear majority in October 1971. The Norwegian voters turned down membership of the EEC by a referendum on 26 September 1972.

9 *Ostpolitik*: the Threat of 'Differential Detente'

1. Kissinger, *The Troubled Partnership*, p. 26.
2. Kissinger, *White House Years*, pp. 132; 410; 528. Kissinger used the terms 'differential detente' and 'selective detente' interchangeably. These terms meant the Soviet efforts to ease tensions with America's Allies while remaining intransigent on global issues of concern to the US.
3. Hans W. Gatzke, *Germany and the United States: 'A Special Relationship'?* (1980) p. 210. Kenneth A. Myers, *Ostpolitik and American Security Interests in Europe* (1972) p. 4.
4. Gatzke, *Germany and the United States*, p. 211.
5. Gatzke, *Germany and the United States*, p. 210; Seymour M. Hersh, *The Price of Power: Kissinger in the Nixon White House* (1983) p. 416.
6. Gatzke, *Germany and the United States*, pp. 211–12.
7. The grand Coalition consisted of the Christian Democratic Union (CDU) and the Social Democratic Party (SPD).
8. Willy Brandt, *People and Politics*, pp. 170–3.
9. Kissinger, *White House Years*, p. 408. On 13 June 1969, Walter Scheel, leader of the FDP (in his talks with President Nixon), argued that the Holstein Doctrine would isolate the FRG from the Third World.
10. Kissinger, *White House Years*, p. 409. In the mid-1960s the FRG had made an 'exception' for the countries of Eastern Europe on the weak excuse that they were not free in their decisions.

11. Honore M. Catudal, Jr, *The Diplomacy of the Quadripartite Agreement on Berlin* (1978) p. 136. The Christian Democrats warned Brandt that the Poles would not settle for anything less than a complete sellout of German interests in the East.
12. Hersh, *The Price of Power*, p. 416.
13. Kissinger, *The Troubled Partnership*, p. 211.
14. Kissinger, *The Troubled Partnership*, p. 211.
15. Kissinger, *The Troubled Partnership*, pp. 211–12.
16. Kissinger, *The Troubled Partnership*, p. 212.
17. Kissinger, *The Troubled Partnership*, p. 211.
18. Kissinger, *The Necessity for Choice*, p. 136.
19. Kissinger, *The Troubled Partnership*, p. 212.
20. Kissinger, *The Troubled Partnership*, p. 213.
21. Kissinger, *The Troubled Partnership*, p. 213.
22. Kissinger, *The Troubled Partnership*, p. 213.
23. Kissinger, *The Troubled Partnership*, pp. 213–14.
24. Kissinger, *The Troubled Partnership*, p. 214.
25. Kissinger, *The Troubled Partnership*, p. 214.
26. Kissinger, *The Troubled Partnership*, pp. 213–14.
27. Kissinger, *The Troubled Partnership*, p. 216.
28. Kissinger, *The Troubled Partnership*, pp. 213; 215.
29. Kissinger, *The Troubled Partnership*, p. 215; *The Necessity for Choice*, p. 132.
30. Kissinger, *The Troubled Partnership*, pp. 215–16.
31. Kissinger, *The Troubled Partnership*, p. 216.
32. Press and Information Office of the Government of the Federal Republic of Germany, *The Development of the Relations between the Federal Republic of Germany and the German Democratic Republic* (1973) p. 22.
33. Catudal, *The Diplomacy of the Quadripartite Agreement on Berlin*, p. 71.
34. Brandt, *People and Politics*, pp. 166; 367. Brandt states: 'my so-called *Ostpolitik* was not first devised in 1969. The Adenauer and Erhard governments had both, in their own way, striven to ease our relations with the Soviet Union and Eastern Europe. In June 1961 the Bundestag had unanimously passed a resolution calling for moves to this end. My own ideas and recommendations had taken shape over a period of many years'.
35. Kenneth A. Myers, *Ostpolitik and American Security Interests in Europe* (1972) pp. 11–12; Kissinger, *White House Years*, pp. 410–11; 531–2.
36. Brandt, *A Peace Policy for Europe* (1969) pp. 26–7.
37. Brandt, *People and Politics*, p. 20.
38. Myers, *Ostpolitik and American Security Interests in Europe*, p. 12.
39. Landau, *Kissinger*, pp. 71; 255. Landau reports that in an interview with Daniel Ellsberg in Cambridge, on 25 February 1972, Ellsberg reported that he learned of this recommendation from Kissinger himself in a conversation at Harvard in the Fall of 1961. Other officials also knew of Kissinger's recommendation. But Landau states

that it remains unclear whether Kissinger ever put this recommendation into writing, or whether he addressed it directly to the President. McGeorge Bundy, the only individual who knows, declined an interview with Landau.

40. Kissinger, *The Troubled Partnership*, p. 69.
41. Kissinger, *The Troubled Partnership*, pp. 69–70.
42. Myers, *Ostpolitik and American Security Interests in Europe*, p. 14.
43. Brandt, *A Peace Policy for Europe*, pp. 24; 29; 70.
44. Brandt, 'Let me Speak of Peace Policy in our Time ... And About What my Own Country Can do', *The Bulletin* (14 December 1971) pp. 339. Also Brandt, *A Peace Policy for Europe*, pp. 29; 105; 151–6.
45. Brandt, 'Let me Speak of Peace Policy in our Time ... And About What my Own Country Can do', p. 389; Also see Brandt, *A Peace Policy for Europe*, pp. 172; 196–7.
46. Brandt, *A Peace Policy for Europe*, p. 78.
47. Brandt, 'Let me Speak of Peace Policy in our Time ... And About What my Own Country Can do', p. 339.
48. Brandt, *A Peace Policy for Europe*, p. 158.
49. Brandt, *A Peace Policy for Europe*, p. 188.
50. Brandt, *A Peace Policy for Europe*, p. 171; Myers, *Ostpolitik and American Security Interests in Europe*, p. 16.
51. Brandt, *A Peace Policy for Europe*, p. 171.
52. Brandt, *A Peace Policy for Europe*, p. 158.
53. Brandt, 'Let me Speak of Peace Policy in our Time ... And About What my Own Country Can do', p. 336.
54. Brandt, 'Let me Speak of Peace Policy in our Time ... And About What my Own Country Can do', p. 336.
55. Brandt, 'Let me Speak of Peace Policy in our Time ... And About What my Own Country Can do', p. 336.
56. Brandt, 'Let me Speak of Peace Policy in our Time ... And About What my Own Country Can do', p. 338.
57. Brandt, *A Peace Policy for Europe*, p. 94.
58. Brandt, *A Peace Policy for Europe*, p. 103.
59. Brandt, *A Peace Policy for Europe*, pp. 115–16.
60. For the West German, American, and Soviet conceptions of detente see Michael J. Sodaro, 'US–Soviet Relations: Detente or Cold War?' (1984) p. 4.
61. Brandt, 'Let me Speak of Peace Policy in our Time ... And About What my Own Country Can do', pp. 338–9.
62. Brandt, *A Peace Policy for Europe*, p. 75.
63. Brandt, 'Let me Speak of Peace in our Time ... And About What my Own Country Can do', p. 338.
64. Myers, *Ostpolitik and American Security Interests in Europe*, p. 10.
65. Myers, *Ostpolitik and American Security Interests in Europe*, pp. 9–10.
66. *The New York Times*, 13 February 1969; Catudal, *The Diplomacy of the Quadripartite Agreement on Berlin*, p. 52.
67. Kissinger, *White House Years*, pp. 145; 406.
68. Kissinger, *The Necessity For Choice*, p. 139.

69. Nixon, *The Memoirs of Richard Nixon*, vol. 1, p. 422.
70. Kissinger, *White House Years*, pp. 146; 407.
71. Brandt, *People and Politics*, p. 194.
72. Catudal, *The Diplomacy of the Quadripartite Agreement on Berlin*, pp. 50–5.
73. On the day of Nixon's inauguration (20 January), the Soviet Union offered to renew discussions with the US on the limitation of strategic arms.
74. Catudal, *The Diplomacy of the Quadripartite Agreement on Berlin*, pp. 55–7; Kissinger, *White House Years*, pp. 145–6. During Kissinger's secret trip to China in July 1971, Chinese Premier Chou En-lai stated that Moscow had deliberately staged the border clashes to provide a diversion while West German parliamentarians travelled unimpeded to Berlin. In Chou En-lai's view the border clashes were manufactured to permit the Soviets 'to escape their responsibilities toward Berlin'.
75. Kissinger, *White House Years*, p. 414; Catudal, *The Diplomacy of the Quadripartite Agreement on Berlin*, pp. 57–9.
76. Brandt, *People and Politics*, p. 156; Catudal, *The Diplomacy of the Quadripartite Agreement on Berlin*, pp. 58–9; Kissinger, *White House Years*, p. 146.
77. Brandt, *People and Politics*, p. 156.
78. Kissinger, *White House Years*, p. 414.
79. Kissinger, *White House Years*, p. 415.
80. Brandt, *People and Politics*, p. 156.
81. Kissinger, *White House Years*, pp. 414–15.
82. Kissinger, *White House Years*, p. 407. Shortly after the President returned from his European trip, Dobrynin saw Kissinger and after mildly complaining about the President's Siemens' Factory speech suggested for the first time there were 'positive possibilities' to negotiate on access procedures to Berlin.
83. Kissinger, *White House Years*, p. 144.
84. Kissinger, *White House Years*, p. 407.
85. Catudal, *The Diplomacy of the Quadripartite Agreement on Berlin*, p. 59.
86. Catudal, *The Diplomacy of the Quadripartite Agreement on Berlin*, pp. 60–3.
87. Kissinger, *White House Years*, p. 408.
88. Kissinger, *White House Years*, p. 408.
89. Kissinger, *White House Years*, p. 408. After the German election of 28 September 1969, President Nixon, that assured the CDU/CSU plurality meant that Kiesinger would continue as Chancellor, telephoned to congratulate him. The Bundestag elected Brandt by 251 votes to 235. Brandt, *People and Politics*, pp. 223–4.
90. Kissinger, *White House Years*, pp. 408–09.
91. Kissinger, *The Necessity For Choice*, p. 132; *The Troubled Partnership*, pp. 215–6.
92. Kissinger, *The Necessity of Choice*, p. 132; *White House Years*, p. 409; Hersh, *The Price of Power*, p. 416. Hersh maintains that

240   *Notes*

Ostpolitik 'became one of Kissinger's obsessions in late 1969 and early 1970'. But 'as Kissinger had to know, the West German initiatives to the East had been repeatedly urged upon the Bonn government by the Johnson Administration'. Kissinger knew, and if Hersh had read Kissinger's writings carefully he would have known why Kissinger had opposed Johnson's support of Bonn's initiative to the East.

93. Kissinger, *White House Years*, p. 411. Kissinger states: 'I thought we should receive Bahr so as to reduce the distrust produced by Nixon's unfortunate telephone call to Kiesinger'.

94. Kissinger, *White House Years*, p. 411; Hersh, *The Price of Power*, pp. 416–17. According to Bahr: 'I made clear we'd inform them in advance of what we would do, but we would do it anyway'.

95. Kissinger, *White House Years*, p. 411; *The Troubled Partnership*, pp. 211–12.

96. Kissinger, *White House Years*, p. 411; Hersh, *The Price of Power*, pp. 416–17.

97. Catudal, *The Diplomacy of the Quadripartite Agreement on Berlin*, pp. 64–5.

98. Kissinger, *White House Years*, p. 530.

99. Kissinger, *White House Years*, p. 530.

100. Kissinger, *White House Years*, p. 44; Kissinger states that Paris opposed *Ostpolitik* but was unwilling to make its opposition explicit.

101. Kissinger, *White House Years*, p. 44.

102. Hersh, *The Price of Power*, p. 416. Hersh reports that Roger Morris, one of the participants in the NSC staff meetings said that '[Kissinger] hated *Ostpolitik* and Willy Brandt for the beginning ... Henry thought the Germans were flirting with historical tragedy; that *Ostpolitik* would be a prelude to internal fascism, a turn to the right, and the emergence of another Weimar Republic'. Robert E. Osgood, who directed the NSC staff's policy planning group, and submitted an analysis that found merit in Brandt's initiatives, reported: '[Kissinger's] great fear and distrust of the Germans, particularly those who wanted closer relations to the East in what he considered a fuzzy-minded and dangerous way'.

103. Kissinger, *The Necessity for Choice*, p. 132; *The Troubled Partnership*, pp. 215–16.

104. Kissinger, *White House Years*, pp. 529–30.

105. Kissinger, *White House Years*, p. 410. Kissinger states: 'It was to Brandt's historic credit that he assumed for Germany the burdens and the anguish imposed by necessity. I cannot maintain that I came to this view immediately. But once I recognized the inevitable, I sought to channel it in a constructive direction by working closely with Brandt and his colleagues'. Brandt, *People and Politics*, p. 284. Brandt reported that his talks with Kissinger at Camp David in April 1970 revealed that 'Kissinger's interest in our *Ostpolitik* was lively but not untinged with skepticism. I gained the impression – one which occasionally recurred in later years – that he would rather have taken personal charge of the delicate complex of East–West

problems in its entirety'.

106. Kissinger, *White House Years*, p. 410.
107. Kissinger, *The Troubled Partnership*, p. 106.
108. Kissinger, *American Foreign Policy*, p. 75.
109. Kissinger, *White House Years*, p. 132.
110. Catudal, *The Diplomacy of the Quadripartite Agreement on Berlin*, p. 96; Hersh, *The Price of Power*, p. 421. Hersh states that a few days after the Berlin agreement was signed, the White House in 'a lackluster "p.r." effort' put out the word that President Nixon had been personally responsible for keeping the negotiations going at critical junctures by intervening directly with Gromyko. In short, he implies that the President had opposed the Berlin talks.
111. Kissinger, *The Necessity for Choice*, pp. 139–41; *The Troubled Partnership*, p. 71.
112. Kissinger, *White House Years*, p. 530.
113. Kissinger, *White House Years*, p. 531.
114. Kissinger, *White House Years*, p. 412; Catudal, *The Diplomacy of the Quadripartite Agreement on Berlin*, pp. 65–6; *The Washington Post* 11 February 1970.
115. Catudal, *The Diplomacy of the Quadripartite Agreement on Berlin*, p. 69.
116. Kohl, 'The Nixon–Kissinger Foreign Policy System and US–European Relations', p. 26; Catudal, *The Diplomacy of the Quadripartite Agreement on Berlin*, pp. 88–90.
117. Kohl, 'The Nixon–Kissinger Policy System and US–European Relations', p. 26; Catudal, *The Diplomacy of the Quadripartite Agreement on Berlin*, pp. 88–90.
118. Catudal, *The Diplomacy of the Quadripartite Agreement on Berlin*, p. 89.
119. Catudal, *The Diplomacy of the Quadripartite Agreement on Berlin*, p. 89; Kissinger, *White House Years*, p. 825; Hersh, *The Price of Power*, p. 418.
120. Kissinger, *White House Years*, p. 532.
121. Kissinger, *The Troubled Partnership*, p. 215.
122. Kissinger, *White House Years*, p. 532.
123. Kissinger, *White House Years*, p. 532.
124. Brandt, *People and Politics*, pp. 284; 288. Brandt states: 'Many people even alleged, though without being able to prove it, that Henry Kissinger voiced different shades of meaning in our absence than in our presence'.
125. Kissinger, *White House Years*, p. 531.
126. Kissinger, *White House Years*, p. 533; Catudal, *The Diplomacy of the Quadripartite Agreement on Berlin*, pp. 136; 157; 166; 198–9.
127. Press and Information Office of the Government of the Federal Republic of Germany, *Documentation Relating to the Federal Government's Policy of Detente* (1974) pp. 13–21.
128. Press and Information Office of the Government of the Federal Republic of Germany, *Documentation Relating to the Federal Government's Policy of Detente* (1974) pp. 13–21.

129. Catudal, *The Diplomacy of the Quadripartite Agreement on Berlin*, pp. 118–19; *Newsweek*, 10 August 1970.
130. Kissinger, *White House Years*, p. 533.
131. Kissinger, *The Troubled Partnership*, pp. 219–20.
132. Kissinger, *White House Years*, p. 534.
133. *The Washington Post*, 7 December 1970; Catudal, *The Diplomacy of the Quadripartite Agreement on Berlin*, p. 139.
134. Catudal, *The Diplomacy of the Quadripartite Agreement on Berlin*, pp. 139–140. Brandt sent numerous emissaries to Washington in late 1970 and wrote personal letters to President Nixon, President Pompidou, and Prime Minister Edward Heath.
135. Catudal, *The Diplomacy of the Quadripartite Agreement on Berlin*, pp. 139–41.
136. Nixon, *US Foreign Policy For the 1970s: Building for Peace*, pp. 39–40.
137. Kissinger, *White House Years*, pp. 817–18; 821; 829.
138. Kissinger, *White House Years*, pp. 731; 828–33; Catudal, *The Diplomacy of the Quadripartite Agreement on Berlin*, pp. 187–9; Dickson, *Kissinger and the Meaning of History*, pp. 130–1.
139. Kissinger, *White House Years*, p. 833.
140. Press and Information Office of the Federal Government, *The Quadripartite Agreement on Berlin* (1971) pp. 12–13.
141. Kissinger, *White House Years*, p. 830; Hersh, *The Price of Power*, p. 420; Catudal, *The Diplomacy of the Quadripartite Agreement on Berlin*, pp. 178–9.
142. Hersh, *The Price of Power*, p. 422.
143. Kissinger, *American Foreign Policy*, p. 75.
144. Kissinger, *The Troubled Partnership*, p. 106.
145. Kissinger, *The Troubled Partnership*, p. 17.

Select Bibliography

Books

ARON, Raymond *The Imperial Republic: The United States and the World 1945–1973*, translated by Frank Jellinek (Cambridge, Mass: Winthrop Publishers, 1974).

BALL, George W. *Diplomacy for a Crowded World* (Boston: Little, Brown & Co., 1976).

BARNET, Richard J. *The Alliance: America–Europe–Japan Makers of the Postwar World* (New York: Simon and Schuster, 1983).

———— *The Giants: Russia and America* (New York: Simon and Schuster, 1977).

BELL, Coral *The Diplomacy of Detente: The Kissinger Era* (New York: St Martin's Press, 1977).

BENDEL, Jeffry R. 'Scholar Versus Statesman: The Record of Henry Kissinger; The United States and Europe', Ph.D. dissertation (University of Massachusetts, 1982).

BINDER, David *The Other German: Willy Brandt's Life & Times* (Washington DC: The New Republic Book Company, 1975).

BRANDON, Henry *The Retreat of American Power* (Garden City, NY: Doubleday, 1973).

BRANDT, Willy *People and Politics: The Years 1960–1975*, translated by Maxwell Brownjohn (Boston: Little, Brown & Co., 1976).

———— *A Peace Policy For Europe*, translated by Joel Carmichael (New York: Holt, Rinehart & Winston, 1969).

BREZHNEV, Leonid *Peace, Detente, and Soviet–American Relations* (New York: Harcourt Brace Jovanovich, 1979).

———— *On the Policy of the Soviet Union and the International Situation* (Garden City, NY: Doubleday, 1973).

BROADHURST, Arlene Idol (ed.) *The Future of European Alliance Systems: NATO and the Warsaw Pact* (Boulder, Col.: Westview Press, 1982).

BRODIE, Bernard *War and Politics* (New York: Macmillan, 1973).

BROWN, Seyom *The Crises of Power: An Interpretation of United States Foreign Policy During the Kissinger Years* (New York: Columbia University Press, 1979).

———— *The Faces of Power: Constancy and Change in United States Foreign Policy from Truman to Johnson* (New York: Columbia University Press, 1968).

BURGESS, Randolph W. and Huntley, James Robert *Europe and America: The Next Ten Years* (New York: Walker & Co., 1970).

BURROWS, Bernard and Edwards, Geoffrey *The Defense of Western Europe* (London: Butterworth Scientific, 1982).

BUTEUX, Paul *The Politics of Nuclear Consultation in NATO 1965–1980* (London: Cambridge University Press, 1983).

243

CALDWELL, Dan *American–Soviet Relations: From 1947 to the Nixon–Kissinger Grand Design*, Contributions in Political Science, 61 (Westport, Conn.: Greenwood Press, 1981).

———— 'American–Soviet Detente and the Nixon–Kissinger Grand Design and Grand Strategy', Ph.D. dissertation (Stanford University, 1978).

CALDWELL, Lawrence T. and Diebold, William, Jr *Soviet–American Relations in the 1980s: Superpower Politics and East–West Trade* (New York: McGraw-Hill, 1981).

CATLIN, Sir George *Kissinger's Atlantic Charter* (Gerrards Cross, Buckinghamshire, UK: Colin Smythe, 1974).

CATUDAL, Honore M., Jr *The Diplomacy of the Quadripartite Agreement on Berlin*, foreword by Ambassador Kenneth Rush (Berlin: Berlin-Verlag, 1978).

———— *A Balance Sheet of the Quadripartite Agreement on Berlin*, foreword by Ambassador Kenneth Rush (Berlin: Berlin-Verlag, 1978).

CERNY, Karl H. and Briefs, Henry W. (eds) *NATO in Quest for Cohesion* (New York: Praeger, 1965).

CHOMSKY, Noam *Towards a New Cold War* (New York: Pantheon Books, 1982).

CLEVELAND, Harold van B. *The Atlantic Idea and its European Rivals* (New York: McGraw-Hill, 1966).

CLOSE, Robert *Europe Without Defense?* (New York: Pentagon Press, 1979).

CROMWELL, William C. *The Eurogroup and NATO*, Research Monograph Series 18 (Philadelphia, Penn.: Foreign Policy Research Institute, 1974).

DAVIS, Vincent *Henry Kissinger and Bureaucratic Politics*, Essay Series 9 (Institute of International Studies, the University of South Carolina, 1979).

DEPORTE, A. W. *Europe Between the Super-Powers: The Enduring Balance* (New Haven: Yale University Press, 1979).

DICKSON, Peter W. *Kissinger and the Meaning of History* (New York: Cambridge University Press, 1978).

DOUGHERTY, James E. and Pfaltzgraff, Robert L., Jr (eds) *Contending Theories of International Relations*, 2nd rev. ed (New York: Harper & Row, 1981).

EAST, Maurice A., Salmore, Stephen A. and Hermann, Charles F. (eds) *Why Nations Act* (Beverly Hills: SAGE Publications, 1978).

EVANS, Rowland and Novak, Robert D. *Nixon in the White House* (New York: Vintage Books, 1972).

FALK, Richard A. *What's Wrong with Henry Kissinger's Foreign Policy* Princeton, NJ: Center of International Studies, Princeton University, 1974).

FLIESS, Peter J. *International Relations in the Bipolar World* (New York: Random House, 1968).

FOSTER, Richard B., Beaufre, André and Joshua, Wynfred (eds) *Strategy for the West: American–Allied Relations in Transition* (New York: Crane, Russak & Co., 1974).

FRANKEL, Joseph *British Foreign Policy 1945–1973* (New York: Oxford University Press, 1975).

GADDIS, John L. *Strategies of Containment* (New York: Oxford University Press, 1982).

———— *Russia, the Soviet Union and the United States* (New York: John Wiley and Sons, 1978).

GARNETT, John C. (ed.) *The Defense of Western Europe* (New York: St Martin's Press, 1974).

GATZKE, Hans W. *Germany and the United States: A 'Special Relationship'?* (Cambridge, Mass.: Harvard University Press, 1980).

GOLDMAN, Marshall I. *Detente and Dollars* (New York: Basic Books, 1975).

GOODMAN, Elliot R. *The Fate of the Atlantic Community* (New York: Praeger, 1975).

GRAUBARD, Stephen R. *Kissinger: Portrait of a Mind* (New York: W. W. Norton, 1973).

HANRIEDER, Wolfram F. (ed.) *Helmut Schmidt: Perspectives on Politics* (Boulder, Col.: Westview Press, 1982).

———— (ed.) *The United States and Western Europe* (Cambridge, Mass.: Winthrop Publishers, 1974).

HARTLEY, A. *American Foreign Policy in the Nixon Era*, Adelphi Papers 110 (London: The International Institute for Strategic Studies, 1974).

HERSH, Seymour M. *The Rule of Power: Kissinger in the Nixon White House* (New York: Summit Books, 1983).

HILL, Christopher (ed.) *National Foreign Policies and European Political Cooperation* (London: George Allen & Unwin, 1983).

HOFFMANN, Stanley *Primacy or World Order* (New York: McGraw-Hill, 1978).

HOOD, Donald Eugene ' "Lessons" of the Vietnam War: Henry Kissinger, George F. Kennan, Richard Falk and the Debate over Containment, 1965–1980', Ph.D. dissertation (University of Washington, 1982).

JOHNSON, U. Alexis and McAllister, Jef Olivarius *The Right Hand of Power* (Englewood Cliffs, NJ: Prentice-Hall, 1984).

JOINER, Harry M. *American Foreign Policy: the Kissinger Era* (Huntsville, Al.: The Strode Publishers, 1977).

KAHAN, Jerome H. *Security in the Nuclear Age: Developing US Strategic Arms Policy* (Washington, DC: The Brookings Institution, 1975).

KAISER, Karl and Schwarz, Hans-Peter (eds) *America and Western Europe* (Lexington, Mass.: Lexington Books, 1977).

KALB, Marvin and Kalb, Bernard *Kissinger* (Boston: Little, Brown & Co., 1974).

KAPLAN, Lawrence S. and Clawson, Robert W. (eds) *NATO After Thirty Years* (Wilmington, Del.: Scholarly Resources, 1981).

KAPLAN, Morton *The Rationale for NATO: European Collective Security Past and Future* (Washington, DC: American Enterprise Institute for Public Policy Research, 1973).

———— (ed.) *SALT: Problems & Prospects* (Morristown, NJ: General Learning Press, 1973).

———— (ed.) *Great Issues of International Politics* (Chicago: Aldine Publishing Co., 1970).

KEGLEY, Charles W., Jr and McGowan, Pat (eds) *Foreign Policy USA/*

USSR (Beverly Hills: SAGE Publications, 1982).
———— and Wittkopf, Eugene R. *World Politics: Trend and Transformation* (New York: St Martin's Press, 1981).
KELIHER, John G. *The Negotiations on Mutual and Balanced Force Reductions: The Search for Arms Centre in Europe* (New York: Pergamon Press, 1980).
KINTNER, William R. and Pfaltzgraff, Robert L. Jr (eds) *SALT: Implications For Arms Control in the 1970s* (University of Pittsburgh Press, 1973).
KISSINGER, Henry A. *Years of Upheaval* (Boston: Little, Brown & Co., 1982).
———— *White House Years* (Boston: Little, Brown & Co., 1979).
———— *For the Record* (Boston: Little, Brown & Co., 1977).
———— *A World Restored: Europe After Napoleon* (Gloucester, Mass.: Peter Smith, 1973).
———— *American Foreign Policy: Three Essays* (New York: W. W. Norton, 1969).
———— *Nuclear Weapons and Foreign Policy*, abridged edn (New York: W. W. Norton, 1969).
———— *The Troubled Partnership* (New York: McGraw-Hill, 1965).
———— (ed.) *Problems of National Strategy* (New York: Praeger, 1965).
———— *The Necessity for Choice* (New York: Harper & Row, 1960).
KLEIMAN, Robert *Atlantic Crisis: American Diplomacy Confronts a Resurgent Europe* (New York: W. W. Norton, 1964).
KOLODZIEJ, Edward A. *French International Policy Under De Gaulle and Pompidou* (Ithaca, NY: Cornell University Press, 1974).
KORBEL, Josef *Detente in Europe: Real or Imaginary?* (Princeton, NJ: Princeton University Press, 1972).
LABRIE, Roger P. (ed.) *SALT Hand Book: Key Documents and Issues 1972–1979* (Washington, DC: American Enterprise Institute for Public Policy Research, 1979).
LAFEBER, Walter *America, Russia, and the Cold War 1945–1975*, third edn (New York: John Wiley and Sons, 1976).
LANDAU, David *Kissinger: The Uses of Power* (Boston: Houghton Mifflin, 1972).
LISKA, George *Beyond Kissinger: Ways of Conservative Statecraft* (Baltimore: The Johns Hopkins University Press, 1975).
LITWAK, Robert S. *Detente and the Pursuit of Stability 1969–1976* (London: Cambridge University Press, 1984).
McNAMARA, Robert S. *The Essence of Security* (New York: Harper & Row, 1968).
MALRAUX, André *Felled Oaks: Conversation with de Gaulle* (New York: Holt, Rinehart & Winston, 1971).
MANSBACH, Richard W., Ferguson, Yale H. and Lampert, Donald E. *The Web of World Politics: Non-State Actors in the Global System* (Englewood Cliffs, NJ: Prentice-Hall, 1976).
MARTIN, Laurence 'The Nixon Doctrine and Europe', in John C. Garnett (ed.) *The Defense of Western Europe* (New York: St Martin's Press, 1974).

MAYALL, James and Navari, Cornelia (eds) *The End of the Post-War Era: Documents on Great-Power Relations 1968–1975* (London: Cambridge University Press, 1980).

MAZLISH, Bruce *Kissinger: The European Mind in American Policy* (New York: Basic Books, 1976).

MELANSON, Richard A. (ed.) *Neither Cold War nor Detente* (Charlottesville: University Press of Virginia, 1982).

———— *The United States and West Germany 1945–73: A Study in Alliance Politics* (London: Oxford University Press, 1974).

MORGAN, Roger *West Germany's Foreign Policy Agenda*, The Washington Papers, VI, 54 (Beverly Hills: SAGE Publications, 1978).

MORETON, Edwina and Segal, Gerald (eds) *Soviet Strategy Toward Western Europe* (London: George Allen & Unwin, 1984).

MORRIS, Roger *Uncertain Greatness: Henry Kissinger and American Foreign Policy* (New York: Harper & Row, 1977).

MYERS, Kenneth A. (ed.) *NATO: The Next Thirty Years* (Boulder, Col.: Westview Press, 1980).

———— *Ostpolitik and American Security Interests in Europe* (Washington, DC: The Center for Strategic and International Studies, 1972).

NATHAN, James A. and Oliver, James K. *United States Foreign Policy and World Order*, 2nd edn (Boston: Little, Brown & Co., 1981).

NEAL, Fred Warner and Harvey, Mary Kersey (eds) *The Nixon–Kissinger Foreign Policy: Opportunities and Contradictions*, Pacem in Terris, III Santa Barbara, Cal.: Center for the Study of Democratic Institutions, 1973).

NEWHOUSE, John *Cold Dawn: The Story of SALT* (New York: Holt, Rinehart & Winston, 1973).

———— *et al. US Troops in Europe: Issues, Costs and Choices* (Washington, DC: The Brookings Institution, 1971).

NIXON, Richard M. *The Memoirs of Richard Nixon*, 2 vols (New York: Warner Books, 1978).

NUTTER, G. Warren *Kissinger's Grand Design*, foreword by Melvin E. Laird (Washington, DC: American Enterprise Institute for Public Policy Research, 1975).

OSGOOD, Robert E. *Containment, Soviet Behavior, and Grand Strategy* (Berkeley: Institute of International Studies, University of California, 1981).

———— *et al. Retreat from Empire? The First Nixon Administration* (Baltimore: The Johns Hopkins University Press, 1973).

PETROV, Vladimir *US–Soviet Detente: Past and Future* (Washington, DC: American Enterprise Institute for Public Policy Research, 1975).

PIPES, Richard 'America, Russia, and Europe in the Light of the Nixon Doctrine', in Richard B. Foster, *et al.* (eds) *Strategy for the West* (New York; Crane, Russak & Co., 1974).

PRANGER, Robert J. (ed.) *Detente and Defense* (Washington, DC: American Enterprise Institute for Public Policy Research, 1976).

ROSENBERGER, Leif Roderick 'The Evolution of the Nixon–Kissinger Policy Toward the Soviet Union: An Analysis of the Cold War Legacy and the Ambivalent Pursuit of Detente', Ph.D. dissertation (Claremont Graduate School, 1980).

RUSH, Kenneth, Scowcroft, Brent and Wolf, Joseph *Strengthening Deterrence* (Cambridge, Mass.: Ballinger, 1981).

SAETER, Martin *The Federal Republic, Europe and the World*, translated by Susan Hoivik, Norwegian Foreign Policy Studies, 31 (Oslo: Universitetsforlaget, 1980).

SCHAETZEL, J. Robert *The Unhinged Alliance: America and the European Community* (New York: Harper & Row, 1975).

SCHLAFLY, Phyllis and Ward, Chester *Ambush at Vladivostok* (Alton, Ill.: Père Marquette Press, 1976).

SCHWARTZ, David N. *NATO's Nuclear Dilemma* (Washington, DC: The Brookings Institution, 1983).

SERFATY, Simon *Fading Partnership: American and Europe after 30 Years* (New York: Praeger, 1979).

SMITH, Gerard *Doubletalk: The Story of the First Strategic Arms Limitation Talks* (Garden City, NY: Doubleday, 1980).

SOBEL, Lester A. (ed.) *Kissinger & Detente* (New York: Facts on File, 1975).

SPANIER, John *American Foreign Policy since World War II*, 7th edn (New York: Praeger, 1977).

STANLEY, Timothy W. and Whitt, Darnell M. *Detente Diplomacy: United States and European Security in the 1970s* (New York: The Dunellen Co., 1970).

STARR, Harvey *Henry Kissinger: Perceptions of International Politics* (Lexington, Ky: The University Press of Kentucky, 1984).

STEELE, Jonathan *World Power: Soviet Foreign Policy under Brezhnev and Andropov* (London: Michael Joseph, 1983).

STEIBEL, Gerald L. *Detente: Promises and Pitfalls* (New York: Crane, Russak & Co., 1975).

STOESSINGER, John G. *Henry Kissinger: The Anguish of Power* (New York: W. W. Norton, 1976).

SZULC, Tad *The Illusion of Peace: Foreign Policy in the Nixon Years* (New York: The Viking Press, 1978).

THOMPSON, Scott W. (ed.) *National Security in the 1980s: From Weakness to Strength* (San Francisco, Cal.: Institute for Contemporary Studies, 1980).

TREZISE, Philip H. *The Atlantic Connection* (Washington, DC: The Brookings Institution, 1975).

———— and Watts, William (eds) *Beyond Containment: US Foreign Policy in Transition* (Washington, DC: Potomac Associates, 1973).

TUCKER, Robert W. *A New Isolationism: Threat or Promise?* (New York: Universe Books, 1972).

VALERIANI, Richard *Travels with Henry* (Boston: Houghton Mifflin, 1979).

WILLRICH, Mason and Rhinelander, John B. (eds) *SALT: The Moscow Agreements and Beyond* (New York: The Free Press, 1974).

WOODWARD, Bob and Bernstein Carl *The Final Days* (New York: Simon & Schuster, 1976).

YOCHELSON, John 'MFR: West European and American Perspectives', in Wolfram F. Hanrieder (ed.) *The United States and Western Europe*

(Cambridge, Mass.: Winthrop Publishers, 1974).
YOST, David S. (ed.) *NATO'S Strategic Options: Arms Control and Defense* (New York: Pergamon Press, 1981).
———— *European Security and the SALT Process*, The Washington Papers, IX, 85 (Beverly Hills: SAGE Publications, 1981).

Articles

ARON, Raymond 'Richard Nixon and the Future of American Foreign Policy', *Daedalus*, 101 (Fall 1972) 1–24.
BARE, Gordon C. 'Burden-sharing in NATO: The Economics of Alliance', ORBIS, 2 (Summer 1976) 417–36.
BERGSTEN, Fred C. 'Mr Kissinger: No Economic Superstar', *New York Times* (12 December 1973).
BRADY, Linda P. 'Negotiating European Security: Vol VI II Mutual and Balanced Force Reductions', *International Security Review*, 2 (Summer 1981) 189–208.
BRENNER, Michael J. 'The Problem of Innovation and the Nixon–Kissinger Foreign Policy', *International Studies Quarterly*, 3 (September 1973) 255–94.
———— 'The Theorist as Actor, the Actor as Theorist: Strategy in the Nixon Administration', *Stanford Journal of International Studies*, 7 (Spring 1972) 109–31.
BRZEZINSKI, Zbigniew 'US Foreign Policy: The Search for Focus', *Foreign Affairs*, 51 (1973) 708–27.
———— 'Recognizing the Crisis'. *Foreign Policy* 17 (Winter 1974–75): 63–74.
———— 'The Deceptive Structure of Peace'. *Foreign Policy* 14 (Spring 1974): 35–55.
———— 'The Balance of Power Delusion'. *Foreign Policy* 7 (Summer 1972): 54–59.
———— 'Half Past Nixon'. *Foreign Policy* 3 (Summer 1971): 3–21.
CROMWELL, William C. 'Europe and the "Structure of Peace"', *ORBIS*, 1 (Spring 1978) 11–36.
FALLACI, Oriana 'Kissinger: An Interview', *The New Republic*, 167 (16 December 1972) 17–22.
FLYNN, Gregory A. 'The Content of European Detente', *ORBIS*, 2 (Summer 1976) 401–16.
GARRET, Stephen A. 'Nixonian Foreign Policy: A New Balance of Power – or A Revived Concert? *Polity*, 8 (Spring 1976) 389–421.
HAHN, Walter F. 'West Germany's Ostpolitik: The Grand Design of Egon Bahr', *ORBIS*, 4 (Winter 1973) 859–80.
———— 'The Nixon Doctrine: Design and Dilemmas', *ORBIS*, 2 (Summer 1972) 361–76.
HOFFMANN, Stanley 'The Case of Dr Kissinger', *The New York Review of Books* (6 December 1979) 14–29.
———— 'Choices', *Foreign Policy*, 12 (1973) 3–42.

KALTEFLEITER, Werner 'Europe and the Nixon Doctrine: A German Point of View', *ORBIS*, 1 (Spring 1973) 75–94.

KAPLAN, Lawrence S. 'NATO and the Nixon Doctrine Ten Years Later', *ORBIS*, 1 (Spring 1980) 149–64.

KISSINGER, Henry A. 'NATO: Evolution or Decline?' *The Texas Quarterly*, 9 (Autumn 1966) 110–18.

———— 'For a New Atlantic Alliance', *The Reporter*, 35 (14 July 1966) 18–27.

———— 'Illusionist: Why We Misread de Gaulle', *Harper's Magazine*, 230 (March 1965) 69–70.

———— 'The Price of German Unity', *The Reporter*, 32 (22 April 1965) 12–17.

———— 'The Essentials of Solidarity in the Western Alliance', *The Conservative Papers* (Chicago: Quadrangle Books, 1964) 18–38.

———— Coalition Diplomacy in the Nuclear Age', *Foreign Affairs*, 42 (July 1964) 525–45.

———— 'Strains on the Alliance', *Foreign Affairs*, 41 (January 1963) 261–85.

———— 'The Skybolt Affair', *The Reporter*, 28 (17 January 1963) 15–16.

———— 'NATO's Nuclear Dilemma', *The Reporter*, 28 (28 March 1963) 22–33ff.

———— 'The Unresolved Problems of European Defense', *Foreign Affairs*, 40 (July 1962) 515–41.

———— 'For an Atlantic Confederacy', *The Reporter*, 24 (2 February 1961) 16–20.

———— 'Limited War: Nuclear or Conventional? A Reappraisal', *Daedalus*, 89 (Fall 1960) 800–17.

———— 'The New Cult of Neutralism', *The Reporter*, 23 (24 November 1960) 26–9.

———— 'As Urgent as the Moscow Threat', *The New York Times Magazine* (8 March 1959) 19ff.

———— 'The Search for Stability', *Foreign Affairs*, 37 (July 1959) 537–60.

———— 'Missiles and the Western Alliance', *Foreign Affairs*, 36 (April 1958) 383–400.

———— 'Nuclear Testing and the Problem of Peace', *Foreign Affairs*, 37 (October 1958) 1–18.

———— 'Military Policy and the Defense of the "Gray" Areas', *Foreign Affairs*, 33 (April 1955) 416–28.

———— 'The Limitations of Diplomacy', *The New Republic* (9 May 1955) 7–8.

———— 'American Policy and Preventive War', *Yale Review*, 44, 3 (Spring 1955) 321–39.

KLEIN, Jean 'European and French Points of View on Mutual and Balanced Force Reductions in Europe: Historic and Current Perspectives', *Stanford Journal of International Studies* (Spring 1979) 53–70.

KOHL, Wilfrid L. 'The Nixon–Kissinger Foreign Policy System and the US–West European Relations: Patterns of Policy Making', *World Politics* XXVIII, 1 (October 1975) 1–43.

———— and Taubman, William 'American Policy Toward Europe: The

Next Phase', *ORBIS*, 1 (Spring 1973) 51–74.

KOSTKO, Y. 'Mutual Force Reductions in Europe', *Survival* (September–October 1972) 236–8.

KRISTOL, Irving 'The Meaning of Kissinger', *Wall Street Journal* (11 April 1974) 12.

LEACACOS, John P. 'Kissinger's Apparat', *Foreign Policy*, 5 (Winter 1971–2) 3–27.

LEGVOLD, Robert 'European Security Conference', *Survey* (Summer 1970) 41–52.

LEWIS, Anthony 'Kissinger Now', *The New York Review of Books* (27 October 1977) 8–10.

MONTGOMERY, John D. 'The Education of Henry Kissinger', *Journal of International Affairs*, 1 (1975) 49–62.

NIXON, Richard M. 'Asia after Vietnam', *Foreign Affairs*, 46 (October 1967) 112–25.

PIERRE, Andrew J. 'The Future of America's Commitments and Alliances', *ORBIS*, 3 (Fall 1972) 696–719.

PLALTZGRAFF, Robert L. 'The United States and Europe: Partners in a Multipolar World?', *ORBIS*, 1 (Spring 1973) 31–50.

SCHAETZEL, J. Robert. 'Some European Questions for Dr Kissinger', *Foreign Policy*, 12 (1973) 66–74.

SERFATY, Simon 'America and Europe in the 1970s: Integration or Disintegration?', *ORBIS*, 1 (Spring 1973) 95–109.

SMART, Ian 'MBFR Assailed: A Critical View of the Proposed Negotiation of Mutual and Balanced Force Reduction', *Occasional Paper*, 3 (Ithaca, NY: Cornell University Peace Studies Program, 1972).

SODARO, Michael J. 'US–Soviet Relations: Detente or Cold War?', paper prepared for the conference on 'Economic Relations with the USSR: American and West German Perspectives', Washington, DC, 25–6 April 1984).

WOLIN, Sheldon 'Consistent Kissinger', *The New York Review of Books* (9 December 1976) 20–31.

YOCHELSON, John 'MBFR: The Search for an American Approach', *ORBIS*, 1 (Spring 1973) 155–75.

———— 'The American Military Presence in Europe: Current Debate in the United States', *ORBIS*, 15 (Fall 1971) 784–807.

Official Documents

The Eurogroup (Brussels: NATO Information Service, Aspects of NATO Series, 1972).

NIXON, Richard M. *US Foreign Policy for the 1970s: Shaping a Durable Peace* (Washington, DC: Government Printing Office, 1973).

———— *US Foreign Policy for the 1970s: The Emerging Structure of Peace* (Washington, DC: Government Printing Office, 1972).

———— *US Foreign Policy for the 1970s: Building for Peace* (Washington, DC: Government Printing Office, 1971).

———— *US Foreign Policy for the 1970s: A New Strategy for Peace*

252 *Select Bibliography*

 (Washington, DC: Government Printing Office, 1970).

Press and Information Office of the Government of the Federal Republic of Germany *White Paper 1975/1976: The Security of the Federal Republic of Germany and the Development of the Federal Armed Forces* (Bonn: The Federal Ministry of Defence, 1976).

———— *Documentation Relating to the Federal Government's Policy of Detente* (Bonn: 1974).

———— *White Paper 1973/1974: The Security of the Federal Republic of Germany and the Development of the Federal Armed Forces* (Bonn: The Federal Ministry of Defence, 1974).

———— *The Development of the Relations between the Federal Republic of Germany and the German Democratic Republic* (Bonn: 1973).

———— *The European Group in the North Atlantic Alliance* (Bonn: The Federal Ministry of Defence, 1972).

———— *White Paper 1971/1972: The Security of the Federal Republic of Germany and the Development of the Federal Armed Forces* (Bonn: The Federal Ministry of Defence, 1971).

Public Papers of the Presidents (Washington, DC: Government Printing Office, 1971).

United States Congress, *Report on the Fifth Meeting of Members of Congress and of the European Parliament*, 93rd Congress, 2nd session, (Washington, DC: Government Printing Office, 1974).

United States Department of Defense *Defense Report: Fiscal Year 1973 Defense Budget and Fiscal Year 1973–1977 Program* (Washington, DC: Government Printing Office, 1972).

———— *Defense Report: Fiscal Year 1972–76 Defense Program and the 1972 Defense Budget* (Washington, DC: Government Printing Office, 1971).

———— *Defense Report: Fiscal Year 1971 Defense Report and Budget* (Washington, DC: Government Printing Office, 1970).

United States Department of State *Department of State Bulletin*, 'The Year of Europe', LXVIII, 1768, 14 May 1973, pp. 593–8.

———— *United States Foreign Policy, 1972: A Report of the Secretary of State* (Washington, DC: Department of State Publication 8699, GPO, 1973).

———— *United States Foreign Policy, 1971: A Report of the Secretary of State* (Washington, DC: Department of State Publication 8634, GPO, 1972).

———— *United States Foreign Policy, 1969–1970: A Report of the Secretary of State* (Washington, DC: Department of State Publication 8575, GPO, 1971).

———— *Department of State Bulletin*, 'North Atlantic Treaty', XX, 507, 20 March 1949, pp. 339–42.

United States House of Representatives, Committee on Armed Services *US Military Commitments to Europe*, 93rd Congress, 2nd session (Washington, DC: Government Printing Office, 1974).

United States Senate, Committee on Foreign Relations *United States Policy Toward Europe And Related Matters*, 89th Congress, 2nd session (Washington, DC: Government Printing Office, 1966).

_____ Committee on Foreign Relations *US Security Issues in Europe: Burden Sharing and Offset, MBFR and Nuclear Weapons*, 93rd Congress, 1st session (Washington, DC: Government Printing Office, 1973).

_____ *United States Security Agreement as Commitment Abroad: United States Forces in Europe* (Washington, DC: Government Printing Office), 1970).

Other Sources

Business Week.
International Herald Tribune, 31 August 1973; 13 January 1975.
Newsweek.
The Los Angeles Times, 30 August 1971.
The New York Times, 9 November 1973; 13 December 1973; 9 April 1974; 13 October 1974.
The Times (London), 1 September 1973.
The Washington Post, 12 March 1974.
Time, 3 January 1972.
Wall Street Journal, 11 April 1974.

Index